WHATTA LIFE

THE INCREDIBLE LIFE & TIMES OF PAT MAGIE

PAT MAGIE

authorHOUSE®

AuthorHouse™
1663 Liberty Drive
Bloomington, IN 47403
www.authorhouse.com
Phone: 833-262-8899

Published by AuthorHouse 07/30/2020

ISBN: 978-1-7283-6586-2 (sc)
ISBN: 978-1-7283-6587-9 (e)

Print information available on the last page.

Any people depicted in stock imagery provided by Getty Images are models, and such images are being used for illustrative purposes only.
Certain stock imagery © Getty Images.

This book is printed on acid-free paper.

WHATTA LIFE

PAT MAGIE

Come fly along with legendary floatplane pilot Pat Magie as he starts his career to owning and operating the largest 135 float plane operation in Minnesota. Become part of the adventure as he tackles the challenges of the Alaska interior on floats, to his adventures around the world making lifelong friends in the process. Learn from his amazing 40,000 + accident free flight hours.

ABOUT THE AUTHOR

The year is 1952 and the U.S. Marine Corps has just turned Pat loose upon the civilian population. Magie heads to northern Minnesota, where he traps wolves for bounty and leads canoe trips into the wilderness. Highlight of this era is a 2 ½ month pilgrimage to Hudson Bay. A menu of porcupine and rice keeps the Hudson Bay explorers alive while they paddle and portage their canoe throughout the North.

During the Hudson Bay trip, Pat developed a keen interest in the far north. To explore further, he concluded that air travel was the way to go, so he bought a Piper J-4 Cub with floats. Flying lessons followed, with solo in eight hours and a solo cross country endorsement obtained aboard a Forest Service Beaver.

For first solo cross-country, Pat decided upon a lake up north with some duck-hunting thrown in for good measure. Timing could have been better however, for this lake froze overnight and takeoff from the remote location was not possible. Pat let the lake freeze hard over, chopped the plane out of the ice, coaxed it onto the ice and took off, floats skating across ice until liftoff speed. Upon returning home, Magie landed on ice with the floats, then switched to skis for winter's duration.

After 485 hours of adventures it was time for the commercial check ride. This required a flight from an airport and Pat's first landing on wheels took place that day.

A series of float planes followed the Cub - a Stinson, Cessna 180, and Howard DGA15. Pat then added the first Twin Beech ever to operate in the U.S. with floats. The beauty of the Twin Beech was that it could carry two canoes at a time and his Wilderness Wings business thrived, opening up vast portions of Northern Minnesota to adventurous canoe enthusiasts. Pat also sold float-equiped Cessnas, and he could get a plane headed north sometimes in the same day the order was received.

Alas, the federal government created a wilderness area which eliminated much of his business, so in 1980 Pat headed north to Alaska, flying for some of the same outfits which bought planes from him earlier.

In 1989, Pat Magie visited Hawaii for the first time and decided the place offered promise. It took years working through bureaucratic thickets, but he and his wife have now established their Island Seaplane business. The Beaver mostly takes sightseers aloft. The Cessna 206 performs this role as well as giving land pilots a chance to earn a seaplane rating. Pat doesn't believe in quicky courses and he'll leave you with an impression of glassy-water landings which may save your life someday. In 2018 the State raised rent 400% thus shutting the business down.

Cover photo by Scott M. Magie on Tebay Lake Alaska
The snow covered mountain is 16,000 feet high and 50 miles away

DEDICATED TO THE MEMORY OF

PATRICK BRIAN MAGIE

My oldest son Patrick (1961-2018) who was flying from the right seat when he could see over the instrument panel. I signed off his original solo flight (on floats) on his 16th birthday and his private pilot check ride (on floats) on his 17th birthday. We froze early on his 18th birthday which made it a week later for me to sign off his commercial check ride on skis. In the next few months I recommended him for multi-engine sea, multi- engine land and instrument rating along with giving him his first job in aviation. He later picked up ATP and CFI at a school on the East Coast. He went all over the world checking out pilots in the Cessna Caravans on floats and accumulated 27,000 hours flight time with by far most of it on floats. He also was the only pilot that I know that has flown a seaplane on every continent of this earth except Antartica where seaplanes are not common. He took a ride with someone else and left us very early. He lived a good life. Gods speed.

WILLIAM THOMAS BAILEY III

Also to my best friend of over 80 years Bill Bailey (1933-2020) whose name come up many times in this book. We shared a lot of fishing and hunting trips as well as adventures between the Caribbean to Alaska and Hawaii. He primarily made a living in the banking business, but had many more exciting things going on the side. He would build houseboats for sale, rebuild sailboats, ride motorcycles and powered parachutes (that occasionally ran into trees), a pilot who owned a variety of aircraft on floats, skis and wheels. He and his wife planned ahead for their retirement (she was in the banking industry also) by buying an island on a lake in northern Minnesota. Then they bought a dump truck and spent winter weekends hauling building materials over the ice to the island. Summer weekends and vacation time was spent building a home. Then they bought a sailboat to make a voyage to Europe, but got into a large storm which diverted them to the Bahamas where they bought another island. Later they built a houseboat, went down the Mississippi River then crossing over to the Bahamas to live on the boat while they built their house. Then they decided against the Bahamas, sold the boat and property and bought a house in Naples, Florida on a canal. Over a few years they rebuilt parts of the house, added a garage, a fireplace and metal roof. Lise still lives there and Bill passed on at a very young age of 87 years when he fell off a sailboat mast. See you later Bill — probably quite a while because two months ago I talked my doctor into giving me another 25 year warranty.

IN PRAISE OF ADVENTURER AND SEAPLANE PILOT PAT MAGIE

Mark Baker, President & CEO, Aircraft
Owners and Pilots Association

A renowned pilot, entrepreneur, world-record-holder, family man and friend – yes, there are many words I could use to describe Pat Magie, but I think *legend* pretty much sums it up.

With 63 years and more than 40,000 hours of flight time, it's safe to say he has earned every one of those accolades.

Over the years, I've been fortunate enough to develop a friendship with Pat and his family, and have treasured every second of sharing our experiences. We've even owned the same Twin Beech at different times.

One thing I have also come to learn is that Pat isn't too keen on tires, as his affinity for skis and floats goes well beyond the average pilot. Then again, Pat is not your average pilot. From Minnesota to Alaska to Hawaii, these pages will put you in the cockpit and take you on a whirlwind adventure.

Those who know Pat will agree that there are far too many Pat Magie stories to fit into one book, but I am sure you will more than enjoy the rich ones that are included here. They certainly bring alive the first-hand tales I fondly remember.

Few people in life possess the innate tenacity for adventure that Pat does, and I am lucky to call him a good friend. Twin Beech 18 Floated by Pat Magie mid 1970 - later owned by Mark Baker

Kevin LaRosa Sr.
Aerial Coordinator

I had the honor to meet Pat Magie in 1996 while working on the movie The Phantom in Thailand. As aerial coordinator of the film I needed a vintage sea plane and a pilot, that is where Pat came into my life. Pat and his wife Debbie flew his beautiful Beach 18, on floats, from their home state of Alaska all the way down the west coast of the United States to California's Long Beach Harbor in Los Angeles. The Beach 18 was then loaded on a ship and brought to Thailand where we were filming. I have worked as aerial coordinator on over 300 films in my career and as a pilot I can honestly say Pat stands out as one of the best. His flying skills made my job easy but not only is Pat a great pilot, but he is also a true gentleman. It was one of the highlights in my career and a true honor to fly with him. When a film is over the cast and crew part ways, but not Pat and I. It has been over 20 years and we still keep in touch, talking about planes and aviation. Pat's knowledge and background is unmatched in the aviation world. All the best with your book...Your Friend, Kevin LaRosa Sr.

Movie Godzilla filmed in Hawaii with Pat and our Twin beech 18. Got to work with Kevin LaRosa again.

CONTENTS

CHAPTER 1

WOW

It was Tuesday June 21, 1994 just a little after 8:00 a.m. and I was standing on the shoreline on Landmark Gap Lake sipping a cup of coffee after eating a large stack of blueberry pancakes. I was standing next to my Twin Beech 18, N1042H, heeled back up on a beach in the northern part of the Nelchina Plateau Alaska. This is the 4th Beech 18 I have owned in the past 30 years since I bought my first one from Joe Marrs of Lake Placid, Florida.

After I finished my coffee, I pumped out the floats, checked the oil and warmed up the engines.

Looking to the south I could see several Caribou milling around and looking North I thought I could see two Dall Sheep about the 5,000 foot level. I just made a note to swing by there as we took off to the north on our departure. We would move slightly east as we flew through Black Rapids Pass at 4,000 feet and watch carefully for buffalo as we descended to the Tanana River Valley to fly to Fairbanks for a refuel stop.

We had another aircraft with us – a Cessna U 206 flown by my son-in-law Tom Prijatel. He was carrying a lot of our camping equipment and our food supplies while I carried a doctor from Bologna, Italy, two of his nephews plus one fellow from the U.S., our camp cook and our personal gear. This was a weekly 7-day aerial tour of the state of Alaska departing every Sunday at noon and returning every Saturday afternoon and would cover about 3,500 miles over Alaska. We would fly approximately three hours per day and land about every hour to fish, visit villages or just view wildlife. We camped out and had the best tents we could buy that were sturdy, watertight, light and easy to put up and take down. We also had very good sleeping bags and 3" foam sleeping pads as well as a pretty neat hot shower that went up most nights. We did all of our cooking over a Coleman 2 burner gas stove, a folding reflector oven and a wood campfire. We did serve pie a couple times a week – usually apple, blueberry or chocolate banana. Every Thursday morning we would make Eggs Benedict complete with asparagus and hollendaise sauce. This would be on Kalisok Lake just above the Kobuk River north of the Arctic Circle in the western part of the Brooks Range. We would always serve the breakfast with the question "Have you ever had Eggs Benedict north of the Arctic Circle before?" and we never did get a yes. Our normal complement of aircraft on this tour was a single engine DeHavilland Otter (DHC-3) and Twin Beech 18, both on floats. The Otter would carry the usual six passengers and their personal gear.

They would make several stops during the day and bring in the catch of the day if we were eating fish that night. At Kalisok Lake the Otter would usually land on the Kobuk River a couple of hours earlier and try to catch a couple Sheefish for dinner. Sheefish is a white colored meat and is delicious – if not Sheefish it would be Arctic Grayling. The Otter would usually arrive at camp about 4:30 p.m. and the cook and I would have the tents up, the shower set up, dinner started and hord'oeuvres laid out. We had a nice beach there and the lake was rather shallow water with 24 hours of daylight, so it was possible to take a quick swim if you wanted to say you had been swimming north of the Arctic Circle and it was pretty comfortable. Almost every night we would have a large campfire to sit around and tell stories even if it was not dark. The next day we would fly just over 500 miles south to Chukuminuk Lake, but land at the native village of Galena on the Yukon River for a fuel stop enroute. The Yukon usually had a pretty strong current so it would be "land up stream" and "takeoff down- stream" and watch closely for debris. Thursday night here it is BBQ chicken, potato salad, corn on the cob and homemade apple pie. We flew this tour for 16 years and were usually booked two years in advance.

Back to June on Landmark Gap Lake and its day's adventure. A few minutes after 9:00 we both taxied out on the lake and pointed north to the Alaska Range. Full power and the bows quickly raised to full up and rotated forward onto the step. Speed picked up very quickly and in about 30 more seconds I could gently raise the right float up from the water and fly. I took a quick look back and verified that Tom and the Cessna were airborne also, so I eased over to the east side of the lake and showed everyone a close look at two Dall Sheep laying on an outcropping of rock just off our right-wing tip. As we passed the north end of the lake I was about 800 feet above ground (AGL) and got to show every one a Brown Bear (Grizzly) fishing in an incoming creek. I could not help thinking that how many pilots get to show their passengers this kind of scenery on take – off and climb out. It sure beats Honda's, Ford's, Chevrolet's, traffic lights and freeways. As we cleared north we made a slight easterly deviation and started up the valley towards the Pass and Delta Junction. While we descended through the pass, we picked up six buffalo grazing along the riverbank. Great morning!

Coming down towards Delta Junction and the Alcan Highway we started a shallow bank to the left and Fairbanks. Fairbanks International Airport has two main runways with a 5,400' X 100' waterway between the two. Transient parking and refueling are both at the South end of 19W. The major problem of the Twin Beech on floats is its gross weight. On wheels the B 18 has 10,200 pound gross while on floats it is only 8,180 pounds. The FAA says that was restricted by smaller 7850 floats. When I did the certification of the D18S in 1970 I expected a gross of 8,725 pounds as the Canadian government has, but came out with only a 1,300 pound useful load after the first test flights. Matt Reid of Bristol Aircraft in

Winnipeg called me in early August of 1970 and told me the FAA finished their flight testing, but was hesitant about giving me the final numbers. When he did tell me the useful load ended up at 1,300 pounds with a gross weight of 7,600 pounds. I exploded and said that I had Cessna 206's that had a larger useful load.

I bought this Beech 18, N6561D, from Bill Britt of Britt Airways in Danville, Illinois about 3 months earlier for $12,500 while I was in Chicago for a sportsman show selling our fishing trips in Northern Minnesota and Canada. A week later I told Wiley Hautala who was a pilot/mechanic for me that he had to go down to Danville, pick up the aircraft and fly it to Winnipeg, Manitoba for float install. Wiley immediately said he did not want to do that because everyone said it was such a squirrely aircraft on wheels. To that I said that four of us have multi-engine ratings, but you are the only one that has a multi-engine landplane rating, so you are the only one who can do it, but I've set it up down there that they will check you out until you are comfortable. Two days later he called from Danville and said that he had done four crosswind take-offs and landings and there was nothing to it, so is it ok to start back.

I could only say "bring it back here". We took it up to Winnipeg two days later and Matt Reid started setting up the FAA portion. A month later Matt Reid called and said the Beech was installed on floats and the FAA was there to do the certification. But he said that they refused to fly the aircraft with two 500 hour engines that had been overhauled for the Civil Air Patrol on a government contract. I could not believe this, but said I would call him back within a couple of hours. I then called Paul Abbott at Covington Aircraft Engines in Oklahoma and explained my problem. He told me that he had two Pratt & Whitney R 985's overhauled and ready to go so I told him to hold them for me for the next hour. I quickly called Tom Grahek in Ely at the Ford dealership and told him I would like to buy a four wheel drive pick up only to have him tell me that there was a 90 day order delay on that. I tried Mike Wienzerel at the Dodge store and he said he would look for a 15 passenger van and called back in half hour with a new 15 pax van at a dealer in Superior, Wisconsin. I said I would take it and fly a couple people down there to pick it up in three hours, then I would stop by his place this afternoon to complete the purchase. I got a couple fellows out of the shop and had them pack quickly and told them we would fly them to Superior then they should drive all night taking turns sleeping – and pick up the two engines to take to Winnipeg. I also called Matt Reid to tell him that he would have two fresh engines the morning after next and start removing the old ones. My guys laid over a day in Winnipeg then brought two 500 hour engines back to us to ship to Paul Abbot as the exchange. I had that van many years after that. The FAA finished up the certification – even though I certainly did not like the gross weight and did not want the aircraft. I did pick up the aircraft later and brought it to Ely, Minnesota. Finally in October I got another FAA guy to come out to redo the single engine requirements again. He was not rated in the aircraft so I had to fly with him and he did need help. We were trying to increase the rate of climb with critical engine shut down and cylinder head temp gauges installed on all nine on the live one to make sure we did not overtemp. We had to square the stall speed and multiply by .02 to find required rate of climb. We did increase the gross weight to 8,180 pounds which I could live with and do some flying over gross. I still envied the Canadians with their 8,725 gross.

Now back to the Tanana River and Fair banks about 15 miles off our right wing tip. Because of the legal useful loads of the Beech 18 I would never go into the float pond with all the passengers at Fairbanks International and maybe get a ramp check. The Beech draws a lot of attention wherever you go including the FAA. So I would fly just about 15 miles west of Fairbanks, land on the eastern side of Minto Lake and drop off the guests plus the cook. We had cleared off a few trees along the shore so that the Beech wing would clear and our cook would feed the guests lunch. They could also cast for some good sized Northern Pike

— catch and release — because we had charcoaled NY Strips steaks, baked potatoes and chocolate banana pie on the menu for that night. Meanwhile I would fly back into Fairbanks, top off the tanks, then back to Minto Lake still barely under gross to continue our flight without any hassle about overloads in front of the FAA. When we departed Minto Lake with the lunch group we would be 2,000 pounds or more over gross, but the aircraft handled it nicely.

This was the first time this year I had been into Minto for the summer and got a surprise when I shut both engines down to drift alongside the shoreline. I came to a very abrupt stop and both bows rose about two feet in the air. We definitely had run aground on something and were stuck. We were all wearing hip boots and quickly got out to unload the lunch fixings and fishing gear. Then hooked a 100 foot line on the floats and we started pulling and pushing with no response. After a few minutes I walked right around the aircraft right next to the floats found there was a fairly large submerged spruce tree under the aircraft that we were stuck on. Evidently heavy snow had caused the tree to fall down during the winter and when the ice went out it sank. I untied the 100 foot rope and retied it so there was 50 feet on each end of the float and then had everyone stand in the water to pull forward. I told them that I was going to run both engines up to full power while they pulled forward. There were trees right in front of us so once the plane was free of its entanglement I would chop the right engine, turn 90 degrees right, then come back up to full power and complete my take-off straight ahead leaving the rope dangling until I landed in the float pond in Fairbanks. It was totally calm and I had two miles of lake for take-off. When I broke free I quickly accelerated to almost 50 knots but it would not go further – and I needed at least 55 knots to fly. I gently nursed the control wheel back and forth, but no go! I was running out of lake so I brought the power off and fell off the step, then cut the mixtures. I must have snagged something with that rope, so I climbed out on the float and started pulling the rope in and immediately realized that the line was attached to something. I kept pulling and could soon see a hip boot. As the boot got closer, I could see someone was in the hip boot. As I pulled him along the float I could not help but saying "Oh S—t, He's Dead". I had dragged him two miles at 50 knots feet first. Over the years I have flown many drowning victims back to town. Many of them have been in the water for awhile and not very presentable – just wrap them up in a tarp or body bag and tie them outside on the top of the float. Depending on the type of aircraft you might put the remains inside if it was a recent drowning. When I pulled this one in, I got him on the rear section of the left hand float and started giving him mouth to mouth and artificial resuscitation – after a few minutes he gave a groan, then threw up. A few minutes later I managed to get him up the ladder and into a seat. It was spooky – dead calm and two miles away we could hear the two nephews groaning and screaming. I quickly slid into the pilot's seat and started up, then reversed course and applied full power. I do not think that I cleared 20 feet AGL going back to Fairbanks and when I turned around the last mountain I called tower and told them that I was "four north for waterway 19, transient parking and need an ambulance!" It was a scrambled moment, but the reply was "Roger 42 Hotel – cleared to land". That came just as I touched down. My son-in-law Tom was waiting there after refueling wondering why I was late. He quickly ran over and swung our tail back on the beach. Just as we tied the plane off the ambulance pulled in. I told Tom to take his Amex card and go along to pay for everything – we do not want any lawsuits. Tell them this is Andrew Scagliorini from Bologna, Italy. I'll get a little fuel and go bring the others in and get some hotel rooms. The ambulance with Andrew and Tom drove off while I called the fuel truck and entered the phone booth there for pilots to use. I got four hotel rooms lined up and I told them to have a van here for pick up in an hour. I put a little fuel in, and took off and headed for Minto Lake again. It only took a few minutes to load the passengers and cook Janice up, and flew back to the float pond, but it took a while to convince everyone that Andrew was still alive and in the hospital. They all said that everyone was just standing there pulling on the rope when I applied the power to both engines when Andrew was suddenly just yanked out of the water and very quickly was pulled away on the end of the rope. I imagine with two 450 h.p. engines going to full power very quickly it would happen "right now". I of course I had no idea anything was going wrong, but the observers were certain he was dead. How many times I have wondered since what would have happened if he had come out of the water dangling below the aircraft with the rope simply wrapped around his left leg and how could I land with him dangling below the aircraft. Then the van showed up from the hotel to pick up these people. I cleaned up both aircraft, pumped them out and tied down. As I finished a taxi drove up and Tom climbed out, but there was Andrew sitting in the rear seat. Tom quickly explained that Andrew had a badly bruised left leg, but other than that he was fine and should spend the rest of the day and night in bed. I found it a bit embarrassing talking to talk to someone that I had killed just a couple of hours earlier so told them to take the cab to the hotel to check in and I would be over shortly. I did call my daughter Katie in Cordova to tell her what had happened. She of course was shocked, but was happy everything was ok now. She did tell me that our camp at Alice Cove on Prince William Sound was empty. We both agreed that would be easier on Andrew staying in a cabin and fishing from a boat instead of crawling out of an airplane several times a day and fishing standing up in the water. I told her to have a couple of our guides there in early afternoon the next day and I would drop them off. Tom took the group out to dinner, told them what we were planning and they thought it was great. The next morning we flew from Fairbanks to Anchorage showing them Mount Denali, Ruth Glacier, over Turnigan Arm, through Portage Pass, slow flight over the Columbia Glacier and landed at Alice Cove about 2:00 p.m. They elected to eat their NY Strip Steak that night, but had fresh Salmon on Thursday and Halibut on Friday. When I picked them up Saturday they all had enough fresh fish and a large box of fish to take home with them. It was a great trip in spite of the accident. I try to avoid that with customers ever since.

When Andrew's group left on Sunday he came over to talk. He told me that he was a Private pilot in Italy who owned a Beech Bonanza and if I were to come to Italy he would fly me "all over the country". I told him "No way, after what I did to you, I would be afraid to fly with you!" This was said with a large smile and we parted as friends. For several years we would get a Christmas card from him and he would sign it off as "The man who lived twice".

CHAPTER 2

THE BEGINNING

The early 1930's found the U.S. in the start of a serious depression. The Stock Market flopped over in 1928, collapsed in 1929 and hard times started for most of the population. Jobs were lost, jobs were hard to find and money was scarce. A fellow named Franklin Delano Roosevelt was elected President in 1932 and quickly came up with some ideas of getting people a job. He organized the (WPA) Work Projects of America and the CCC (civilian conservation corps) which created many thousands of jobs.

The first few years of my life I saw a lot of the camps. This was sort of a quasi military operation. Young men were given uniforms, got three meals a day and a barracks to live in plus $19.00 per month for their labors. The CCC's were primarily located in areas of wilderness – this was before we had much in "Wilderness Areas" of today. These young men built roads, bridges, camp grounds and quite a few buildings – including their barracks. Nobody realized it at the time, but it did make a simpler transition to actual military life that started to grow in 1940. The drums of war did end the depression.

As April 29,1930 rolled in there was a very uncomfortable young woman in the maternity ward of St. Marys Hospital in Duluth, Minnesota. Right at 2:00 a.m. she gave a loud scream – which could have been either pain or pleasure as I left her womb to enter the world. Very quickly I was slapped on the butt, had some snipping and cutting and cleaned up with a towel, then laid down on the bed with the woman who I would call "Mother" for over 79 years. My birth certificate lists her as Lucille McNally Magie at age 21 and a housewife living at the Carter Hotel. My Father was William Henry Magie, age 28 years and an aviator living at the same hotel. I was also excited to see on my birth certificate that I was "legitimate" – that was proof that my parents were positive about having a family and not just passing thru the night. I was followed by four sisters later and still have problems with taking orders from women.

The next couple of years saw my father going bankrupt in 1932 when he had two Lockheed Vega's on floats hauling mail around Lake Superior. His original pilots license was #8 signed by Orville and Wilbur Wright in the early 1920's. His last license was #229 in 1930 signed by Orville. This was long before there was a FAA or CAA and was issued by the Federation Aeronautiqe Internationale. It was a United States of America Annual Sporting License. He was grounded for a while during the 1920's for doing a loop passing under the aerial bridge in the Duluth Harbor in his Jenny with a girlfriend in the back seat.

He also became the first pilot to land on the Duluth airport. He had his Jenny parked in a local farmers field, but was evicted one day for disturbing the livestock. He had heard that construction had started on a airport on top of a hill above the city and proceeded to fly over there to take a look. He found two teams of horses plowing the new to be runway, so he buzzed the plow teams to clear the runway and landed. He later – much later, was presented to the public on the 50th anniversary of the airfield as the first pilot to land on it. His father, my grandfather, was a medical doctor in Duluth for many years and was pretty well to do for those days. He had finished medical school in Indiana during the 1880's and hitchhiked (by wagon I guess) to Duluth, Minnesota. He then approached the two doctors in town and asked if they would object to his starting a practice there. An offer was quickly made that he could join them if he would stay over the winter. They were alternating between themselves that one would go out for the winter while the other stayed in Duluth. My grandfather stayed in Duluth year around and did very well financially. He built a large brick covered home at the end of the car line on Superior Street. That is still there and has his name engraved in the concrete of the entrance. My father said that as a young hunter he could walk just aways north of the house to shoot deer. Now you have to go quite a few miles to hunt deer, but they say that is progress. My father had quite a few problems because of his father's money, owning airplanes, a Stutz Bearcat convertible and attended several fine colleges in the East. VMI and Princeton were two of the learning institutions that invited him to leave after a few months because he had a reputation as a playboy. He finally finished his higher education at Lawrenceville, Virginia as a civil engineer and promptly got a job flying airmail. Those were pretty hairy days of aviation – no radios, no navigation assists, no instruments – just a lot of guts. In later years when I started flying we would compare many methods used then and now. I do not remember my first flight because I was only four months old. It was August, 1930 and mother had me on her lap in a wicker laundry basket wrapped in blankets in the back seat of an open cockpit Waco 10 flying from Duluth to Wausau, Wisconsin where he was based.

A few months later he left the U.S. Mail and purchased a couple of Lockeed Vegas and installed them on floats. This allowed him to get a mail contract between Duluth and Fort William on the north shore of Lake Superior and many towns and villages on the south shore of the lake. Then one of his pilots had to land near Split Rock Lighthouse on Lake Superior due to bad weather. He did not properly tie up the aircraft and it sank before morning. Meanwhile the stock market had completely crashed and his father was broke. This was a real come down, His father (Dr. William H. Magie) had removed John D. Rockerfeller's appendix in a rail car in the Duluth harbor, sent a bill for $50.00 and got a check for $5,000.00. Dr. Magie had also loaned some money to Will and Charley Mayo to start their famous hospital in Rochester, Minnesota. My father and mother, myself and my brand new sister Sally moved into my grandfather's house on Superior Street. That's where my name "Pat," came in – as there were three "Bills" in the house and Bill #3 did not cut it, so I became "Pat", a good name for a Irish lad.

Shortly later my grandfather passed away which put us on the move again. I do not remember any of this, but we spent some time in Schroeder and later on the North shore of Lake Superior. Then my father got hired as a foreman at a CCC camp in Grand Marais, Minnesota.

CHAPTER 3

MOVING ON

My mother's father was a timber cruiser at that time who did a lot of walking through the woods of NE Minnesota picking out marketable trees to be harvested by the logging companies. My very first memory comes from 1933 when I was just barely over three years old. My father and my Grandfather McNally were standing opposite each other pumping a speeder- handcar on the railroad tracks heading for my grandfather's cabin on Flour Lake north of the Gunflint Trail. My mother and Grandmother were sitting on a log bench holding my one year old sister Sally while I was just taking everything in.

Surprisingly a timber wolf came out of the woods and started running down the track right behind us. A speeder car is not very speedy – all dependent on how fast you were pumping – maybe 5 or 6 miles per hour. This wolf stayed about 25 feet behind and just loped along for about 3 miles. This was the first wolf I had ever seen, but found out that they can be a very curious animal. Many times since then I have crossed a frozen lake to find my snow shoe tracks from a couple of days earlier to find where a wolf had approached the tracks at a 90 degree angle. Sometimes he would turn left, walk a couple hundred yards to the left, then go back to the right and decides he cannot get around the tracks in either direction. This might lead to going back where he came from, or take a running leap to jump over the tracks and proceed on his way. Occasionally he will simply step into the track and keep walking as this is easier than walking in deep snow. There will be more on wolves later on. To this day I think that a pack of wolves howling at night is a wonderful sound that few people get to hear. Later that night we had a great meal of walleyed pike before going to bed. I was in a small sleeping bag on a cot with a window right over my head. During the night my grandfather heard the screen being ripped open and when he looked at the window he saw a bear climbing in. He rolled out of bed, grabbed his 30-30 Winchester while thinking to himself "if I shoot the bear it is going to fall right on Pat and if I don't shoot him he will step on Pat" KaaBom! The impact of the bullet did push the dead bear back out of the window. This was to be my first, but not the last of my many encounters with bears.

In early 1934 we lived on Grand Marais Hill over looking Lake Superior. We had a brown and white springer spaniel named "Tippy" who started barking furiously one day. My mother took me out on the back porch to show me a large bull moose standing about 100 feet from us. I was four then and can remember that vividly. I have seen many thousands of moose since then – and it is still my favorite red meat to eat. Later in 1934 we moved to Isabella which was a small logging village about 30 miles west of Grand Marias and a small CCC camp there. I remember one Sunday morning I was splitting firewood. I also split my left foot between toes 2 and 3 about two inches into my foot. My very bloody and painful foot was all that kept me from a severe spanking. Axes were hard to find around the house after that. 1935 also saw a new sister Joanie. The three of us already here were born in St. Mary's Hospital in Duluth where my grandfather Magie had worked for many years and where my mother had taken nurses training. We were in Isabella at the time and my parents started driving down the north shore for Duluth, but only got to Two Harbors, Minnesota before Mickey arrived.

Late 1935 saw another transfer to Camp 711 (CCC) on the Echo Trail and the Portage River about 30 miles NW of Ely, Minnesota on a narrow one lane road so that when you met another vehicle one of the vehicles had to back up to a wide spot where you could pass. We moved into a 2 story log cabin on the NE corner of Big Lake and about 25 miles from Ely and the only place on the lake at that time. No electricity, no running water. Water came from the lake in pails through the ice during winter, a wood range for cooking, a sauna (steam bath) for bathing or a large tub on the kitchen floor, oil stove for heat, a telephone on the wall in a wood case with a crank handle (2 longs, 2 shorts was our ring), oil and kerosene lamps and a outhouse. I had another sister added while in Grand Marais and she was one year old now – Katherine (Mickey). She had more happenings. In the spring the ice went out of the little creek passing the house on its way to the lake and Mickey fell in and got swept downstream very until she got hung up under a bridge. I yelled for my mother and she ran out, dived in under the bridge and came up with Mickey. It was a cool day – about 30 degrees and lots of snow on the ground. Later that winter she was almost two and was running around the living room slipped and fell against the oil stove putting a three inch gash in her cheek. Luckily mother had completed nursing school just before marriage. It was 20 below and a blizzard and 25 miles to town on a one lane road. No way – so she patched up Mickey.

1936 saw the family in the same cabin and my mother was starting to teach Sally and I how to read and write. We were way too far away from any school. My father killed any moose or deer that wandered thru our yard and I helped him net fish at night. We ate pretty good for the days of the depression and everyone picked a lot of blueberries. My father would occasionally bring home a bag of flour or fruit that he would trade with the camp cook for fish or venison. My mother had accumulated a few apples one day and baked a pie. It was a hot day, so she put the finished pie on the counter and left the back door open to cool down the kitchen after baking on the wood range. Not long after there was a lot of yelling, screaming and swearing coming out of the kitchen. When I got back there she was chasing a bear around the kitchen beating him with a broom because he had eaten the cooling pie – he did escape out the door, but we had no dessert that night. I also saw my first seaplane that summer in 1936. It was a very dry summer with many forest fires. That was another duty of the CCC's and my father was gone a lot. He came home one day after being gone for almost three weeks and went out to the sauna to clean up. While he was doing that Bill Leithold landed on the lake in a Curtis Robin on floats. My mother ran down to the beach to help him ashore and was not happy when Bill said he had come to pick up Dad to take him to another fire on Lac La Croix. Mother did stall them long enough to feed them some sandwiches and coffee. We watched them take – off, swing north to the fire and it was about ten days before he got back again. He had bought me a $29.00 Iver Johnson .22 caliber rifle at Montgomery Wards so that I could shoot rabbits and partridge for dinner. I also did a lot of walking along the shoreline catching fish. It was a busy life – hauling in water and firewood, hunting, fishing and some schooling every day. We did not have a car, but one of the other foremen, John Cann, had a Packard and once in a while the two families would make a trip to Ely to shop on Saturdays. I have to say that single shot .22 really made me a good shot because I had to hit the target in the head so no meat was wasted.

1937 saw another transfer to a camp on Side Lake, a little north of Chisholm, Minnesota. Another log cabin, but we got electricity, running water and a one room school house. My father bought a Packard automobile, so we could go to the grocery store, doctor or whatever. Late in the summer of 1937 my father took me in the car and we rode to Hibbing, Minnesota. Here I got my first airplane ride. that I can remember. An old buddy of his from the airmail days was in Hibbing for a day of barnstorming in a Ford Trimoter. I spent the whole afternoon in a wicker seat right behind the co-pilot's seat. My father spent the afternoon in the right front while he and his buddy swapped stories of "the good old days". I think it was 20 minutes or so for $6.00 or $7.00 and I got to see quite a few take-off and landings. Very nice, but noisy. I also remember my father spending quite a bit of time listening to a three foot high wood encased radio trying to keep track of Amelia Earhart's last flight attempting to fly around the world. He had met her years before somewhere and had a pilot's interest in her trip and disappearance.

My sister Sally and I were in school and sister Mickey was just about ready to start, so 1938 saw a move into Hibbing. We first had an apartment called Caruther's right in town. Electricity, running water, flush toilets and a school two blocks away on one side and a hospital two blocks away on the other side. My dad was home every night now, so my mother started working night shift at the Hibbing General Hospital 11:00 p.m. to 7:00 a.m. and that brought some more money in to make up for not being able to shoot a moose. No bears in the kitchen either. I also get my first shotgun – a Winchester Model 24 double barreled 20 gauge for duck hunting. I was getting to be a pretty good shot by then. All I heard was "hit them in the head – don't waste the meat". This was to be to my advantage several years later when I enlisted in the Marine Corps.

1939 saw another move to the west side of Hibbing -3109 Second Avenue West – into a cedar house. It was built by a logger by the name of McCusick which was built of vertical cedar logs with the bark still on. It had four bedrooms, 2 baths, a garage and a large hedge around the front half of the lot. Cobb Cook School was about two blocks away and myself, Sally and Mickey were quickly enrolled and the Springer Spaniel "Tippy" would usually walk us to school. Joe Beretto, a professional hockey player lived in the next house on the west side and Glade Lenz who owned a drug store downtown on the east side.

Four years later I would work for him. I was a soda jerk, shelf stocker and offer after school and weekends. Many friendships were made at the Cobb Cook School that would last for many years. The last part of 1939 brought the sounds of war to much of Europe. September 1, 1939 Hitler's German troops swept into Poland and swiftly took over the country. This brought on a declaration of war on Germany from Britain and France and the Second World War was off and running. This was quickly followed by German attack on Denmark, Norway and then Belgium and Holland. They quickly caved in.

CHAPTER 4

A NEW DECADE

By the beginning of 1940 the depression was over and jobs were becoming more plentiful, but the noise of cannons and bombs throughout Western Europe proved to be a even more serious problem.

During June of 1940 German troops marched into Paris and British soldiers and airmen sent to aid the French were rapidly pushed back westerly to the English Channel. Here at Dunkirk they were looking at certain capture and annihilation, but the British Navy and hundreds of privately owned English boats pitched in and ferried thousands of troops with gear back to British shores so that they would be available to fight again. Now Hitler had control of Western Europe except for Switzerland, Spain and Sweden. Hitler had poised his troops along the French coast in preparation to physically invade England, but then decided they should first eliminate the air power of England. Herman Goering said that his airforce could accomplish this in a few weeks. This started the aerial "Battle of Britain" with many day light raids on English airfields and military installations as well as the civilians of London. This put a lot of pressure on the highly outnumbered Spitfire and Hurricane fighter pilots who somehow held on until Mid-September when the German raids stood down except for their night bombings of London.

President Franklin D. Roosevelt saw trouble coming, but as a neutral nation could not sell arms and war supplies to the British. Instead he worked out a Lend Lease Act that allowed the U.S. to lend 50 Navy destroyers to England in exchange for military leases from Britain to build U.S. bases. Later the Lend Lease Act was put to use to provide aircraft to Russia to be used in their defense from Germany.

Meanwhile during the late 1930's the Japanese were starting a expansion in the Pacific and signed a mutual defense pact with Germany and Italy. They all thought that the U.S. would stay neutral and not get involved in a two front war with Axis partners. China was invaded and British Malaysia picked out for takeover as well as Burma. When Japan took over Northern Indochina, President FDR then shut off the sale of scrap metal and aviation fuel to Japan.

When in July 1941 Japan stationed troops in Southern Indochina, Roosevelt froze all Japanese assets in the U.S. and shut down all shipments of oil to Japan. Nobody in the U.S. wanted to get involved in a world war and simply buried their heads in the sand so that we became isolationists.

This all changed just after 0800 on Sunday morning, December 7, 1941 when scores of Japanese aircraft attacked Pearl Harbor on the island of Oahu, Hawaii and destroyed a large piece of the Pacific fleet and killing over 2,000 Americans. Heads came out of the sand and Monday December 8th saw thousands of Americans standing in line at military recruiting stations to "join Up".

About 1:30 p.m. December 7th I was in bed with a cold at the house at 3109 Second Avenue West playing "pick up sticks" with my sister Sally when my mother came running into the room saying the Japanese have just bombed Pearl Harbor. That really did not mean too much to me as I did not even know where Pearl Harbor was. But it certainly was on the radio on every station and EXTRA issues of the newspapers were out by late afternoon in many places. Of course then there was no TV, smart phones or "breaking news" with reporters there while it happened – just radio and newspapers.

It did not take very long for things to change because of the war. Soon after the declarations of war came gasoline rationing, speed limit reduced to 35 mph to save fuel and tires, scrap metal drives to provide materials for manufacturing the needed articles of war, blackouts along the eastern coast especially. The Coast Guard began patrols along the beaches and shoreline looking for saboteurs dropped off by German submarines and even "Victory Gardens". The city of Hibbing opened up many large plots of land to allow residents to grow produce needed by the families. We were a family of six and got a pretty large garden area two blocks from our house. Every day after school we would spend a couple hours growing potatoes, carrots, lettuce, onions, radishes, cabbages and other vegetables for our use. I remember doing corn, but we did have some trouble with that. This all started the summer of 1942 and I was 12 years old then, Sally was 10, Mickey 8 years and Joanie was 6. The garden took up a lot of our time and did convince me that I did not want to grow up to be a farmer. All of this farming was done with a pick, shovel, hoe and rake — no tractors, combines or other mechanical assistance. Dad was a foreman in the Hull-Rust Iron Mine just north of Hibbing at that time and was working much overtime mining the ore that was needed in the steel plants and factories that were making the machines of war – tanks, trucks, ships, aircraft, rifles, cannons, bayonets, ammunition, bombs for pilots and even hand grenades. FDR had promised in December 1941 that we would produce 50,000 aircraft per year and about 1943 it actually happened. "Rosie the Riveter" had to leave the house and kids and pitch in, but she might have thought it was a salvation being in the outside world and getting paid for it.

Even though Dad was working 50 to 60 hours a week, he still got out hunting for deer and ducks for food. I had started duck hunting at 8 years old with my 20 gauge shotgun and got to go along with him on those excursions which were more for food than fun. It was not too serious of a deal if we happened to shoot over our limit. There was the occasional trip to Squaw Lake for some exceptional duck hunting.

Late in December, 1941 the Japanese invaded the Philippine Islands and there were savage battles until April 9, 1942 when 78,000 Americans and Filipino troops surrendered and started the Bataan death march to their prison at Camp O'Donnel where 16,000 would die of malnutrition, malaria and bayonets.

Meanwhile Wake Island and Tarawa were taken by the Japanese.

CHAPTER 5

MAKING ICE

April 18, 1942, a desperate air raid led by Jimmy Doolittle was made on Tokyo and Yokohama by 16 B – 25 Bombers from the aircraft carrier "Hornet". They did very little damage, but this was primarily done to give hope to Americans. A lot of the aircraft were lost and several of the aircrews were captured and beheaded. Many Chinese who tried to assist the crews that crashed landed in China were also murdered. June 2, 1942 the islands of Kiska and Attu in the Aleutians were invaded and taken while the U.S. Military installations at Dutch Harbor Alaska were bombed and the U.S. Continent was actually attacked. This turned out to be mainly a diversion for a planned invasion of Midway on June 4, 1942.

Luckily the U.S had realized that Midway was going to be attacked and sent a naval force to intercede, got very lucky and sank four Japanese aircraft carriers causing the invading fleet to retreat. This was the first major win for the U.S. and slowed the occupation of the Pacific. Two months later the 1st Marine Division invaded Guadalcanal in the Solomen Islands on August 7th – the first campaign changing the U.S. to the roll of the aggressor – and captured a Japanese airfield just before it got operating fully. Use of this airfield would definitely have exposed the shipping of war materials from the U.S. to Australia and New Zealand. It took a little over five months of bitter fighting to gain absolute control of the Solomen

Islands, but finally the Marines were withdrawn for R&R – a very ill and tired bunch – who now had to rest and prepare for their next invasion.

Back in America people were getting used to more wartime activities – scrap drives, bond drives and gold star banners starting to show up in the windows of some houses that signified a member of the family being killed on duty. I was now 12 years old and started seventh grade that fall of 1942. This was the last year of my life without working for some kind of job.

1943 saw my father pulling some strings with Frank Knox who was Secretary of the Navy (a college buddy) and entering the U. S. Marine Corps in spite of his age and family. At that time no one over 38 years old and no more than 2 children was supposed to enter the military. Several years later, he pulled some more strings with Frank Knox to get me in the USMC when I could not pass my eye exam. Dad went to Parris Island, South Carolina for the engineers. Mother was still working as a nurse and received part of dads Dad's paycheck from the USMC. The car was sold, busses used a lot – and a blue star was put in the window.

Late in June of 1943 my mother got a call from a friend wondering if I would be interested in going to work for John Nelson at his fishing resort on Crane Lake, Minnesota for the summer. With my fishing partner away in the USMC, life was rather boring with just the family " Victory Garden" to tend daily. It did not take to long to find out that I much preferred fishing to farming.

A day later I packed up one of Dad's Duluth packsacks and caught a bus from Hibbing to Virginia, then on to Orr, Minnesota and grabbed a ride with the mailman to John Nelson's Lodge. I felt at home right away being on the water and dock plus hauling firewood and ice to the guest's cabins. Usually the last job daily was cleaning out the boats. Then I would seek out a 16 foot canoe for a evening paddle around the bay. A canoe was a pretty common form of transportation at this time. Amazing how fast the summer went and I soon found my way back to Hibbing, school and the "Victory Garden". Our next door neighbor was Glade Lenz and he owned a drug store downtown and I soon found a afternoon and weekend job as a soda – jerk and shelf stocker. This certainly eased up on the farming.

During the winter I heard of a job at Canadian Border Lodge on Moose Lake out of Ely, Minnesota. The big attraction was that they would teach me how to drive while doing my other chores – applied and reported to work June 1, 1944. The lodge had over a dozen cabins scattered along both sides of a bay with a narrow and bumpy road that was traversed by a 1928 GMC flatbed truck that rarely came out of first gear or went over 3 or 4 miles per hour. It also had a log chained on up front rather than a bumper. A stop merely necessitated an abrupt turn into a tree when you need to stop quickly.

Firewood, chunks of ice and coleman fuel were distributed daily to each cabin. We also had a small water dam in a creek used to house many dozens of minnows to be used by our guest fishermen. I would service this chore every other night with a 16 foot wooden Thompson boat sawed off to 12 feet and powered by a 16 hp Evinrude Light Twin outboard motor. This would make about 20 mph and carry four or five 55 gallon barrels of water with 30 to 40 dozen minnows that would be trucked over to the holding dam. This would take me down Moose Lake, New Found Lake to Sucker Lake to Prairie Portage in the dark, purchase the minnows from Leo Chosa and his daughter who had a ½ mile truck portage between the Moose Lake Chain and 28 mile long Basswood Lake. They would haul quite a few people and their gear across a short road, sell minnows, outboard fuel and even some unlicensed beers.

There was a fair sized water fall between the two bodies of water and a Canadian Customs Officer on the other side of the river. This boat trip was usually done in the dark except for the longest summer days. I did kill my first bear during August of 1944 because we had one prowling around the camp at night and scaring some of the guests. In fact I actually bumped into him while coming out of the bunk house door one night in the dark. Several of the camp guests were talking about leaving and going home because of this night prowler, so I went to our garbage dump that night with my .35 caliber Remington and solved that problem. I have probably killed 20 bear in my lifetime, but never just to hunt one, but only to solve a problem chasing off tourists or damaging equipment. My first canoe I owned a year or so later was a really nice 16 footer canvas covered Canadian White. I worked hard to save up enough money to buy that and one night a bear ripped all the canvas off of the canoe. This was a fairly common happening if the canoe was left laying on the ground upside down. I suppose they thought it was a log and they could tear it open to get at any critters or insects inside. Later on in Alaska I had a couple of brown bears (Grizzlies) take too much interest in my being the main entrée For dinner that night. The bear I shot in the garbage dump when I was 14 was the only bear that I ever skinned out to make a rug. This is a messy and smelly job that I swore I would never do again. I did take the carcass down to the icehouse on the back of the truck, put a gunny sack over it's head and hung it from a log rafter. A bear that is skinned out looks very much like a naked human, so I put a pair of chopper mitts on his front paws and a pair of rubber overshoes on his two back feet. The next morning at 6:30 I showed up in the crew dining room and told all the girls on the Kitchen and dining staff that our caretaker – Old Elmer — hung himself in the icehouse the night before. Everyone ran out of there and down to the icehouse where a lot of screaming started. No one went close enough to make an exact identification and were very upset when "Old Elmer" showed up later in the day. I did not eat too well for a couple of days.

People today do not think of ice houses – today's hotels can make several tons of ice each day. Back in the 1940's just after the lakes froze up people would take a three foot long, 1"x12" piece of lumber and attach a six or eight foot 2"x4" piece of lumber to it and put on a pair of ice skates. As soon as there was enough ice to hold them, they would skate the snow off a patch of ice maybe 100' by 200' long and keep the snow off to allow the ice to freeze two feet or so thick. Usually during the Christmas holiday everyone that worked for the lodges would donate a couple of days to "make ice". First would be a few holes cut in the ice with a large ice chisel, then a five foot ice saw would be inserted and then saw in straight lines. Ideally the ice would be cut into 30"x30" x 24" blocks which would weigh about 100 pounds each. These would float loose when separated, then pushed or pulled over to the icehouse which was always built as close to the lakeshore as possible. Several 2"x12" x20' planks would be put in place and watered down to make ice ramps leading into the structure. The blocks would usually be winched up by a hand winch with a long rope and a set of ice tongs. Each lodge operator would start calling on all of the local sawmills during late summer making arrangements for all the sawdust they could get. Each layer of ice blocks would usually have six to eight inches of sawdust surrounding it. The walls and roof of the house would normally be two layers thick of sawdust and moss which would keep ice right up to the annual event of "making ice". Later on the ice chisels and saws were replaced with ice augers and chain saws with 24 inch blades. But it was always a two or three day annual party (depending on the size of the icehouse) with lots of venison stew and drinking choices. These last choices were always necessary because it always was a wet job with the temperatures normally below zero. Winter also meant school and catching up on the war.

1942 saw the Marines taking Guadalcanal in August and the Army invading North Africa in November to assist General Montgomery hold off Rommel. 1943 saw the Marines start moving across the Pacific invading Tarawa, New Guinea, then followed by Guam, Saipan, Iwo Jima, Okinawa and the Philippines while the Army took over North Africa and Sicily, across the channel to Italy. A long hard battle up the length of Italy brought about the European invasion at Normandy France on June 6, 1944, D Day. A few months of bitter fighting found Germany and Italy surrendering to the Allies in the spring of 1945. Japan follows suit during September of 1945 and signed the Peace Treaty aboard the battleship Missouri. The winter passed quickly and I was working at the drug store again. I think it was during the fall of 1944 that one of the neighborhood brothers, Chuck Evenson who lived two doors down from our house came into Lenz's drug store with a young woman. They sat down at the ice cream counter and ordered milkshakes. As I put together the order I could hear Chuck telling the woman how he saw her fiancé shot down in flames in a Pacific battle a few months earlier. They left with Chuck leading her out the door crying her heart out and two untouched milk shakes on the counter.

CHAPTER 6

GROWING UP

1946 saw me back guiding day fishermen at Canadian Border Lodge at Moose Lake out of Ely. Occasionally we would tow a couple of canoes up the whole Moose Lake chain – Newfound, Sucker and Birch Lakes and make five portages into Knife Lake for some bass fishing and camping out. I really enjoyed this and got to know Dorothy Moulter (known as the Root Beer lady). She was a nurse from Chicago who came up to take care of Bill Bergland who was getting too old to take care of himself. She stayed with him several years on an island on the western end of Knife Lake until he passed away and left the property to her. This was her year around home and was 25 miles plus 5 portages from the nearest road or telephone. She would get quite a few visitors during the summer months from canoe party traffic but only wolves and deer during the winter months and its -40 degrees below weather. She did help the summer pass by with her medical knowledge. There were several magazine articles in such as Saturday Evening Post, Woman's Day and even Time Magazine once – especially during the 60's and 70's when the USFS was trying to get her removed from the Boundary Waters Area (BWAC). This Wilderness Act was signed by Harry Truman in December, 1948 establishing a no flying area over a large portion of NE Minnesota below 4,000 feet above sea level (MSL). This law took effect in June 1, 1953 and Ely Minnesota was flooded by U.S. Marshals who arrested many pilots who were flying for the commercial seaplane operators on Shagawa Lake in Ely. There will be much more on this as I moved into aviation three years later.

In the summer of 1947 I worked for the USFS (United States Forest Service) over on the Gunflint Trail east of Ely. Probably the most exciting thing of this summer was sitting at the table next to Gypsy Rose Lee, then the world wide famous stripper – at a restaurant on the North Shore of Lake Superior. The next year 1948 I returned to guiding and worked for Martin Skala who operated a fly-in fishing lodge on Lac La Croix, right on the Canadian border. I got to do a couple of 7 day canoe trips around the Quetico Park that summer. This was a lot more interesting than just sitting in a boat dragging a lure around all day. The following summer I established myself as a free-lance canoe guide. I handled trips for Wilderness Outfitters, Borders Lake Outfitters and Bill Rom's Canoe Country Outfitters. I liked that Bill Rom let you pack your own food so that I could specialize in some meals and ended up doing his trips exclusively. That winter of 1949 I assisted Bill by going all over the country selling our trips at sport shows in Chicago, Milwaukee, Minneapolis, Omaha and Des Moines. This brought a lot of guided canoe trips for me and I really utilized this to get into different lakes that I had not seen before and learned many good fishing holes.

I had graduated from high school in May of 1948, I enrolled in Junior College that fall after hunting season ended. Later I was offered a job driving a 20 ton Euclid truck hauling iron ore out of the open pit mines that are numerous in Northern Minnesota, the Iron Range. I worked the 11:00 p.m. to 7 a.m. shift, showed up at school at 8:00 a.m. and got to work again at 11:00 p.m. You would park the truck under a large shovel and it would take 8 to 10 buckets of ore to top you off and you would start your haul up 1,000 feet of altitude to the top from the edge of the dump. There were no lights, so there would be a "dump man" with a flashlight signaling you to back up, stop and dump your 20 tons of ore.

One night it was almost 2:00 a.m., black as can be, blowing 20 mph, snowing very hard. The dump man probably had his head buried in his parka and kept waving his flashlight until my truck backed right off the edge starting down 300 feet. The minute I felt the rear wheels start to go over the edge I just launched out the door and saw the lights go end for end the first few feet. This usually happened to someone almost every month during the winter months, but I got an immediate 5 day pink slip – a 5 day vacation without pay. One day the following winter I finished the shift and I turned my truck in at the shop and told them the brakes were pretty soft and should be checked. The next night I came to work and found my truck idling in the yard. These trucks seldom got shut down during the winter unless they were in the shop for maintenance. I just threw my lunch bucket in and drove over to the shovel for the first load of the night. Soon after the shovel operator blinked a light and gave a blast of his horn telling me I was loaded. This was at the time one of the deepest open pit iron mines in the world with a steep narrow road carved out of the wall of the pit. I got about a third of the way up and the transmission jumped out of gear. It was a straight shift gear and I think it had 6 speeds forward.

Naturally I hit the brakes and got no response. I then yanked on the Johnson bar (parking brake), still nothing and I am starting to seriously roll backward — time to bail out! Cranked the wheel hard right so the vehicle would hit the steep bank on the right instead of another 300 foot drop to the left and I left the rig. I know there was another truck coming up with a load. My rig rolled just enough to pick up speed, hit the bank and rolled on its side spilling the load. Another 5 day pink slip – although I insisted it was the fault of the shop. I did lose my interest in a truck driving career.

The summer of 1950 started off with a couple of great trips early in the season. The first one was 2 couples for 10 days that started over the Memorial Day weekend. We went around the Hunters Island route which is really enjoyable with a ten day trip – great fishing, great scenery and very comfortable with the ten days to do it. This was followed by another ten day trip to McIntyre and Kashapiwi Lake for some serious lake trout fishing with three fellows from Nebraska. I next went for seven days on theU.S. side to Thomas and Kekekabic for more trout fishing. When I returned to town I found out that the world had returned to one of its favorite pastimes — WAR. At 4:30a.m. on June 25th North Korea had invaded South Korea and a understaffed U.S. Army of occupation. Japan had taken over Korea years before and U.S. and the Soviets had taken the country back just before the Japanese signed the peace treaty in September, 1945. The Soviets took over North Korea and the U.S. supplied the occupation of South Korea. This lasted until late June of 1950 when a North Korean force armed by the Russians tried to take over South Korea.

I realized that this would probably not affect my life in the very near future, but it probably would in the upcoming months, meanwhile I was booked up right to fall. I went over it with Bill Rom and settled it up that if anything official looking came from the draft board to send a plane to pick me up so I could enlist in the Marine Corps — where my dad served in WWII — before I was drafted into the Army. The law established the no fly — wilderness area had passed, but was not in effect yet, so there were quite a few seaplanes based in Ely. One rainy morning in late August I camped on the south end of Kashapiwi Lake serving breakfast when I heard an airplane coming from the south. A couple of minutes later one of Elwyn West's cabin Waco's showed up in the rain, but continued northward and gave me my breath back. A few weeks later – the last weekend of September – four of us were enrolled back in Jr. College and were duck hunting at one of our favorite spots. It came up by the campfire that night that we all thought college was pretty boring. It was mentioned that maybe entering the Marine Corps would give us more shooting, free ammo and no hunting license, so a week later a friend "Shaver Strand" and I enlisted in the Marine Corps. Our parents drove us down to Minneapolis where my father was very well acquainted with the two Recruiting Sergeants there on recruiting duty. The enlistment was handled very quickly, but I did not pass my eye exam. My father told one of the sergeants to call Frank Knox, the Secretary of the Navy, and he would talk to him. The sergeant sort of gasped that "sergeants do not call the Secretary of the Navy", but my dad just said to tell him that Bill Magie from Minnesota wants to talk to him. A few minutes later my dad was handed the phone and he told Frank Knox that "my kid wants to join the Corps and they say his eyes are too bad, but he can hit a running deer in the head every shot". Then minutes later Shaver Strand and I were at attention with our right hands up and now in the U.S. Marine Corps. Our parents then took us to dinner at Charlie's, one of Minneapolis's better restaurants before dropping us at the train depot for a 3 day trip to San Diego, CA and boot camp.

CHAPTER 7

USMC

We arrived in San Diego about 9:30 p.m. three nights later. Our orders said to report to the USMC Recruit Depot by no later than midnight, so we decided to go get a couple of drinks. Neither one of us were 21 years old yet, but when we showed our orders to report to the Marine Base we were bought a drink by almost everyone. This was a mistake. When we did show up at the gate, we had to do a couple of hours of paperwork, a preliminary issue of clothing, sheets, blankets, etc. and finally got to bed – the rack they called it. And very shortly thereafter at 5:00 a.m. the bugle sounded reveille and even though we proclaimed that we needed more rest what the Marine Corps wanted came first. It was probably one of the longest days of my life – hung over and we learned there was very little walking in the Marine Corps – you ran everywhere! We also started to get broke in for saluting, how to assemble in formation and most important you received your rifle. You knew its serial number and lived with it. You were taught that it was a working tool and how to care for it. It was also used as a instrument of torture by our Drill Instructor – D.I.- who would often make us run a mile with the M1 held high over your head or stand at attention with the weapon held up straight over your head until you started sticking your stomach out to ease the pain – then the D.I. would sink his fist into your stomach — and God help you if you dropped your rifle on the deck! You learned how to disassemble and reassemble the weapon in the dark or out in the open in a pounding rain. The rifle was loaded with a 8 round clip that was ejected after the 8ᵗʰ shot and the breech remained open for a quick reload. The M1 Garand semi-automatic replaced the 1903 Springfield bolt action, with 5 shots that used to be the standard. This was a surprise to the enemy – especially the Japanese in the early Pacific operations of WWII. They would count off five shots incoming and then rise up to attack only to find 3 more shots coming immediately. The Garand M1 quickly proved to be a pretty trouble free weapon which served well and it was really pushed on to us to take care of it. Finally that long, long, long first day came to an end at 10:00 p.m. with the bugle blowing

"TAPS". After that everyone pretty well fell into a pattern – up at 0500, a short run, calisthenics and then breakfast, quite often S.O.S. – creamed hamburger on toast. Then again there would be a day of marching, running, exercises, class work and weapon familiarization that would finally end up with bugle and "TAPS" again. It was a war time schedule so it was like that 7 days per week. Boot camp was condensed to 10 weeks to speed up delivery of troops to Korea sooner. We would have a 10 day leave after boot camp, then 12 weeks of combat training that ended up in a boat ride to work in Korea. We had timed our enlistment so that we would be home for Christmas – we thought.

One of the Marine Corps practices was to quickly train the troops to do what they were told to do and not to hesitate when told to take out that machine gun on the side of the hill. The Corps wanted a "Yessir, we'll get them" and go do it without thinking of getting hurt. It seemed to work. You and your rifle would clamp down your steel helmet and do what had to be done. The most important rule was to not let down your buddy.

After four weeks of the preliminary training, we were trucked up North of San Diego to Camp Mathews for rifle range work. Now we were working with live ammunition in our rifles, got to fire some light 30 caliber machine guns and even had to crawl across a stretch under a live fire machine gun that was anchored firing a stream of fire 36 inches above ground. This evidently was to get you used to being shot at while advancing. Naturally there was a lot of talk about what everyone was going to do if they ran into a rattlesnake eye to eye as they crossed this stretch under live fire. We were also introduced to hand grenades which I really took to. One busy week at Camp Mathews saw our return to San Diego.

By now we were starting to draw Guard Duty at night – usually 2 hour stretches which came out of our sleep time. I liked the roof top duty because the Marine Corps base bordered the San Diego International Airport and a large aircraft manufacturer, Convair, was located there and they were building the B-36 Bomber. This was a six engine piston powered aircraft that was first designed in 1941, but did not fly until just after WWII ended. It hung around in several variants – including eight engines at one time – and was still being built because it could take off in the U.S., fly to Europe, drop a 72,000 pound load of bombs and return to the U.S. without refueling. It was called the "Peacemaker". It never did become a major weapon, but I always was happy to see it right across the field as the worlds largest aircraft.

Our 10 weeks in boot camp went by very quickly and we were given one stripe to sew on our sleeves with a 10 day leave to go home as a PFC. We thought we had it all planned that we both would go back to Minnesota together, but we found out that the military does not think as we do all of the time. We got our new orders and Shaver Strand was given leave over Christmas, then was ordered to report to electronic school in San Francisco on his return. My orders gave me 10 days leave over New Year's and then report back to Camp Pendelton for combat training. My folks got a round trip ticket for me with the last connection out of Minneapolis on North Central Airlines. I arrived in Minneapolis just after dark on New Years Eve. My flight with North Central was in a Lockeed 10 an hour later to Hibbing, but I was the only passenger and the weather was not very good. I overheard the crew talking whether they would fly the trip or scratch it. They held on right to the departure time to see if anyone else showed up and then said "what the heck, lets go so this guy gets home for New Years". So I landed in Hibbing at 10:00 p.m. and was picked up by my family. The return was Minneapolis, then on a DC-3 to Denver and San Diego with a bus connection to Camp Pendleton. Then I was assigned to Tent Camp II and picked up my locker box, seabag, helmet and rifle and settled down to two months of graduate work. Most of this was the use of BAR, the bayonet, light machine guns – both 30 caliber and 50 caliber, 61m.m. motors, flame throwers and working with tanks and air support. Days were fast and busy, but we did get a two hour break for Church on Sunday morning. We did go offshore in LST's and did a couple of amphibious landings on the beach. We each shot several hundred rounds from our own rifles, some more in the .45 Thompson submachine gun and both the M1 and M2 Carbine. I had done a lot of hunting in my short life for deer, ducks, geese and partridge, so I did enjoy the shooting. The 15th of March, 1951 came up and we, were trucked down to the San Diego docks to board ship for a trip to Korea as the 7th Replacement Draft. We had to spend a couple of hours standing on the dock waiting to board the ship when I heard my name being paged and raised my steel helmet in the air. A woman wearing a Red Crossband on her arm came over to me carrying some paperwork. After showing her my dog tags she informed me that mother was hospitalized in serious condition and might not survive this. She had a 10 day emergency leave for me but needed some papers signed. She also asked if I had any money — which just leaving for Korea I did not. She then gave me $200.00 and more papers to sign. This would all be covered – the airline ticket, a bus ticket to Los Angeles that afternoon and would come out of my paycheck later. After all I was making $21.00 as a PFC per month tax free. I pulled out a set of greens uniform and other stuff I would need from my seabag and packed everything else in my in my foot locker which she said would be at Pendleton with my rifle and helmet when I returned. The lady did give me a ride to the bus depot and very quickly I was on my way.

It was not too long and I was at the LAX Airport only to find it fogged in. I sat there several hours and I was bussed to Burbank which was just outside of the fog. This cost me a ride in a DC-4 with extra seating and put me in a DC-3 which earned us an apple and a cheese sandwich along with an Army blanket when we boarded. Shortly after daylight we were circling Kansas City in a snow storm trying to get in on an instrument approach. Finally we got on the ground and got refueled, then had to go thru a lengthy de-icing system before we could leave again. We finally arrived in Chicago late in the afternoon as the last flight for the day was leaving for Minneapolis with every seat already filled. The agent in charge of the counter looked at my orders for an emergency leave and asked if anyone would give up their seat to a Marine in uniform who needed to get home for an emergency problem. Right away a fellow standing a couple of people in front of me said that he would stay over and catch the first flight in the morning. I tossed him a quick salute and climbed on board for Minneapolis and got there in time for the last flight to Duluth. From the airport there I bummed a ride to downtown Duluth to the Greyhound Bus Depot. I was there only a few minutes and Art Clausio came in and asked if anyone wanted a 70 mile ride to Hibbing. He was the Dodge car dealer in Hibbing who was in Duluth for a late evening meeting.

This was a common practice in those days, Greyhounds last departures were usually 7:30 to 8:00 p.m. and the last arrival at midnight from International Falls so the depot remained open and many Iron Range folks would stop to see if anyone needed a ride. He took me right to my house.

I guess I had never seen a week go by so fast! Very quickly I was on an airplane back to Los Angeles, but my mother was doing well. I caught the bus up to Oceanside and Camp Pendleton where I was assigned to Casual Company. I had been there only a couple of days when we were trucked to San Diego's North Island Naval Air Station to help offload wounded flying in from Korea. When we got there I found out that most of them were from my company of the 7th replacement Draft of March 15th that I did not sail with. They had got hit shortly after they off loaded ships and were moving to the front lines to be spread out between the outfits that needed replacements. One of the fellows I knew pretty well, Mike Tostata, had lost both legs below the knee. Another was a young fellow from Alabama who had taken 2 burp gun rounds in his face and lost part of his jaw. All of these guys were between the age of 18 and 21 years and they gave me the names of several who were KIA. This really brings the realization of war to you.

CHAPTER 8

TOP SECRET MISSION

A couple of days later back in Casual Company at Pendleton I was called into an office and asked if I wanted to be an F.O. (Forward Observer) for the artillery. I thought that sounded interesting calling in fire from Artillery and mortar companies and even getting involved in air cover strikes. The next day I was transferred across the road to Camp Del Mar— the artillery training center. The next few weeks were very busy with a lot of classes and firing 105 mm Howitzers, 155 mm howitzers and both 60 mm and 81 mm mortars. June 15, 1951 we were again trucked down to San Diego Harbor to sail with the 10th replacement draft to Korea, but as artillerymen instead of infantrymen. About 10:00 p.m. I went to bed stacked up in the fourth tier of bunks scheduled for a 4:00 a.m. departure. At 2:00 a.m. a sergeant shook my shoulder and asked my name, then told me to grab my rifle, helmet and seabag and to report on deck. In five minutes I was up there and found 27 more enlisted men standing there equipped as I was. The sergeant led us over to four 6x6 trucks and loaded us in and a chain secured across the backend on each and an armed guard in the right front seat. We drove the rest of the night and a good share of next day with a few pit stops and a quick meal at March Air Force base. It was mid afternoon when we reached our destination and we knew we were in the desert because it was in the mid 90 degrees. We were immediately moved into a barracks and locked in with an armed guard at the door.

No one would answer any of our questions about what was happening, so we took a nap until a guard with a rifle woke us up. Evidently everyone had already eaten, so we were marched into a empty mess hall and given our evening meal with a armed guard observing, then marched back into our lock up for the night. We did figure out it was a Navy base as the food was very good. We went thru seven days of this and kept asking each other if we had done something very wrong. By now if we had not been yanked off the ship, we would have been in Korea. A little after mid day on the seventh day a captain and a gunnery sergeant came in and got our attention. His first words were " I suppose you are wondering what is going on here". He then explained that we all had been going through a FBI security check and we all passed. He and the gunny and the 28 of us were forming a 30 man Marine Detachment that would be working for a group of civilian scientists who are wanting to investigate the use of Atomic Artillery and the fusing of the ammunition. He said we would start doing a lot of firing with 105 mm and 155 mm Howitzers and press on to 8 inch, 12 inch and probably 16 inch cannons. He also stated that we might work several days straight and not fire again for a few days while they tried to straighten some problems out. We were going to move into a separate building where just our crew would be quartered and we could eat at regular mess hours unless we were busy firing.

Two days later we set up four 105mm gun positions, but the civilians decided it was to hot at desert level to be safe with the critical ammunition and we would have to move to a cooler higher elevation. A search of Federal Land in the Panamount Range showed a miner had a mining lease at about 7,000 foot elevation. He quickly lost his lease and moved out leaving a small metal shack with a kitchen/living room, bedroom and a garage for his jeep. We were trucked up there 85 miles on a gravel road in 6x6 trucks again making us covered with dust!

The next day we did the bumpy, dusty ride again and told we had to dig four ammo pits. The day before we tried digging with a pick and shovel and the sun dried dirt was almost like concrete, so I suggested that we cut down some of the numerous Joshua trees scattered all over the area. I grabbed a axe, walked to a tree, wound the axe up and took a mighty swing – and the axe bounced right back. This was a total surprise to a woodsman who had cut down a lot of trees. The trouble was the trunk was like a sponge to retain the little water that fell on them. I had told our gunnery sergeant about this the day before and asked him to bring along a case of hand grenades and a coil of prima cord which is normally used to make fuses for explosives. We would use a pick to make several small holes in the ground and stick a grenade in each one. This would loosen up the dirt so we could dig down a couple of feet. We needed almost four feet, so we then wrapped prima cord around a tree trunk in several loops and lit the fuse which cut the tree trunk right off. Each of these activities needed a short sprint when it happened, but we did get it done that day. We made the 85 mile ride back to the base that night which I hated that with a passion. We were scheduled to our first firing mission the next day with the scientists so we felt a little better about the upcoming ride up the mountain.

In the morning the captain gave us a pep talk about dealing with the civilians and also gave us the news that the FBI wanted six armed guards up there at all times with a radio. I quickly informed him of my guiding days and that I was a pretty good cook. I volunteered to stay up there as camp cook and guard. We had some extra vehicles going up in the morning – two more 6x6's with a work crew, squad tents, six cots, a small propane refrigerator, propane stove, heaters and enough tables and chairs to accommodate the guard detachment. All six of us had our M1 rifles plus several M2 carbines and a jeep with a .30 caliber light machine gun. At all times when there was no firing going on we had to have one armed guard circulating around the compound and one man on the radio making hourly check – ins with the main base. We had 4 hours on and 8 hours off. I would take the 8:00 p.m. to midnight outside and the 8:00 a.m. to noon inside so I could cook. We did not have the trucks and crew coming up from the main base every day, but usually three or four times a week at least. We did not have much storage space, so I would keep sending lists with the downhill trucks. Because of the short storage space, we ate a lot of steak, chicken and roast and I baked quite a few pies. About once a week the Captain and Gunny would stay for the evening meal – usually when it was steak and apple pie.

We were doing pretty well on the shooting and after a couple of months they hauled away our 105's and replaced them with 155mm weapons. We had a lot of wild burros and coyotes around there all the time and way too many rattlesnakes. Being from Northern Minnesota I had never seen a snake other that an occasional garter snake and here we were killing several rattlers a week. The guys from the southern states would usually grab them by the tail and give them a very strong whip snapping motion that would often break their necks – or use a bayonet to chop their heads off. I much preferred to shoot them – especially when coiled. Everyone had figured out how much I hated snakes. One night as I came off the 8:00 p.m. to midnight guard duty I went into the main living area of our shack, talked a bit to the guy on radio watch while I made a ham sandwich and then took my trusty M1 and walked out to the squad tent. We had an extension cord running out to the center pole of the tent with a light bulb there for use at night. Being a half hour past midnight I did not want to wake up the four guys in there and just backed up to my canvas cot, leaned my M1 up against the cot, put my hands out as I sat down and my right hand came down on a coiled snake. I suppose I rose two feet, turned around grabbing my rifle and shot 6 or 7 rounds as fast as I could pull the trigger pointing almost vertically down at the snake. By then I had realized that the other 3 guys were all on the floor yelling "stop". The breech of the rifle was still closed, so I know I did not fire all 8 rounds, but when we turned the light bulb on the snake was totally chopped up – as was my cot, pillow and sleeping bag. I shoved the mess outside the tent, grabbed one of the unoccupied sleeping bags and went to sleep. In the morning when the Captain arrived he was very unhappy saying "how am I going to explain this to the Brass". Later we had a snake shooting that was more dangerous.

One morning when the Captain came up in his jeep he waved me over to the vehicle and told me that I had taken a test when I was at Camp Pendleton and done very well on it. Now I was being offered a chance to attend Officers Training School at Quantico, Virginia. In six months I would come out a Second Lieutenant and would have to extend my enlistment for one year. When I asked him if I could go to Korea then, he said no because of the secret project I could not leave the U.S. for five years. With that rule I told him I was not interested. The duty I had was pretty good for military life. I only went into the main base about once a month to get a haircut – no inspections or parading. We had a jeep with a mounted .30 caliber machine gun that we would chase coyotes with and managed to kill a couple deer (with our rifles) that were promptly cut up and served for meals.

One night the four of us off duty persons plus the one on radio watch were engaged in a poker game. All five of us were sitting at a table when I glanced down and saw a rattler about four feet long sliding under the table between everyone's feet and I yelled "Snake". The fellow sitting next to me on my left side was from East Alton, Illinois and evidently was more afraid of snakes than I was as he jumped up, overturned the table and grabbed a M2 Carbine out of the rack behind me. We usually had a somewhat surprise FBI inspection every few weeks to insure that our personal weapons were always fully loaded.

The M2 usually had a 30 round clip, but we usually loaded them with 25 rounds because they tended to jam with 30. They were also a very light weapon with a definite tendency for the muzzle to climb if you squeezed off more than 3 rounds. He held the trigger down until the clip was empty and of course most of them went through the ceiling – luckily. I will never understand why no one got hit with that many shots fired in such a small area. Naturally our captain was put out. He kept inferring that maybe it was better taking our weapons away. At least I had realized that the danger from the rattler was minimal when stretched out to full length.

We spent almost a year on this project and two things were pretty evident. The peace talks were starting to sound serious and the civilian scientists were sounding pessimistic about atomic artillery. The sidewinder missile was being worked on at the next range over from us and they thought the missile could get further away with the radioactivity. There were quite a few projects working at the Naval Weapons Center, just before we were to shut down the captain called me in and said that I had been a Corporal for almost a year now and if I extended to July 1 I would get my third stripe and become a Buck Sergeant – which was a pretty good rate for the Marine Corps for those days. He also said the duration of the war enlistment I had to spend some time as a Reserve Marine and if I were called back the third stripe would be nice. Other than that I would be out before the end of April. Seeing as fishing season and the guiding season opened in early May, I opted to go back to my previous career – which I really liked. I dropped a note to Bill Rom of Canoe Country Outfitters that I would be available in May and ready to get back into the woods.

CHAPTER 9

BACK TO THE BUSH

April 11, 1952 it became official and the Marine Corps decided they could get along without me somehow. I grabbed the first train back east to Duluth, Minnesota where my parents lived now. Before I had left our mountain camp at China Lake I had managed to divert 6 hand grenades to an off base hideaway and I picked them up. I had mailed them in three packs to my uncle who was only four years older that I and in the Marine Corps at the Air Base in El Toro on the southeast side of L.A. but lived in an apartment in Newport Beach with his new wife. He had joined the USMC in 1946, got out in 1949 and called back in 1950. I sent him the three packages that I picked up when I left Camp Pendleton. I picked up a used Buick Special upon getting back to Minnesota a few days later and went to Ely to prepare for the season. That was one good thing about being in the desert – I could not spend any money on the week -ends and could now afford the car.

My first canoe trip for 1952 started during the second week of May. I was guiding three fellows from Milwaukee, Wisconsin and they wanted to catch lake trout. The fishing season did not open for another few days in Minnesota, so we decided to enter the Canadian side where it was open. The Canadian Customs was not in place yet, but the Ontario Ranger was there and could issue fishing licenses and travel permits. It basically was a wilderness area on both sides of the border so there was not much of an opportunity to do any smuggling. Basswood Lake, one of the boundary lakes between Canada and the U.S. and was 28 miles long. U.S. Customs was located on the main street of Ely and everyone returning with a border crossing slip was supposed to stop at the office in town and check in. I could not help chuckling to myself. Not quite a year earlier I had declined an opportunity to go to Quantico, Virginia to attend the Marine Officers Candidate School (OCS) and become a Lieutenant. When I asked the Captain who made the offer if I could go to Korea as a platoon leader after completion and he said that because of secrecy of the artillery project we were involved in I could not leave the U.S. for 5 years and risk capture. I had said "NO" because a good share of my life was spent in Canada guiding and I wanted to return to that when I was done with my USMC service.

They were scheduled for a 7 day trip so I suggested that they rent a 3 h.p. outboard with 6 two gallon cans of fuel seeing as they were more interested in fishing and this would allow us to head for McIntyre and Sarah Lakes and get some excellent lake trout fishing for a little over four days. In previous years I had caught many lake trout between 15 and 20 pounds and a few over 25 pounds which are a pretty good sized in that area. We had two 17 foot Grumman aluminum canoes with a front and rear seat and three thwarts. One thwart in the center balance point with two shoulder pads each for carrying the canoe over portages plus one each behind the front seat and one in front of the rear seat. Then we would tie one eight foot pole across the front and rear thwarts each, making the two canoes into one unit about 8 feet wide and bolt a outboard motor attachment on the left side of the RH canoe. This made a very stable vessel and we could make a pretty fair distance without too much of a fuel burn. By having 6 two gallon cans we could stash a fuel can every time we ran one dry and not have to carry it all in and then back out. We could separate the two canoes for fishing.

The first day we made almost 30 miles and three portages to camp on the upper end of North Bay of Basswood Lake. The second day we made almost 20 miles and five portages and we set up camp on McIntyre Lake in time to catch a lake trout for dinner. The next days were terrific – sunny skies and fantastic lake trout fishing. At noon on the sixth day we broke camp and started back to North Bay of Basswood Lake again. Our last day saw a portage into Sunday Lake followed by a three mile run down the lake and another portage into Bayley Bay of Basswood Lake. From there it is about another six miles to a short portage of just under 20 rods. This was Prairie Portage on the north side of the waterfall.

There was a ½ mile long truck portage on the south side (U.S.). This was used to travel from Basswood Lake (28 miles long and Sucker Lake) which was part of the U.S./Canadian border water route of canoe traffic going back almost a 100 years that was used by the early voyagers and trappers. The truck portage was operated by a native named Leo Chosa and his daughter. They hauled people and their gear, boats and motors, camping gear and sold minnows and bait. When I was younger I made a lot of night minnow runs there – usually getting 40 to 50 dozen for our guests at the lodge.

When we hit the sand beach on the west side of the portage we quickly lifted out the pack sacks, unhooked the outboard motor from its rack and unlashed the two poles connecting the two canoes to other and made a couple of trips across the portage. From there it was an easy two hour ride to Moose Lake and the road back to Ely.

CHAPTER 10

1955 HUDSON BAY

I was back in College for the past three years after my USMC break. I was a lot more serious about it this time. My first year after graduating from high school ended up in my being asked to leave the College because I was playing cards a lot and my grades showed it. This time my grades have been good and I have been able to work with a lot of the professors to leave a little early in the Spring and start late in the Fall — just have to pass all the tests. I had just finished a short canoe trip in May and was going back for the exams when Bill Rom told me he had a phone call that morning from two fellows in Texas who wanted a tough trip for an 18 year old boy who was starting college that fall and wanted to go out for football. One was the biological father and one was the step father. I told Bill that I was pretty well booked for the summer, but I could change that if they would allow a couple of months to paddle to Hudson Bay. Most of those parties I was booked with were old parties that knew that my life's ambition at that time was to paddle that route. I had read a typewritten story of Alec Puera of Winton, MN who had in 1932 driven to Sioux Lookout, Ontario and then paddled down the Albany River to Fort Albany – a Hudson Bay Company trading post. These posts were scattered all over Northern Canada to trade with and support the local native population. There he and his partner waited for a week and caught the company supply vessel to Moosonee on the south tip of the bay. Moosonee had a railway train once a week. It did all get put together with the would be football player, Jim Sterling, and we left with the beginning of June on our adventure.

I have made the border route from Ely to Lake Superior several times including the nine mile long Grand Portage. If you have to make a second trip to complete the portage it makes a 27 mile walk on Grand Portage. I had planned on a little over two months at least, but it ended up at two and a half months. We had a Grumman 17ft canoe and six #3 Duluth packs of gear and food. One each for us with personal gear, sleeping bags, air mattresses, toilet articles and clothing, another for a tent, equipment and a couple of tarps, camp and cooking gear, plus three food sacks. One of the food sacks was filled with ½ Macaroni and ½ noodles. Another was ½ instant mashed potatoes and assorted dehydrated vegetables. We also had two canned hams, several slabs of bacon and some flour. We were counting on fish for most of our meals. To avoid Grand Portage we took my car over to Lake Superior and up to Nipigon River. We then put the canoe in the water and started north. This was all upstream until we hit the Ogoki River. I had planned on a week to do this stretch, but it turned out to be two weeks because of the current. There was also a lack of portage trails. We literally had to cut our way when we had the portage around a set of rapids. I think it was on the Little Jackfish River one day when we had to portage. I put on one of the Duluth Packs on my back and the canoe over my head and just bulled my way through the bush until the canoe was just hung up in the trees and brush. Then I would crawl out from under it and take the 30 inch bow saw and open the way ahead. I was really looking forward to reaching the Ogoki River and spending a few hundred miles going down to the Albany River. Then it takes another couple of hundred miles to the salt water.

After a few days we hit the Ogoki River and got started downstream. We found out very quickly there were a lot of rapids and no portage trails. I did some shooting of rapids back in Minnesota and the Canadian Quetico Park, but they had well developed and used portage trails – complete with canoe rests where you put the forward end of the canoe up on the rack and get out that from under it for a few minutes. Also the rapids back there were usually pretty short so you could walk down it and size up the route through the rocks and not wreck your canoe, but the rapids here would often run a couple miles. We saw a seaplane overhead on the third day out and again on the second to last day so it would be hard to get help. We had two Hudson Bay company outposts ahead where they had radio contact.

Those two were the only outside contact for over two months. We did see one canoe with a native family on Ogoki Lake about twenty days out. They were across the lake from us so we did not speak. Almost a week later we were making good time down the Ogoki River and it was a beautiful day. Light wind, not a cloud in the sky and probably in the high 60's temperature. We were in a fairly wide and slow section of the river and as we came around a bend a bull moose entered the water on our right side and started to swim across the river. I quickly told my bowman to paddle as fast as he could and come behind the moose on his left side. I told him that when we got alongside I was going to jump on his back. My father years before had a picture taken on him riding a swimming moose on Basswood Lake. When we got in position I jumped on and everything was fine — for a few seconds. The moose immediately made a 30 degree turn to the right and started coming out of the water on a shallow sand bar. I very, very quickly fell off his back end and started swimming back to the canoe – with a very P.O.ed moose stomping around the sandbar. We paddled a couple miles down the river and pulled over to shore where I shed my wet clothes and laid them out to dry on top of our packs.

A day or so after that we came to Ogoki Post which was the Hudson Bay Company trading post. There was a young Scottish fellow there alone because his wife had been flown out a week before to give birth. He was a bit lonely and said we could sleep on his porch that night if we stayed for dinner. He broke open a couple cans of Caribou and prepared a great meal. He told us about a couple of good spots to catch some speckled trout. The next morning we left, wished him well on his growing family and started down the river again, planning on reaching the junction of the Albany River which would take us to salt water. Two days later and about 50 miles down stream we were shooting a fairly long rapids and when we came around a corner, I could see a drop in the tree line ahead. That meant waterfall and I yelled at Jim to work over to the RH shoreline. There was a nice smooth large granite shelf there that we could run up on and off load to make a portage around the falls to better water below. It was a warm sunny day and when the bow of the canoe came up on the granite shelf Jim stepped out- paddle in hand to walk away about 10 feet to look at the falls. That brought the bow of the canoe up and the very strong current immediately took the stern downstream and over the waterfall. I had time to get one stroke of my paddle into the water and straighten out the canoe so that I would not turn sideways, then I threw myself forward laying on our packs and dropped almost 15 feet.

I hit the river below and filled the canoe full of water, but it did not sink. The canoe floated down stream about 50 to 60 feet where I was able to drag it shore in a shallow spot. I then got all of the gear out and emptied the canoe of water. The waterfalls make enough noise that Jim and I could not hear each other, but I motioned to him to walk downstream beyond me and I would bring the canoe over to pick him up. This took almost another hour to get accomplished. All of our gear – tent, sleeping bags, clothing and food supplies were all wet and even though it was barely noon, we would stop at the first usable place to camp and dry everything out. The worst thing was that we had one 41/2 foot fishing rod and reel and small box of tackle which were laying on top of the packs – along with two trout that were to be dinner that night. Here we were not even halfway and we lost a way to get our main source of food. A few miles down stream we found a fairly level and open spot where we spent the night.

Everyone had cautioned me before we started this trip to avoid camping where you could see that someone else had camped. Northern Canada had an outbreak of Tuberculosis (TB) that affected many of the native people because of unavailability of medical aid. Most of the villages were only accessible by aircraft or boat (snow mobiles in the winter). The young fellow running the HBC post of Ogoki had mentioned this while we were there. All dried out we got an early start the next morning determined to get on the Albany River in the next three or four days. We ran into another waterfall and had to make a mile and a half or so portage (with no trail) which cost us almost another day. But we were finally on the Albany River which was a larger river with a little less current and was wider and deeper. It also got a little more traffic than the Ogoki River so there would usually be some kind of trail around the rapids.

Who knows – we might see some people along the way. The map shows about 300 miles to Fort Albany in a straight line, but we know that we can add quite a few miles for all of the curves and bends in the river. I was so thrilled to be on the Albany. This was one of the major rivers in Ontario and basically ran in an easterly and westerly direction and did allow some of the natives and settlers to reach salt water and some of the trade items from across the Atlantic Ocean. The river also opened a means of peddling their furs and help them to make a living.

We had gone several days now without any meat except our dwindling bacon, but I remembered something my father had told me years before. He said not to ever kill a porcupine unless you absolutely had to. He said you can survive very easily on porcupine if you were short on food. Basically any vegetarian animal is edible. I saw a porcupine during one of our first days on the Albany and took my axe and tapped it on the head with the back side of the axe. Then very carefully I flipped it over on its back to skin it out. We found that one porcupine would feed the two of us for two days. Some times we would broil a couple of quarters over the coals or cut it up for stew, but that was our staple meat for the next month. The first couple of days down the Albany River went pretty easy. There was not the continual run of rapids full of rocks like the Ogoki.

When we did hit a major rapids we could quite often get thru without to much trouble. The country kind of flattened out as we progressed down stream. We were getting short of food, so I started staying up paddling all night on every other night and Jim would sleep in his sleeping bag in the front end of the canoe. As we went along the map showed a small village at the junction with another river. When we reached the spot it was deserted. I suppose that was the result of Tuberculosis outbreaks, but we did investigate. Another couple of days and it looked pretty certain that we would arrive at Fort Albany and the Hudson Bay Store. We were looking forward to buying some more food supplies. That morning at daylight I had been paddling all night and as we came around a corner I could see a rapids ahead. I could see down the entire length and could not see any rocks to avoid. It did not register that the rapids were a lot narrower at the bottom then the top. I suppose it was about a ½ mile long. I had pulled over to the shoreline on the left and started down. As soon as I got into the fast waters I heard a very whining sound which kept getting louder. We figured out later that as the rapids narrowed the velocity of the water increasing created the whining sound. I yelled at Jim up in the bow just after we started down to lay still, do not get up. Then the very whining faded away. We pulled over to shore and got our sleeper out of his sleeping bag and decided that we would never go down a rapids again unless we were both up and working. We did take the time to make some oatmeal for breakfast — then back in the canoe headed for Fort Albany. There we should be able to get some food and the hardest part of the trip would be over — we thought.

We made the last twenty miles and found the trading post on one of the channels of the Albany about 4:00 p.m. and pulled the canoe up on shore next to the cabin. The post was run by a young couple from Scotland. In those days Hudson Bay Company was known as one of the largest chain of stores in the world – in the number of units. They were scattered all over Canada ranging from small outposts of a cabin or two to large mall type of stores in the larger cities in the southern part of the country. There was a large portion of the Scottish people that were running the smaller village outposts, with the lure of adventure and free travel with HBC – as well as free lodging and food. Naturally they were very excited to get visitors. This did not happen very often. They were on their third year there and we were the third party of travelers, but definitely came the farthest. They said that the others were dropped off by air a couple of hundred miles upstream on the Albany. There were several of the natives from the village wandering around. We spent almost three hours talking about our next leg going to Moosonee which was 110 miles south, but I was determined that we were going to finish up on our own power. I thought I understood tides, but I was going to learn a lot in the next week. We did decide that they were making dinner and we could sleep on their porch. We went out to get our gear, but the canoe and gear was not there where we left it. We went to the post and told them that it was missing and they immediately said "the tide is coming in and we will get one of the Indians to tow it back here. They will know right where it is". Ten minutes later a couple of the villagers came back in a Chestnut Freighter canoe towing our little (by comparison) canoe and all our gear. In the north an aluminum canoe was a rarity. Most of the people up there used either Chestnut or Peterborough canoes that were canvas covered cedar strip, square stern canoes, usually between 20 to 25 feet long, fairly wide and were called freighters. You would hardly ever see an Indian paddling a canoe, they all used motors. Every HBC post had many barrels of aviation and regular fuel in their yard and usually hand pumps and hose for transfer. We had a lot of discussion that night about tides. We were now in the last part of July and sunrise would be about 4:30 a.m. and sunset about 9:30 p.m.

We had quite a discussion about tides again during breakfast. That day the high tide was at 9:30 a.m. and again just over 11 hours later. They told us that because the shoreline was so flat and muddy that most days you usually could get ashore or depart the shoreline only at high tide so plan your day around that. They also tried again to talk us into staying another few days and catch the company supply vessel when it goes south, but I really wanted to do it on our own. Now I've been there and done that so a day and a half and staying dry seems sensible.

In the morning we repacked everything and got it down to four #3 Duluth packs – our personal gear, one camp gear and one food. They were pretty short on quite a few food for the next few days until the supply vessel arrives. We did buy a couple cans of spam, some beans and flour and the lady of the post spent half the night baking us bread which was well needed. I had been making bannock (basically fried flour and water) and we both had our fill of that. We paddled out into the saltwater about 10:00 a.m. just past high tide. We were told to keep paddling out so that the tide did not pass us and leave us high and dry until it came back in. Sure enough by mid afternoon we were high and dry. It was just mud and even though we were wearing 12 inch high leather boots, we could not walk anywhere, just sit in the canoe and wait for the return of the tide. It was a little more than three hours until we started to float again. We had thought that we should be back on solid shoreline by 8:30 p.m. to make camp for the night. This started our next lesson. We had a light westerly wind and the tide did not go into the solid shoreline. It was just before dark, but we started out to sea with the tide and resigned to another all night of paddling.

About 3 hours later the tide passed us up again and we were stranded high and dry again. We had been watching some lightning and it moved right in on us and it started raining. We dug out our raingear and a tarp which we draped right over us and the canoe. This was really miserable and then it got worse. The lightning started again but it was traveling horizontally 3 to 4 feet above the water. This immediately brought to my mind that it is usually the tallest tree in the meadow that get struck by lightning. This caused me to ponder that we are sitting in an aluminum canoe — are we grounded?

Daylight came an hour or two later and shortly thereafter the tide started coming back in which allowed us to start for shore. We did find some good solid ground and quickly gathered some firewood. This brought along coffee and oatmeal. While we were doing this one of us had to keep pushing the canoe offshore so we would not get stranded again. This worked well – we were able to get out of the canoe for a bit, get fed and a bathroom break. We were getting smarter and paddled south all day without getting high and dry. Now as it was getting closer to high tide again we started planning. It would be nice to get a decent sleep tonight. There was a long narrow point coming out from shore ahead of us and we started aiming for it. This really worked out well. We got there right at high tide to give us about a thirty minute slack tide to unload. We quickly got the tent erected and went out to collect firewood. There were a lot of dead trees just above the high tide mark and we had plenty of wood in a few minutes. I cooked a gourmet meal of boiled noodles and fried spam and we went to sleep planning on a early departure.

Morning came and by the time that I had finished up the pancakes a rather strong easterly wind had come up with some heavy waves rolling in. It was just over 200 miles from the far shore and the waves were six feet, so we decided we would wait a bit to see what happened. We took a nap to catch up on some of our lost sleep, woke up a couple of hours later and found 25 knot winds and 10 foot waves. We then walked around and found the entire point very rocky, but we found a more protected spot and moved the tent and canoe. A quiet day and early dinner gave us the promise of an early start on the morrow, but the wind howled all night so we spent another day hiding from it. The wind laid down during the second night and we ate breakfast, then loaded the canoe and pushed it into the water just as the tide switched to run out. We probably paddled about 100 feet offshore when the wind started to blow about 20 knots and switched to the west. I quickly decided we did not want to be out in the outgoing tide and a strong offshore wind when it is 200 miles to the next shore. I yelled at Jim and we swung the canoe around to go back to shore. I yelled at Jim again to "paddle as hard as you can, but don't break your paddle. If we don't get back to solid ground, we will die out here". We did make a little head way and my paddle touched the bottom – instantly I was over the side and waist deep in water pulling the canoe ashore. When we got everything out of the water and the tide went further out, we just collapsed and thought about the last 30 minutes. Then we found a protected spot for the tent with the westerly wind. We did not know for sure, but I am certain that some of the gusts ran 50 to 70 knots.

That southern part of the bay is very flat with few large trees or anything to break the wind up. We spent another day hiding from Mother Nature and I decided that there would not be any more night moves—as this weather changes too fast and was extremely wild. We did see a seaplane fly over late that afternoon. The wind did lay down during the afternoon, but I had just decided no more night travel, so we were surely ready to go in the morning. I thought that we had two more days to Moosonee and I was more than ready to get it over now. I had dreamed of this trip for almost ten years, but we have had a lot of problems lately.

The next morning came without a cloud in the sky and a light northerly wind and away we went. We had figured the high tide for about 7:30 that morning and that was our departure. We made good time until about noon and the wind picked up and started blowing 30 to 40 knots but from right behind us. It was low tide so I did not want to try to get to shore. The waves were getting pretty large, but we quickly learned how to handle them. I could look right behind us and we probably had a ten foot face of the wave. We would have to paddle as hard as we could, then go down with the bow and the bowman would lean to the stern as far as he could so that the bow wound not submerge – then paddle full open to get back up. The wind was perfectly aligned with our course so we were making good head way.

Seeing as we could not get ashore with these waves we did not get too concerned. Right about high tide the wind laid down quite a bit and we entered a mouth of a river. This was the Moose River and it ran right through the town of Moosonee – almost there! Of course we were traveling upstream again and it was a strong current. It got dark and we were only about half way to the town. We kept going and finally saw a light ahead and pulled the canoe ashore. There was a four room hotel there, but it took awhile to find someone to get us a room. There is no road to Moosonee other than the railroad which brings one train per week and they occasionally get a ship hauling freight and fuel. At that time there was no airport – all air traffic was either a seaplane or a skiiplane. I think at that time there were 350 to 400 people living there with at least half of them government.

We had to wait three days for the next train, but we did get to sleep in a real bed and really enjoyed a hot shower rather than a quick in and out of the water to clean up. There was even a small Café that did not offer porcupine. Three days later we caught the south bound train to connect with the Canadian National west bound. This was trans-continental rail, but it was quite common that they would stop and drop you and your gear – including canoes, rafts or boats – anywhere you desired. In fact, it worked on the other end also – if you wanted a pickup on a river that crossed the track you would simply get everything stacked up by the track and have one person walk about a half mile in the direction of the arriving train and hold up a sign requesting pickup. This gave them advance notice to slow a little more gradually. The loading was done in 5 minutes or so. You would never see that today though. Time is too important.

We had one more railway change late that day and finally got back to my car, loaded up the canoe and gear. It was a little after dark, but we drove the rest of the night. Of all the ways we could have been killed on the trip we almost ended up hitting a moose going 80 miles an hour (us not the moose) on the way home to Ely. But we made it!

CHAPTER 11

AFTER HUDSON BAY

It was mid — August when we got back to Ely. I did pick up a couple of canoe trips to do some more guiding and I found out that there was not a lot of adventure when I paddled out in Bayley Bay of Basswood Lake. Five to six miles of water that used to be a large piece of water now seemed to be a river. The well trod portages also seemed like a park. I did not realize it at this, time but I had set myself up or a drastic lifestyle change.

I did pick up a canoe trip in late September with two newspaper writers – a man and a woman. We had seven days, so I took a tow up the Moose Lake Chain to Prairie Portage, cleared Canadian Customs and paddled across Bayley Bay and it was raining. I decided that we would camp right there on the portage next to the Canadian rangers Station. That way they could interview Gerry Payne, the resident ranger there for many years. I was also sure that he would invite us in to cook our dinner – especially when he found out that it was steaks and we had one for him. He did have a wood kitchen range with a roof over it. The next morning the weather was a lot better, so I cooked breakfast over our campfire before we broke camp, then we carried everything right across the portage. Back in the water we paddled up to North Bay of Basswood Lake with two portages and went up the river to Isabella Lake for the night. The next day we made five short portages and six hours of paddling and we were on McIntyre Lake which is one of my favorites. A very pretty lake and good fishing for walleyed pike, northern and lake trout. Several years before I had cleared out a campsite that was in a dead end bay and was not on the main route. There were many advantages to this. Number 1. is that if it was a hard and miserable day I could be assured that there would not be anyone on the campsite when I got there. Number 2. I could leave a supply of firewood there and expect to find it still there when I arrived. It is always a common courtesy to leave enough firewood for one meal when you leave, but it is uncommon to actually find it there. Number 3. is that you can leave all of the tent poles and tarp poles that you need when setting up and the site had been used before. The three of us arrived at our site about an hour before dark and it was raining. The first thing was to get the parties tent up so they could get out of the rain and get unpacked, blow up their air mattress and lay their sleeping bags out. Their tent was a 7 foot x 8 foot "A" frame and took less than ten minutes to unpack and erect. Another ten minutes to put up the tarp to cover the cooking and eating area and get a fire going. The coffee pot and our largest kettle for hot water for cooking and dishwater went on the fire while I put up my 3 foot x 7 foot 6 pound tent.

After this I cleaned 3 walleyed pike for dinner and poured the first cup of coffee. Not bad – we have a 12 foot by 16 foot tarp over the cooking and eating area and dinner will be ready in 15 minutes. We have a log table that I had built ten years or so earlier, plus a couple of log benches to sit on next to the fire.

Once dinner was eaten and the dishes done I decided to get some campfire wood for sitting by and warming. Another advantage of your own campsite, was I knew there was a dead spruce tree about eight feet tall behind our camp and I had been saving it for over a year just for a night like this – rainy, dark and cold. It was about 150 feet behind the camp, but I quickly found it and chopped it down. Then I hooked my ax over a bough at the base and towed it back to camp. Then I took my bow saw and cut it into several pieces then used the ax to make smaller pieces and started a separate fire away from the tarp. I threw on a couple pieces of the dead spruce which quickly flared up brightly — followed by a loud scream. The woman was pointing at my left foot and there was a spray of blood coming out of my boot. I kept my Hudson Bay ax very sharp and must of grazed my boot which did make a deep cut. I had felt the ax hit my boot but did not feel that it had cut me. I did sit down, unlaced my boot and pulled it off. Now I could see a three inch gash in the top of my left foot with a lot of blood shooting out. I put a pot of water on to heat, got a towel and wrapped it around the foot and got the first aid gear out. As soon as we got the wound cleaned up, it was really hurting, so I crawled into my tent. We had a cut a section of a 10 inch log and I kept my foot raised on the log which seemed to reduce the bleeding some.

It was not a good night, but I did get a little sleep. My tent was only a few feet away from our rock firepit and a little after daylight I got a fire going for coffee and warm water. I could not get my boot on and simply crawled around. Bandages were changed and scrambled eggs made. By then I had spotted a couple of small birch trees along the shoreline. I gave the fellow my 30 inch bow saw and had him cut down the trees and bring them back. They were just over one inch in thickness. It didn't take to long and I had a pair of crutches made and we all decided to start back to a hospital – about a three day trip.

We then got the camp dismantled and everything loaded back in the canoe. We back tracked across McIntyre Lake and hit our first portage to Sarah Lake. This was a short portage of seven rods (a little over 115 feet), but very steep going down. It was planned on the man carrying the canoe and I would crawl, but he fell down in the first 10 feet which made me decide that we would not go far with a hole in the canoe. So I did drag the canoe down the hill. We paddled about two miles and hit the portage to Tuck Lake. This was about 75 rods, but very flat and a grass covered trail. It took an hour, but I dragged the canoe across while crawling. As we paddled across Tuck Lake I could see smoke off our right side and I was sure that it would be Hollis LaTorelle who was another canoe guide. When I got there it was Hollis and his son Jeep. They were each guiding a canoe party and each were customers of different outfitters.

There were just over a dozen outfitting companies in Ely, but only a half dozen professional guides and of course we knew each other. It was overcast right then with a light rain when these two ran into each other and were sharing a noon fire and coffee. We paddled over to their campsite and they were very surprised to see my crutches. Hollis was going to be there that day and the next, then he was headed back to Ely. He was going south right over the Kett Lake mountain which had a mile and one half portage and a couple of short ones which put you right in Basswood Lake. He had two guests, a 17 foot square stern canoe with a 3 h.p. outboard motor. We could make Ely in one long day from there. He asked which way I was thinking of taking and I told him – west to Robinson Lake and then south to the U.S. Forest Service cabin on Crooked Lake next to Lower Basswood Falls. Hollis said that if I could be at Upper Basswood Falls by 1:00 p.m. he would tow me, and help me across the last two portages and take me to the hospital. Jeep said he was traveling to Robinson Lake that afternoon and would help me on those two portages. That would leave me with one more short portage to the cabin and there would be 3 short portages and one long one going up the river, but they had pretty smooth trails thanks to USFS portage crews. This really sounded great as my foot was really bothering me, so we got started. About three hours later we were on Robinson Lake and Jeep and his customers left to set up his camp for the night. Another three hours and we had gotten back to the U.S. side and the Forest Service cabin. There was no one there so we just moved in, and got a fire started – then dinner. After we had eaten, I want through the first aid kit there and found some Epson salts. We heated up some water for soaking and added some salts. I had not been able to lace up my boot all day because my foot was so swollen, but we got the boot off and cleaned up the wound as well as we could. Then I started soaking the wounded foot in Epson salt and the bleeding started again pretty heavy and every time the gal went out to dump the water off the porch she threw up. We had a good supply of bandages and tape and got it well wrapped.

By morning I felt much better and could almost walk on it, and did walk with the crutches. When we left the cabin we paddled 200 yards to the first portage – Lower Basswood Falls and a short portage. Here I found I could walk with the left crutch and carry a canoe – left hand on the crutch and balance the canoe with my right arm. I did need to have someone turn the canoe upside down and raise the bow until I could get under the portage yoke. The we paddled another one and a half miles and took the portage around Middle Falls of Basswood with a 12 rod portages, followed by a little longer portage around a rapids. Now we have one portage to go around Upper Basswood Falls which is in the one mile category. I got started and made it halfway, then left the canoe sitting on a canoe rest. We got to the east end of the portage just as Hollis pulled in with his canoe and motor. I told him about the canoe so he went right down and got it. Then we were on our way to town and some medical aid for my foot which was very painful again. We had two portages which went very easily being with Hollis. He dropped his guests off and took me to the hospital where they kept me for a couple of days and put a light cast on. My personally built crutches were replaced by a hospital type equipped with rubber foot pads. Another adventure of many finished.

CHAPTER 12

WINTER 1956

The winter after the Hudson Bay trip, I went to Sport Shows in Chicago, Milwaukee and Minneapolis selling canoe trips – and my guiding services. At Chicago a fellow and his son came up to the booth to chat. I had guided them and another father and son on a ten day canoe trip and had some excellent fishing and a fun trip. They wanted to talk about the trip I had the previous summer and the fishing I had seen. Of course I could only tell them about the first half of the trip because we lost all of our fishing tackle going over the falls. I did tell them about some of the speckled trout we had caught on the Ogoki River. The father got really excited to hear about catching three to five pound speckles. He said that he had fished speckled trout for several years he had never seen one over a pound and a half and wanted to try that. I suggested that we could drive up to Long Lac, Ontario and then get flown to Speckled Trout Rapids on the Ogoki River. We had spent a night there the year before and had some very good trout fishing. He was intrigued and asked me to look into the cost and availability of such a trip. A few weeks later they booked a weeks trip for three fathers and three sons for mid – June. I was excited about going back to the Ogoki River and just get dropped off right at the campsite without two or three weeks of hard work to get there. We got flow in by two Noorduyn Norseman each with a 17 foot canoe tied on, all seven of us and most of our gear. The Norseman was a 10 seat high wing aircraft, a 600 h.p. Pratt

& Whitney R 1340 engine, Edo 7170 floats, just over 900 built, 52 foot wingspan, fabric covered. One of Canada's greatest gifts to aviation. We had another Norseman coming with the last canoe and gear in a hour. I got a fire started with a couple of pots of water on the fire for coffee and dish washing. We also turned to fishing and pretty quickly had dinner set aside and cleaned. I even set the reflector oven up to make some biscuits and threw several potatoes in the coals for baking.This started a great week with lots of sun and fishing, but no worrying about tomorrow's rapids.

Late afternoon of the seventh day we disassembled the camp and started to listen for the aircraft coming from the south. Shortly thereafter the first Norseman circled, landed and taxied to our camp. It took fifteen minutes to load half the gear four passengers and tie one of the canoes on. Just as we taxied out the second one landed, got another canoe, three passengers and the rest of their gear. One more would come in for the last canoe, Great trip!

The next morning the two pilots that flew us in and out came into the restaurant while we were having breakfast and sat down with us. We did start talking about airplanes because I was thinking this was a great way to see more of the North Country. They told me about what you have to do to earn a pilot's license and some about the aircraft used as seaplanes. One thing I will always remember is the way they praised the Cessna 180 which was first produced three years prior. Once they talked about that I said " I must have one"! Now I have owned about 100 Cessna 180's. This trip was the last nail in the coffin of my future.

CHAPTER 13

THE BIG STEP

The fall of 1956 I had airplanes on my mind. I kept looking at maps of Ontario, Quebec, Manitoba and the Northwest Territory. Minnesota claimed 10,000 lakes, Ontario 100,000 lakes and NW Territories says 1,000,000 lakes and at that time I had not even considered Alaska and its 3,000,000 lakes — you add all the rivers to it and there is a huge amount of water on this earth. Much more water than there are airports. Everywhere I wanted to go would need a seaplane. So I got busy calling every flight school in the northeast half of Minnesota — telling them that I wanted to become a pilot, but wanted to do the whole course in a seaplane. I was surprised that no one would even consider it. They said I would have to buy my own aircraft and find an instructor who would do it that way. They brought up the fact that the FAA required night flight time to qualify to take a check ride exam and that was not usually done on floats. The more I thought about it, I felt that I would buy a seaplane. I was 26 years of age with my military time behind me. I would be graduating from University of Minnesota, Duluth Branch (UMD) — early at the end of the winter quarter in a few months with a Business Major and Journalism minor. I had a good reputation as a canoe guide, was doing well financially and buying a new Buick every other year. I owed a bank in Duluth $800 on the last Buick I bought, so I went in and paid it off. Then I went up to the Duluth International Airport and found one airplane for sale – a Stinson

Gullwing with a round 300 h.p. Lycoming engine for $2,500. This looked like it would be a good aircraft for running around the North, but the fellow who had it had more sense than I. He said go buy a Cub or Champ, learn how to fly, then come back for the Stinson. So I drove down to Lake Superior seaplane base at Park Point. They had a short paved runway and several docks, but was iced over at this time of year. A young fellow was behind the counter and answered my questions about airplanes for sale and took me outside to show me a Piper J4E Cub Coupe. He said that a woman that lived a mile down the road had it for sale at $1,000.00. He told me to drive down there and offer her $850.00 and she would take it. He also said that it would cost another $25.00 for an annual inspection. At that time I knew absolutely nothing about airplanes and halfway believed him. I did tell him that the U.S. Forest Service in Ely had a piper J4A with a 65 h.p. Continental Engine that they had used for fire patrol and liked it. We both agreed that this one with the 75 h.p. should be theoretically 15% better with the engine upgrade, but my aviation knowledge was going to start. I did drive down the street and made the $850.00 offer which she accepted. I told her I would go get the money and be back in an hour. I went back up town to the bank and told Percy Pascoe that I wanted to refinance the Buick again for $900.00 to buy an airplane. He shook his head but quickly made out the paperwork so I could start making car payments again. Then I took the $850.00 back to the lady owner, collected the logbooks which I took back to the seaplane office and told him to do the annual inspection.

Three or four months went by and no annual inspection, so I had not started flying lessons. I had started checking around and Bill Koski 50 miles north of Duluth in Eveleth said he could do it and to just bring it in. Late in April I ran into David Powers who I had met in college at UMD. He told me that just that morning he had passed his commercial pilots check ride. I quickly told him that I would give him his first flying job if he could ferry my Cub from Duluth to Eveleth so I could get the annual inspection. I said I would drive to Eveleth, and bring him back to Duluth and give him a bottle of whiskey of his choice.

We got that done the next day. Ten days later I was driving up to Ely to settle in for another season of guiding – about six months. As I drove into the airport I saw a set of floats out on the grass, so I stopped and talked to the owner of the operation, Art Tomes, and asked about them. He told me that they were Edo 1320's and had complete Piper Cub gear with a price of $1,200.00. I told him I would take them and wrote a check to him. Bill Koski was out for the day, but I could see that he was working on my aircraft. The fabric needed rejuvenation, so I told him to color it in cream and a deep red. This had been done and was looking good. I left him a note that I bought a set of floats from his boss and to install them. I also told him that I would be back in a couple of days. I did get back there three days later and Bill Koski told me that my J4 was not FAA approved on floats and I promptly told him the US Forest Service in Ely had a Piper J4 on floats for several years. Then he explained to me that they must had a J-4A while mine was a J-4E. He did not know the reasoning, but told me to call the FAA Maintenance and Engineering office in Kansas City and ask why the difference in the Piper J-4A versus the Piper J-4E.

A couple of days later I did call and luckily reached a fellow originally from Eveleth, Minnesota and actually knew a couple of the operators. We spent almost an hour on the phone while he was looking up previous approvals and said he could not find any difference other than the engine. He also said that in1952 a Mr. Richard Gloss from Detroit Michigan had gotten a onetime FAA approval on a Piper J-4E on floats. He said that if I would pay for a collect telegram he would make an approval of the installation on my aircraft. I drove down to Eveleth to give Bill Koski the wire (before e-mail) and he was very surprised.

He brought up more bad news that the floats I bought had struts and wires for a Piper J-3 which was a narrow width compared to the side – by side J-4. He was sure he could shorten some of the struts, but I might have to purchase a couple. A week later he called me and said we also needed the fuselage fittings because of the width of the fuselage. So I called Edo Float Company in New York and ask if they had the four blocks that I needed. I reached Wade Weathers and we had another long winded phone call while he was researching their records. He got the information that they only built and sold 90 sets of those fittings and it would cost $695.00 to manufacture another set. I could not see that paying over ½ the value of the set of 1320 floats for four blocks that I could hold in one hand was a good deal.

Weathers told me to call Bill Martilla four miles away on Ely Lake. At that time he probably did most of the seaplane maintenance in the northern half of Minnesota. I did that and he said that he thought he did have the float fittings, but he had given a fellow a pail of float blocks to see if he could come up with what he needed. He did call me back two days later saying he had them in the bucket and price was $90.00. With no hesitation I told him I would mail him a check immediately if he could get the fittings over to Bill Koski. Finally in late July I got a call saying the airplane was completed and I sent Bill Koski a check for $380.00. I also asked if he could find someone to fly it to Ely and I would get him back to Eveleth. While the work went on the J-4 I got introduced to "Trade-A-Plane". Which was 30 to 40 pages of aircraft and parts for sale nationwide and published three times a month. I had found a advertisement for a brand-new metal propeller for sale. This was listed as a McCauley 7159 (71 inches long and 59 degree angle of pitch on the blades) for $79.00. My mechanic, Bill Koski told me to replace the wooden 7159 propeller when the floats go on the aircraft as the wood propellers take a beating from the water spray. I had bought one and had it shipped to Bill. It was installed on the aircraft now.

Also Bill Rom had introduced me to Chick Beel who was one of the U.S. Forest Service pilots and a flight instructor. He had told me that he would be happy to train me for my pilot's license. It was the beginning of a life long friendship. He had experience in the Piper J-4 and also thought it should be a little better with the 75 h.p. engine. The Forest Service had given their J-4A to a local school system for teaching students how to fly and use it as a career opportunity. I knew about this and had checked with the school, but it was down for a fabric replacement and engine rebuild with an estimated year to finish.

Also I really could not be considered a high school student anymore as I had a college degree. The U.S. Forest Service in Ely had a Cessna 180 on floats and skis, a Noorduyn Norseman and just got their first DeHavilland DHC-2 Beaver. A couple of years later another DeHavilland Beaver replaced the Norseman and later on the Cessna was replaced by the third DeHavilland Beaver. They still operate three Beavers today – floats in the summer and one or two on skis during the winter. The summer months are mostly involved with forest fires – water bombing, hauling fire crews and fire patrols.

FINALLY – the aircraft showed up in mid August and I was to meet Chick Beel at Rolando's dock at 5:00 p.m. to start my new passion. Naturally the first task is to teach me how to preflight the aircraft. We started with pumping any water out of the floats, check the amount of fuel and draining all of the fuel sumps, check the oil and engine compartment and then all of the control surfaces and their fasteners. I had installed six feet of ½" nylon rope on both bow cleats and the bottom of the rear struts of each float for tying up at the docks. Once the preflight was completed Chick stood on the RH float behind the propeller and hand propped it to start the engine running. We taxied around a little to let me get the feel of the water rudders, then headed into the wind, retracted the water rudders and opened up the throttle. This made a lot more noise and we started to move a little faster – but we could not get on the step and could not fly! We had a long, slow taxi back to the dock. Chick thought that the prop was the problem and said to call Kenny Maxwell who had the prop shop in Minneapolis to explain the problem. I was so disappointed – I had owned this airplane for the better part of a year, spent what I thought was a lot of money on it and had not flown it yet.

I did call Kenny Maxwell at the prop shop in Minneapolis at 8:01 a.m. He agreed that it was the prop and the solution would be to have a flatter pitch to get more RPM's. He checked and said that he had a metal 7165 in stock and how did I want it shipped. I asked him to put it on the Greyhound bus and I would have it at 5:30 p.m. and try it out that evening. This was 1956 and there were not a lot of credit cards out other than gas companies, but on my promise to send him my propeller and pay any difference he shipped a new one to me. I had it the next afternoon. Chick and I removed the one that did not work and installed the new one – which did not work! Two more bus arrivals in the next two days and we had not got off the water yet. That made it the fourth try to fly, but another pilot stopped by our dock to asked what going on. He was Keith Mackie and he had a 65 h.p. J-3 on floats. We told him of the problem and he said that he was going to take his prop off right then and we could try that. He was back in 15 minutes and we put it on the J-4 and taxied out. When the power was applied the nose came right up and we went on the step AND WE FLEW! We flew around for a few minutes then took Keith's prop back to him. This was a McCauley 7443 (74" long and 43 degree pitch) and this is what I needed. I will make my daily call to Kenny in the morning, but now I knew what to order for the propeller of the day.

The next morning I talked to Kenny and told him what I wanted, but he said "NO, it is illegal. You have a 75 h.p. Continental and maximum length you can put on is 71 inches". I replied "if I stay legal, I will only have a boat, not an airplane". Finally after a heated discussion, I agreed that it would be illegal to install and sign off the propeller, but would it be illegal to sell me a 7443 propeller. I did ask him if it was illegal to sell me the prop that he would receive a call in the next 30 minutes from someone else who wanted the 74 inch prop. I did have a 7443 prop on the bus that afternoon and on the aircraft for my flight instruction that evening. Chick

Beel remarked that we will keep water right under us for a while. I did a lot of business with Kenney Maxwell for many years after that and probably had a hundred props overhauled at his shop.

Every night at 5:30 I would be at the dock for flying, but it seemed to me that we had a lot of interruptions. Some nights Chick had to fly late for the Forest Service and other times it might be too windy or rainy. I kept telling Chick that we would just have to follow the Mississippi River south to Louisiana as the ice formed. The god's finally got their act together and on the first sunny Saturday of October I got my first solo flight. Chick and I went flying at 11:00 a.m. and spent a little more than an hour and returned to a large vacant dock at Sandy Point. Then he said the attention getting words "give me three take-offs and landings by yourself right in front of me". WOW! It was perfect day sunny with a westerly wind that just left ripples on the water. He did warn me that the aircraft would be quite a bit lighter without him and I could plan on getting off the water somewhat quicker. It really felt good to be alone, but slightly scary. After the third full stop landing we flew a mile down the lake to our dock where he said to go out for another hour to practice and build some time. He also said that on the morrow, Sunday, he had an afternoon fire patrol in a Beaver and he asked if I wanted to go along and navigate the flight then he could endorse my student pilot certificate for solo cross country. Naturally I jumped at this opportunity and he gave me a USFS map with the route marked out to study overnight. We spent two hours in the Beaver the next day and I couldn't believe I could be flying a Beaver when I barely had ten hours flying time. Of course Chick did all the actual flying, but I did get to steer the Beaver for the two hours of flight and got signed off for solo cross country in the J-4. The way the rules have tightened up over the years, it will never happen again.

In early November I took my first cross country flight to the west end of Pelican Lake for duck hunting. Bill Rom and Dr. Ed Ciriacy drove over there from Ely and my friend who enlisted in the U.S. Marine Corps with me a few years earlier, Shaver Strand, picked them up by boat and brought them to his family island camp. I flew in there just excited to make my first cross country flight to Pelican Lake. I was a serious duck hunter in those days and the birds were starting south in large numbers. Pelican Lake was a fair sized lake, but was shallow with quite a few bays so there was a lot of food available for the ducks and they evidently used it as a rest stop on their southbound flight. The first couple of days the shooting was good and we had roast duck for dinner two nights. The third morning was overcast and a few flakes of snow falling and I decided that I should get the airplane out of there before I got frozen in.

An hour later I was in the air headed east and it was snowing a little harder. It was basically a water route back to Ely. 6 miles across Pelican Lake, then 7 or 8 more miles of land until 30 miles of Lake Vermillion, 4 miles to Burntside Lake, then Little Long Lake and Shagawa Lake. I left Pelican Lake at 1,000 feet and started across the 8 mile stretch to Lake Vermillion showing 75 mph. I had almost 20 hours of flying time then, but I did know that I had a 20 mph. headwind and the snow was getting thicker.

So before panic set in, I did a 180 degree turn to start back to Pelican Lake. I was down to two miles visibility when I landed back at the island. I tied the aircraft up and Dr. Ciriacy and I went out to another small island and had fantastic shooting. It started snowing a lot harder. There must have been a few thousand ducks dropping in to sit out the snow – mostly large northern bluebills – and they kept landing in our decoys. It did not take long to fill our limit. We just sat there watching a hundred or so blue bills land right in the decoys, then we would stand up and wave our arms to make them fly off. A few minutes later another flock would land. Finally we got cold just sitting there in the snow with no shooting, picked up the decoys and boated back to the cabin. I found almost four inches of snow on the airplane and had to sweep it off. Once the snow piles up on the tail surfaces the weight sinks the heels of the floats until they are underwater. This allows the water to get through small leaks on top, and there always are some. Just walking back and forth seems to loosen up some rivets or maybe screws would not get really tightened down enough after pumping out. This can be pretty serious and there are quite a few seaplanes that get sunk late in the fall. I really learned a lot about 20 years later in Cordova, Alaska. In Cordova we could fly floats all year around down in the saltwater harbor and you could often get a foot of snow overnight. People had several different ways of coping — the most common was running a 5/8 inch rope under the floats between two docks. Back at Pelican Lake it was still snowing and the temperature was falling pretty fast late that night, so everyone decided to pull out in the morning so they did not get frozen in. I had to get up for aircraft sweeping every couple of hours all night. The cabin was built with a boat house underneath it and it was fairly large.

The next morning as everyone was getting ready to leave I decided I had to stay to take care of the airplane. We looked at the boat house again and figured out that we could turn the aircraft sideways so it would fit inside. When we tried it the plane was too high so we pumped some water in the floats and sank it a few inches — then pumped the floats out again after the aircraft was safely inside. Now I decided again to monitor it until I could get it out, fly it back to Ely and have use of it all winter on skiis.

I had a good supply of food and I would keep my limit of ducks, so I felt pretty secure when the boat pulled away. Later that afternoon the snow quit and at sunset the clouds disappeared leaving clear skies. When I got up in the morning I was surprised to find ice right across the lake and the thermometer showed – 5 degrees below. There even was skim ice throughout the boat house under the roof. Now I knew that I was stuck for a week – or maybe two! We had turned off and drained what there was of the water system and the outhouse was put back in use — which meant putting a kerosene heater inside. There was no electricity, but several oil lamps, a wood fired kitchen range and a large wood fired heat stove in the living room, so I just had to keep a supply of wood available. In the next few days the temperature dropped to minus 20 degrees and the ice thickened quickly. Each morning I would cut a hole in the ice to check thickness and had four inches by the sixth day so now I started my plan for escape.

First I put a plank over the top of the floats, placed the outhouse heater on the plank with a section of stove pipe over so it directed heat into the engine compartment. It took the better part of a day to get the engine started and warmed up, then I draped a sleeping bag around the engine. I started it up every day (warm up and hand propped) and run it up. Meanwhile I had to scrape and cut off ice that had accumulated all over the wings, floats and fuselage. I had taken a chain saw and cut out a 20 foot X 20 foot piece of ice right outside of the boat house where the airplane had been put in the boathouse as well as a 15 foot wide channel to move out 6 feet from the boathouse. Once I got it nosed out of the boat house I hand propped the warmed engine and *applied* full power to climb up on top of the ice. It took almost three days to get it out of the boat house and sitting on ice. It was another three days to clean up all the ice accumulation and thaw out the floats so they could be pumped out. It had warmed up slightly with daytime temps about 15 degrees above zero and the night about zero. Tomorrow I am out of here was my thought that night. Shortly after daylight I moved the outhouse heater to the plank on the floats and it took almost four hours to get the engine running. I ran it up, checked the magnetos several times and thought about the takeoff. This is going to be something we had not practiced or even talked about.

I got my clothes, shotgun and sleeping bag stowed away in the aircraft and got everything locked up. I had cut a couple of holes in the ice and froze tie down ropes in place. Now I untied these and cut them off right above the ice and threw them into the plane. Hopefully I will not need them at the other end in Ely. I will not even think about the landing until I get in the air and I will have an hour to ponder on that. Looking back at that now it was scary to do, I had never heard of anyone taking off and landing on ice with straight floats. Now I have done it a hundred times at least as well as landing on wet grass. The main thing is to keep your altitude pretty flat so you do not drag your heels and remember the steerage is primarily your air rudder. No brakes on the landing and if it is smooth ice you will have a long run out. Once the ropes were in, I jumped up on the float, hand propped the engine, climbed in and headed into the wind and pushed the throttle in all of the way. It seemed very fast and I was flying!

An hour later the landing went very well, but it took a while to figure out how to taxi into the bay. I left it parked on the ice tied down to a dock just in front of my mechanics hanger. When I got home I called him, told him where it was and to put skis on. I called Chick Beel to schedule a check – out on skis, but found out he was on a freeze up vacation and would not be back for a couple of weeks. I walked around, sat in the plane and finally checked myself out and was fairly proficient when Chick got back. As Chick later wrote in a newspaper article about me " I have created a monster". He said it with love and respect and maybe just maybe a little frustration.

CHAPTER 14

1961

In mid — April the U.S. financed an invasion of Cuba to overthrow Fidel Castro who was the dictator. He had overthrown the military dictatorship of Batista a while before. President John Kennedy along with other government officials were concerned with Castro's friendly outlook with Russia. The idea was probably good, but the planning left a lot to be desired in the military sense. The U.S. government did not want to have it known that they were backing the invasion and hid behind the supposed work of the CIA. Eight B-26 bombers were turned over to the CIA and they did make one raid just before the invasion that was supposed to destroy the Cuban Air Force, but then the B-26's were grounded so that the U.S. intervention would be played down. The invasion force itself amounted to slightly less than 1,500 men and they were only escapees that had fled Cuba — not trained soldiers while the Cuban Army was over 200.000 men and they had a depleted some what Air Force that was still able to operate against the landing force. They also did not do well on the point of landing because several of the ships of the invasion force ran up on coral reefs. It turned out to be a two day war with about 1,000 invaders taken prisoner and just less than 200 killed. Shortly after that I started hearing that the Marine Corps was going to start recalling some of the inactive reservists to active duty. Several months later in September I received a letter from the USMC concerning my current status in life and availability. I replied that in 1952 I was released from active duty and returned home to start college. 1956 I graduated from college. 1958 I got married and 1959 my first daughter was born. 1961 we lived in a two bedroom log cabin 10 feet from the lake and my wife was carrying my first son to be in her baggage compartment, ETA late October. I did take a profile picture of the wife and the two year old daughter, another of our three year black Labrador, the two bedroom log cabin and my third airplane, a Cessna 180 on floats, and a new business. I guess they figured that all made me not qualified as I never heard back from them again.

October 30, (Halloween) our first son, Patrick, showed up as a "trick or treat". He would carve out quite a career in aviation. I owned one Cessna 180 at that time, N4636B. Late in the summer Jim Pascoe and I jointly bought a Howard DGA-15P and put it on a set of 6470 floats. Of course this was financed by Percy Pascoe of the Duluth bank. The following year Jim bought into Wilderness Outfitting Company and I took over his half. The Howard was an interesting airplane. We installed six Cessna seats inside the cabin and it carried 151 gallons of fuel, but it only had a wingspan of 38 feet and small flaps — compare that to 36 feet of wing span on the Cessna 180 and 48 feet on the Beaver. This did make a pretty smooth ride in turbulence and the oversized 6470 floats smoothed out rough water take-offs and landing. The length of the float also put the water rudders below the tail group which gave it excellent steerage taxiing on the water. The Howard became known as the "poor man's Beaver". The oversized floats also helped it to get on the step fairly quick, but the short wing gave it a long take off run.

Early in 1963 I sold the Howard to Roger Holt of Greenville, Maine and agreeing to take a Cessna 180 on trade. A day on the phone, the price was agreed upon along with a meeting place halfway — Burke Lakefront Airport in Cleveland, Ohio. The morning I was scheduled to leave it was it was fog right to the ground, so I did not get to Cleveland until late afternoon. There I met Roger's son and one of the ugliest 180 Cessna's I had ever seen. I told him it was not a deal and got back in the Howard to go home. He did stop me until he called his father. It ended up that we both stayed there overnight ending up in a strip joint and writing out a contract on a napkin that they would pay me an additional $750 on July 1ˢᵗ and another $750 on August 1ˢᵗ. All of this took place while a barely dressed woman was walking back and forth on top of the bar over our heads. I did get that Cessna N9459C back to Ely for a new paint job, glass, interior and a new engine mount. It took a month and several thousand dollars, but it got back in the air.

About three years later, I was walking out of a bank in St. Paul, Minnesota where I had just financed three new Cessnas when I met Pat Covington and his wife going into the bank. I knew Pat who owned two Cessna 206's on wheels used to transport caskets and their passengers all over the U.S. for different undertakers. We stopped to talk for a minute and he said they were on their way to Maine to buy a Howard on floats. He said "yes" when I asked him if he was dealing with Roger Holt. Then I told him that I still held the title to that airplane because Holt had never paid the additional contract so I did not give him a bill of sale. It turned out that they flew the Howard for a couple of months in Maine, had a serious scare in it and pulled it out of the water. Sure enough — ten days later I got a check for $1,500 from Pat Covington.

CHAPTER 15

CHERRY LAKE 8-23-63

It is Friday night and I am working at Bill Rom's Canoe Country Outfitters. We have quite a few canoe parties starting their trip in the morning. For most of them it would be their first time trying this. The rate then was $6.00 to $7.00 per person per day which included their canoe, tent or tents, sleeping bags, cooking utensil's and food supplies. Either Bill Rom, John Pechek or I would spend an hour or so with each party and discuss what they want to do while they are in the wilderness. Some are big on fishing, some just want the camping and traveling while some others seeing wildlife is the most important part. We would usually spend at least one hour going over a map, showing them campsites, portages and water to avoid in bad weather. It is 9:45 p.m. and I am just gathering up my stuff to go home across the lake for dinner and sleep when someone yells at me to get the phone. It is Bill Anderson who owns the resort at the end of the road on Moose Lake — 20 miles east of Ely. He said that he had some guys I should talk to and handed the phone to another fellow. He told me his name and said there were six of them camped on Cherry Lake and one of the six went rock climbing that morning and had taken a fall. He said the climber fell 50 to 60 feet and landed on his head in a rockpile. He was unconscious and bleeding pretty bad, but the others got a sleeping bag and carried him back to their tent. Two of the group stayed with the injured kid and the other three started paddling for help. They made two portages into Knife Lake – almost 20 miles long – and found Dorthy Moulter on the west end of the lake. She told them to take her canoe and outboard motor and explained to them how to wade and lower the canoe down five different rapids and save time over the portages. She had lived on a island there in Knife Lake for 20 years and had to do this every couple of weeks to get to town. From the last rapids it would be less than a two hour run to the first dock, road and buildings on the left side – and the first telephone which belonged to Bill Anderson. It was late August and had been dark for over two hours already, so he knew he would not catch anyone at the Forest Service, but he tried me because he knew I owned a couple of aircraft. The fellow I was talking to said they had left the injured fellow 10 hours previously and he was unconscious and bleeding from the nose, mouth and ears. I found out which campsite they were at and told him that I had been to Cherry Lake several times – by canoe, not by air – and I would start looking for help, but I would go up there.

The first call I made was to Chick Beel, who was a U.S. Forest Service pilot and had taught me how to fly. He said that there was no way they could take out a government seaplane after dark and that he had been into the lake. He said it would be tough at night because there are some high hills around the lake and the available water was very narrow. I ended up telling him that I was going to go up there and take a look. I then called Dr. Ed Ciriacy and told him about the accident and he said he should get up there as soon as possible. I explained to him about the lake and narrows that I could not remember if the wings would fit through, but I did tell him that I know I could always land in Knife Lake, borrow a canoe from some campers and I would take him in by canoe to Cherry Lake – two portages and maybe 8 to 10 miles of paddling or we could leave in the dark at 4:00 a.m. and be there waiting for daylight about 5:00 a.m. He said that he doubted that the fellow would be alive by then. I told him I was going down to the dock and I would have an airplane fueled and warmed up in 20 minutes. He said he would get his bag and couple of quarts of blood and would be there. A few minutes later we were off the water at Shagawa Lake and climbing to the north east. It was 80 miles and took 45 to 50 minutes. This was really flying in those days (and nights) and I was flying a 1955 Cessna, N4636B, equipped with a Narco MK 3 omnigator, a small VOR needle, 27 transmitting channels and a Lear 12 ADF, but there basically was no one to talk to or hear. 122.8 was the primary frequency we used to communicate with our office or other locations to request U.S. Customs when it was needed on an inbound flight. We had four Canadian Custom stations, but none of them had a radio or telephone – just taxi up to the dock and present yourself. No clearances, no assigned altitudes – wonderful.

We went past Wood Lake, Moose Lake, then down the length of Knife Lake and did a left turn into Cherry Lake. I made three attempts at landing to the west in case I could pick up after glow from the sunset, but that did not help. It is usually no wind or very light wind at night so the basic rule is not to use your landing light as it will reflect over a large area and is very confusing to judge your height. A night landing on water is basically a glassy water landing and settle in carrying a little power to touchdown. Should you have breezy conditions –20 knots of so — there will be white caps and you can safely use your landing lights while doing a normal power off landing.

We swung out to the southeast to look at the South Arm of Knife Lake, but went right over Hanson Lake where I noticed a fairly open stretch of water. A quick 180 degree turn, 20 degrees of flaps and slowed down to 60 mph and go one minute of open water – or one mile. That will work! Another let down until the wing tips meet the tops of the trees and you know what altitude you need on a go- around. The setup is good and Dr. Ciriacy says he did not even feel the floats touch the water. Now the landing light comes on and we taxi down the shoreline to find the portage to Cherry Lake, l find it and tie the bows to trees on the shore. Then we walk across the portage, yell at the fellows in the camp and one comes over in a canoe to take us to the camp.

It is now 11:45 and the doctor quickly checks the victim and tells me that he is still in shock and needs some heat on him. They have a 12'x16' wall tent, so I empty it out, take it down and set it again as an open "A" frame. Then I built two fires that threw their heat into the tent. Next I built a pot of coffee and told the doctor that we had coffee when he wanted. He told me that he wanted me to help shave the fellow's head so he could assess the skull damage. He had a hole in his skull and about 3:00 a.m. we sat down to a cup of coffee and the Dr. asked me if I could get back to Ely to pick up some items he needed at the hospital. More blood, bandages and medications. I told him that was no problem landing at my base and I got paddled back to the portage. 4:00 a.m. found me back on Shagawa Lake and soon on my way to the hospital. When I got back to the base I found Chick Beel waiting for me. He lived out on Cedar Lake and heard me when I flew into town. I told him that it was a 17 year old boy who was still unconscious, had a fractured skull, probably a broken neck and possibly other spinal problems. At that time I only owned two Cessna 180's and knew that getting a stretcher inside with someone in that shape would be a chore. I asked Chick if he could bring a USFS Beaver up there to fly him out. A larger door would be much easier to load, so we agreed on late morning. I then took off and went back to Cherry Lake getting there about 15 minutes before sunrise—so I just circled and landed right at the campsite on Cherry Lake about 5:30 a.m. A couple of hours later Dr. Ciriacy asked if I could go to the hospital again to get a full body traction stretcher – and away I went. I called Chick Beel when I got to the hospital and said 10:30 a,m, would be good for the pickup. This gave me time to get the stretcher up there and the injured fellow on it.

Chick arrived as scheduled and we loaded the victim in the Beaver. I could not help but think maybe it had been better to leave him here to pass away peacefully. He had been unconscious for 24 hours and the doctor was certain there would be spinal problems as well as all the known damages. I took off right behind Chick and the doctor and was slightly faster, so I had landed at my base and drove a mile down to the USFS dock and base. Chick pulled up to the dock and we loaded the wounded fellow into the ambulance. There was another fellow standing on the dock that I did not know. It turned out that he was a FAA employee who was in town on another matter, but heard about my night flight. He did tell me that he was filing a violation on me for taking off and landing on an unlighted surface per Part135. I told him that I would probably only charge for the fuel I used, but that made no difference to him. Milt Nelson, the chief pilot for the USFS air operation for many years, said that "Pat did a dam fine job. He risked his life and his airplane and saved the kids life". But the government is always right?

Six or seven years later someone that knew about the incident sent me a newspaper clipping from a Minneapolis newspaper with a story about the young fellow from the Cherry Lake incident saying he had a severed spinal cord and was paralyzed from the waist down, but completed law school in a wheel chair. He had just married a young lady who was a lawyer and was paralyzed from the waist down and in a wheelchair, so it worked out very well and was worth doing in spite of the FAA. I flew for over 60 years – mostly by far in seaplanes – and practically everyone says there shall be no operations in the dark. Most operators say to go to a lighted airport and land on a lighted runway. I think that is not only expensive, but ridiculous. The fellow that taught me how to fly said if you are going to make a career of bush flying, you are going to get stuck out late due to weather or emergency's or spend a lot of nights sleeping in a drifting seaplane, so he showed me how to take off and land in the dark. I would guess that I have made over a thousand landings after dark on water and never had a problem. It is always more comfortable if you are familiar with the landing area as to rocks, reefs or other possible dangers. If it is a lake or waterway with a fair amount of habitation I would recommend a low level pass with all your lights on to get the attention of canoeists or kayakers that are not equipped with running lights. If there are lighted boats running around, remember that they probably cannot hear you over their motor. I had hired my first full time pilot, David Hangartner, earlier that summer.

CHAPTER 16

1966

In 1966 I owned four aircraft — a Twin Beech 18, two Cessna 180's and a Piper PA - 12 that had a Lycoming 135 h.p. engine with all of them on floats. I had bought the PA-12 the fall before from its owner in International Falls, Minnesota with Edo 2000 floats, Federal 2500 skis and wheels for $6,000.00. This was used primarily as a trainer and some light charter. After freeze -up we put the skis on and had several persons signed up for Private Pilot flight training. As the winter went on I found myself wishing I had 2000 skis instead of the 2500's. The month of January would quite often see a high of 20 degrees below zero. The 2500 skis were a little heavy and would crack the landing gear tubing and it seemed that about every other night would find a couple of us laying on the ice at 30 degrees below zero welding the landing gear up so we could fly in the morning. People have asked me for years "why not put the airplane in the hanger?" When I bought the place I got 37 acres, 3,300 feet of shoreline and a unheated and uninsulated 60 foot X 60 foot hanger. I did dig out the back side and made it a 60 foot X 80 foot hanger and traded out a moose hunting trip for a cement hanger floor. This was followed by insulation and I installed a furnace. I also built on the south side area a two story office, waiting room plus a coffee bar, restrooms and even a shower so returning parties could clean up after a week or so in the bush. On the north side I built a 12 X 24 foot work room that we could easily heat for working on a float or wing with a separate heat system. But to open the 60 X 16 foot main door when it was below zero would require 12 hours or so to recover the lost heat. Our skis were mostly straight skis with no wheels so we would also have to shovel snow inside on the hanger floor so we could slide the aircraft in. It was much easier to freeze a rope in the ice and tie the aircraft outside. We had Stewart-Warner 50,000 BTU and Herman - Nelson 250,000 BTU gas powered heaters on toboggans to take out to the aircraft for warm up and starting. At night the heaters would be brought into the heated work office so they would start in the morning. The coldest morning I remember was 57 degrees below zero with no wind chill. I had 12 ice fishermen scheduled to fly out that day to heated fish houses we had on the ice on several lakes. One fellow had a bad heart, so I did not fly him out — but the others went and I picked them up a little before dark. The last week of March we had four pilots take their Private Pilot checkrides in a PA-12 on skis. They were Carlo Palombi, Pat Ferderber, Joe Skala and Flossie Carlson. Four check rides in one day. Carlo and Pat later worked for me after getting their commercial check rides.

Carlo Palombi, Pat Ferderber, Joe Skala and Flossie
Carlson ready for their check rides.

When the ice went out in May everything went back on floats. The first trip this PA-12 made on floats had a 16 foot boat tied on its side and the engine burned out. We pulled the engine and sent it out for overhaul. We got the Lycoming back in the latter part of July and reinstalled on the aircraft. The next two weeks were a nightmare with that engine. Finally I got fed up with it and called a dealer, Bob Leaders in the Minneapolis area and told him I might get interested in a brand- new Cessna 172, on floats that had been sitting in the show room of Walston Aviation in St. Paul for several months. And they were the Cessna distributor for the northern Midwest. After a couple days of negotiating I bought the Cessna 172 with a $18,000.00 price and traded the Piper Pa-12 in on it. This was N4252L with a pretty white, black and red paint job mounted on a set of brand-new Edo 2000 floats. We got the aircraft picked up, tied to our dock in Ely and started flying our current students. Everyone really enjoyed the brand-new airplane and we picked up three new Private Pilot students in the next two weeks. This got me thinking, and I went into town and talked to the banker. Then to the local newspaper and bought an add saying we were offering a Private Pilot course for a down payment of $495.00 and the bank would loan them $500.00 for twelve months at $50.00 each. This did bring almost ten students in the next three months. This aircraft was a 1200 hour time between overhaul (TBO) at that time and by the later part of March we had over 850 hours on it — in eight months. One of the major advantages happened in late October when a Cessna 150 landed at our base on Sandy Point. This was a surprise as I didn't know the Cessna 150 was approved on floats. Two occupants got out and introduced themselves as working for Walston Aviation, our Cessna Distributor on the South St. Paul airport. They said Cessna had installed a set of Edo 1650 floats with a one time approval on this 1966 Cessna, but 1967 models of the Cessna 150 would be approved as a seaplane in the spring. They offered me the chance to go try it out, so a friend, Jim Kobe and I jumped in and taxied back the length of Sandy Point. We had a light westerly wind giving us a bit of cross wind. Both fuel gauges were showing almost full and there were two suitcases in behind the seats, but we very quickly got on the step and then flew right off. We flew it for about 15 minutes, shot a couple more take-off and landings and then returned to Sandy Point. I was very pleased and excited about the performance and passed that on to the two gentlemen from Walston Aviation. It was getting late in the afternoon and they said they wanted to spend the night and talk to me about a business proposition. I drove them uptown to the Forest Hotel and said I would come back at 6:00 for dinner. During dinner they asked if I wanted to become a Cessna Seaplanes Only dealer.

This was quite a surprise and they explained the procedures. There would be a 20% discount on the aircraft and floats and 25% off the cost of ARC avionics. They also would take my check for a retail sale of an aircraft and hold the check until I got paid from the customer. They would also help me setting up financing for any aircraft for my own use. All I had to do is sign a contract for an order for a new 1967 Cessna 150 on floats for spring delivery. We spent a couple of hours discussing this but I ended up telling them that I would give them my answer at breakfast. Then I did sign the contract, became a Cessna seaplane dealer and could sell any new Cessna that had a seaplane kit installed on it — with or without floats. Later I was buying and selling quite a few sets of floats and started dealing direct with the float manufactures and getting 25% to 40% discounts — plus we got a fair bit of shop work assembling and installing the floats. Dick Johnson and Bob Bogert were the two that made the pitch to me and we were friends for quite a few years after that. Within two weeks later I sold Dr. Ed Ciarcy a brand new Cessna 180 and the next spring a new set of floats for it. An interesting thing showed up later. The 1967 Cessna 150's on floats did not perform near as well as the 1966 model they threw together. Three years later Lee Gilligan of Crystal Shamrock Aviation in Minneapolis got an STC (Supplemental Type Certificate) and installed a 150 h.p. Lycoming engine in the Cessna 150 floatplane. I actually ordered a kit from him, but shortly thereafter I cancelled the order. I thought it wiser to buy a 150 h.p. Lycoming in a Cessna 172 and have more uses for aircraft — including sightseeing and light charter. In 1968 Cessna stopped producing the Cessna 172 with the Continental six cylinder engine and replaced it with a Lycoming four cylinder 150 h.p. 0-320-E2D engine that had a 2,000 hour TBO (Time Between Overhaul). The first one I bought that spring of 1968 was N8425L a pretty polished aluminum aircraft with an orange and white stripe. I used to purchase all my new 172's with polished metal basic paint job because it saved 40 pounds of weight with less than one half of the aircraft covered with paint. I also always ordered the child's seat after the Lycoming versions came out. This way we could haul two normal adult passengers plus one or two children for sightseeing. We operated all of our airplanes with a 30 minute fuel reserve in the right hand tank and the fuel we needed in the left. This kept our working weight down so we had decent performance. With the Lycoming engine we also started using Pee Kay's 2300 float. These were a little heavier, but we sure liked the flat top for walking on — especially if you had a canoe tied on or on rough water. We often would carry two normal sized passengers, a 17 foot canoe and maybe 175 - 200 pounds of gear for shorter flights staying within 50 or 60 miles from the base. In 1977 Cessna brought out the 172XP (Extra Power) with a 213 h.p. engine, a constant speed propeller and a higher gross weight. This unit really worked well on the P-K's or the Aqua 2400's. I usually kept one or two online and sold quite a few as retail sales. The last few years in Ely I usually had four Cessna 172's working on floats in the summer and on skis in the winter. We were not working off an airport, so if someone bought a Private Pilot course it would be done on floats in the summer months and on skis in the winter months.

We did plow out a runway on the ice during the winter months. We would start as soon as we had about one foot of ice with a 3,000 by 100 ft runway — which by spring would usually be reduced to 2,500 by 50 feet with fairly high banks. We also laid out two ski runways that we kept smoothed out by dragging a log up and down the area with a snowmobile. When Christmas ended and everyone threw out their Christmas tree, we would pick up a hundred or so to mark the perimeters of the landing areas to give us more definition when it was snowing. In the spring when ice went out we could see the whole runway of five foot thick ice floating down the lake.

Taking on the Cessna dealership as a seaplane only sales turned out to be one of the best things I ever did. I would buy a batch of new airplanes in the spring — Cessna 180's, 185's, and 206's, and install a set of new floats, flew busily all summer and then sell the aircraft over the winter for close to our purchase price. Another benefit that there was very little maintenance except 100 hour inspections and changes of oil or spark plugs — Cessna even paid us for the first 100 hour inspection. And naturally our customers liked the idea of flying in new equipment. I made a lot of trips to Wichita, Kansas to the Cessna plant and delivery center where sitting to watch the bridge rusts was the main entertainment. To buy a drink you had to belong to and go to a club. It ended up with Bob Munroe of Kenmore Air in Seattle as a Seaplane only dealer for the Northwest, Dick Folsom Air in Greenville, Maine for the Northeast portion of the country and myself of Wilderness Wings Airways in Ely, Minnesota for the upper Midwest. I actually did quite a bit of business in Louisiana where seaplanes serviced much of the oil business before the takeover of the helicopters.

CHAPTER 17

HAND PROP

I don't know – and could not even guess about the number of pilots who have hand-propped an airplane. I learned how to fly in a Piper J-4E Cub Coupe on floats. It had a continental 75 h.p. engine instead of the original J-4-A which had a 65 h.p. engine. I thought having an additional 10 h.p. would be an advantage – but learned differently as I went along. The J-4 did not have an electrical system at all – no lights, no starter, no radio. I paid $850.00 for the aircraft out of annual, bought a set of floats, installed them and got an annual inspection and started a wonderful career in aviation. But every time I flew I had to hand prop to get the engine running. Because it was side by side seating my instructor taught me how to do the propping from both the RH side and the LH side. Normally we like to dock the airplane with the pilot side to the dock so that he can step out and catch the aircraft and tie it to the dock. Also the pilot likes to be the last one to get in right after he unties and pushes off. While on floats you have to be behind the propeller to hand prop – wheels or skis you would normally be in front of it. A lot of seaplane pilots stand behind the prop even when on solid ground – then you are not in the way if the aircraft moves forward when it starts.

This makes me think of one of my best friend – Bill Bailey of Minneapolis. He was in the upper end of the banking business and had a nice home on the north shore of Lake Minnetonka just northwest of

Minneapolis. In mid November I had two multi – engine seaplane students going in Ely and both needed a couple of more hours of training and a checkride. They both lived within 100 miles of Minneapolis. We would normally freeze up mid November in Ely and Minneapolis about two weeks later. I called Bill early on a Sunday and told him that we were forecast to go below zero that night and that would finish our summer. I asked if I could bring the Twin Beech (N6799C), park it on his shoreline and finish up the training Saturday and Sunday of the next week - end with their FAA check ride on Monday. He said to bring it in as he had the floats taken off his Cessna 172 just two days earlier, so he had lots of room.

I sent one of the dock hands to Minneapolis with one of the vehicles, topped the Twin Beech off with fuel, put another four full barrels of fuel in the cabin plus 10 gallons of oil in 5 gallon cans plus about 200 feet of rope. I had put the beaching gear in the vehicle that was already moving south. I thought everything was in good shape no matter what happened and I would be able to finish the two students and get paid by the VA without waiting for the next summer. This would be several thousand dollars to start the winter with. It was a two hour flight to his house. I got back to Ely that evening and got busy arranging flight time with the two students as well as getting on the FAA schedule for Monday with a backup for Tuesday. I guess we have all learned that in real life plans do not always work. Bill Bailey called Thursday and told me the lake had frozen over the night before. He said that he had gotten a fellow with a loader and they got the Twin Beech out of the water. I told him that I would try to get down and fly it off the ice when it hardened. Later he called again and said he had the Twin Beech tied down on the ice as well as his Cessna 172 on wheels. The two aircraft were tied parallel to the shoreline about 150 feet apart facing each other. He also told me that he and three other friends of his had each chipped in $500.00 and bought an Aeronca Champ on skis to play with during the winter. The Champ was tailed into the shore and had plenty of room to taxi around and between the Beech and the Cessna so I did not have to move the Beech until spring. Just before Christmas on a nice sunny Sunday Bill decided to go fly on skis, so he preheated the engine and untied the Champion. Then when he thought the engine was ready he opened the door, turned the fuel on, gave it several shots of prime, exercised the throttle and positioned himself to pull the propeller. Unlucky for him it started – at full throttle and rapidly started moving forward. On a Piper J-3 the door is split and opens ½ up and ½ down, but on the Aeronca Champ the door opens fore and aft and when the engine went to full power it blew the door shut. He could not get the door opened with the propeller blast, so he slid out until he had hold of the outboard end of the RH lift strut. The ice was very smooth and had some snow cover, but his heels were dug in and the Champ was turning in circles at full power. Somehow he missed both the Twin Beech and his own Cessna. After several turns he realized that he could not keep this up until the engine ran out of fuel, but being fast on his feet and a quick thinker he decided he would let go when the circle was pointed to the southwest. The highly populated area of Minneapolis/St. Paul was east and south of his location, St. Cloud and a dozen small towns strung out to the northwest along Interstate #94. To the west and southwest the terrain was flat and mostly lightly populated farm country and could probably absorb an airplane crash without a lot of injuries. But plans do not always work out and this time when it was turned loose it continued its turn to the right while picking up speed. It finally straightened out and headed directly towards Bill's house and picture window with his wife and two sons standing in the window watching all this excitement. The tail came up in the air as the speed built up to almost flying speed, but the shoreline rose a couple of feet and the skis hit it converting it to a gearless champ that could go even faster. Who knows how fast it could go now, but fortunately it was deflected a few degrees from the previous course it had toward the house. It struck a large tree right on the hub of the propeller. This of course stopped all forward motion, spared the house and wrapped the wings around the tree and destroyed the aircraft — no insurance, so Bill bought out the others. Charlie Kehoe was a captain for Braniff Airlines at that time living next door to Bill Bailey on Lake Minnetonka and he and his wife saw the entire happening. I do not know if it is true or not, but they say a dozen neighbors added picture windows facing a view of Bill's house. If you are going to hand prop an aircraft, do not untie the machine until after the engine is running and always check the position of the throttle TWICE before starting. Quite a few times when I am alone, I will turn the fuel selector off – the engine can run for a few moments and then I turn the fuel back on.

The first winter I was flying was 1957 and I went to Duluth for a few days over Christmas to visit my parents. One day I drove up to the airport and stopped to talk to Ray Walberg who was the local operator. Like all airport offices there always seemed to be a few people hanging around and this was true that day. There was a North Central Airlines DC-3 on the ramp loading passengers for a flight to Minneapolis. We had watched him start one engine, but nothing happened on number two Then the young Captain came out and into the office asking if he could use a telephone. We all could not help to hear him when he got someone in their office in Minneapolis to send another aircraft with a mechanic and a starter as he had one that would not turn over. There was a fellow in the office there who jumped up and said "Hold on, we can hand prop that one and you can leave on schedule". His name was Hilding Anderson and I knew him slightly as he had been a Norseman pilot for the U.S. Forest Service in Ely a couple years earlier. The North Central captain looked at him and laughingly said "You do not handprop DC3s. Hilding said to stand by a minute, and went in back to the hanger and returned with a leather boot that fit over the prop, with a 20 foot rope attached. Hilding told the captain to get back in the cockpit, "give me 8 or 9 shots of prime, crank the throttle and I will start your engine for you". By now there were a dozen watchers as Hilding put the boot over the end of the prop, had one fellow give him a hand on the pull and it started on the first pull. The boot of course flew off as the propeller started to move and I have never forgotten that sight.

My second airplane was a Stinson 108-3 with a Franklin 165 h.p. engine and I learned how to prop that one pretty quick. A Cessna 180 followed the Stinson and it had a poor battery which I was not told about. I ferried that one on floats back to Ely, Minnesota and ended up landing after dark in Northern Wisconsin just before a thunderstorm hit. The next morning and my third start for the airplane I had to hand prop it with a dead battery. I had never flown a Cessna 180 before this, but Chick Beel could not get away, so he gave me an oral check ride and said that he would check me out thoroughly when I got back. I had left Austin Lake at Kalamazoo, Michigan and started across Lake Michigan to Green Bay, Wisconsin, but ran into fog to the water just before halfway. I returned to Michigan and followed the coast up to the narrows between northern Michigan and southern Michigan then west to Wisconsin. I was planning on landing at Boulder Junction to spend the night and there was a seaplane base there for fuel. I was probably 10 to 12 miles from Boulder Junction when it got dark, but I could see the lights of the town. Just then a bolt of lightning passed in front of the propeller and heavy rain appeared on the windshield. Five minutes earlier I had flown by a large dock with a bright light on it and I did a quick 180 turn and started back to it. The lake was not large, but definitely workable. As I swung around I could tell that I had a cross wind from the right front at approximately 20 knots and could not help thinking that here I am making my first landing in a Cessna 180 at night with a crosswind and heavy rain – and no insurance! It went well though and as I taxied up to the dock, a fellow walked out there to help me. As we tied the aircraft down I asked if this was a resort and if it was could he put me up for the night. He said yes and walked me up the hill and showed me a cabin and pointed out the dining room which had already closed. But he said to be there in 15 minutes and his wife would feed me. A nice chicken dinner a good nights sleep, breakfast with a charge of $10.00 but I gave them $20.00. That probably doesn't happen much anymore. The next morning was sunny, but very windy and the battery was dead. So I hand propped the airplane and took off for Boulder Junction and a fuel stop. A cold front had gone through during the night and it was blowing 25 knots, but the wind direction made it workable. The short flight getting there did charge the battery just enough to barely get a start when I left Boulder Junction. I flew from there to Duluth and listened to the control tower with reported gusts to 45 knots so I decided to fly straight to Ely and then fly down to Bill Martilla's to buy a new battery later. The windsock was standing straight out and snapping when I got to Ely, but I had no trouble landing behind Sandy Point and parking. Two years before while I had the Stinson I signed a lease on the property from the mining company. There was an underground iron mine ¼ of a mile away and it included a large dock and 60 ft by 60 ft hanger with no insulation and a gravel floor. I called Chick Beel and told him I was back with the Cessna 180. He said that the USFS had a lightning strike start a fire when that cold front went through and it was about 80 miles east of Ely. That made USFS air arm pretty busy flying fire crews and supplies, but in a day or so he should be able to check me out. I told him no problem, I have already flown the aircraft into a fog bank, into a thunderstorm, landed at night in a strong crosswind, flown a 300 mile detour and in some pretty strong winds and had hand propped the aircraft. I probably had 600 hours of flying time then. A few months later he asked me to submit a bid on a U.S. Forest Service fire patrol contract to help out when they had a fire or two going. 1,000 hours flight time was the minimum and I had just slightly over 800 hours, but he said to write in the required 1,000 hours. He said that they had two different pilots who each had a Stinson 108 that Chick did not approve of. He said that not only was I a safer pilot, but I was very familiar with the area after years of canoe guiding.

So I got a FAA Part 135 certificate which was pretty simple then. A FAA examiner flew the airlines to Duluth, took a taxi cab five miles to the west end of Pike Lake just as I landed there. He looked at my pilots license, my logbook, the aircraft logs and a five minute inspection of the Cessna 180 and mailed the Certificate to me. Now I had both the FAA 135 certificate and a USFS contract and the money came in easier.

I learned the P&W R985 engine was simple to hand prop when needed. In bush flying you would quite often be out for a few days or a week and not be within a couple of hundred miles of an aircraft service operation so you learned to be self-sufficient. Some of those batteries on larger radial engine aircraft might weigh close to 100 pounds. The first time I had to had prop a Beech 18 it took me a while to figure it out. I had flown 250 miles to Armstrong, Ontario and landed for fuel. I had another 190 miles to go and pick up five passengers and two canoes at 1:00 p.m. on the Albany River and then make a non stop flight back to Ely. This was one of Orville Wieben's Superior Airways bases manned by one pilot – and a Bellanca Senior Skyrocket with a 600 h.p. P&W R1340. He showed me the propeller hub on this with a notch in it. He said that you put a knot in the end of a rope, place the knot in the notch tie it on a pick-up and drive away and the engine would start. The Beech did not have a notched prop hub and the failed starter was on the RH engine – out over the water. The bow of the floats stuck out about 12 inches in front of the prop, so there was not enough room to swing the propeller and go anywhere if the engine started. The prop blades were right over the float with a six inch clearance. I finally remembered Hilding Anderson and the DC-3 — we did not have a prop blade boot, but took a six foot piece of ½ inch rope, tied a five inch loop on one end, stood on the RH wing between the engine nacelle and the fuselage. I then manually adjusted the prop blade so that the lower end was straight below me, primed the engine, carb heat off, magnetos on, prop control adjusted, mixture rich and lowered the loop of the pull rope down until I snagged the lower end of the propeller. Then a strong pull upward, the lower end would come up, the rope would slide off of the blade and usually the engine would start. It did that day – first pull. Every time we put a Twin Beech on floats we would remove the LH generator and battery which eliminated about 150 pounds, but usually at the end of the second season the battery would grow old and we would have to hand prop a few times. I always hated to buy a new battery and then have it sit unused all winter.

The first time I hand propped a single engine Otter was an experience. I was ferrying a DeHavilland DHC-3 from Ely Minnesota to Cordova, Alaska. I usually flew to Ft. Peck, Montana for fuel, then to Polson, Montana for another fuel stop in case I could not get through Snoqualmi Pass and had to divert south on the Columbia River to Portland to follow the coast north to Seattle. I had a passenger riding in the right seat – Tom Grahek, Sr. from Ely and headed for Ketchikan, Alaska to visit his son Tom, Jr. who was flying for a seaplane operator there. Tom Jr., a year later became my son in-law Tom 2. I ended up with two son in-laws who both were named Tom making them Tom 1 and Tom 2. Tom senior and I spent the first night at Fort Peck and the next morning started for Polson, Montana. As we entered the east end of Marias Pass the wind picked up blowing 40 knots plus and it got turbulent. I did not relish the thought of spending the next hour going through a very narrow steep sided canyon where the wind could easily gust 50 knots or more especially with my passenger holding on to his seat very hard, so I turned and got out of the pass and headed north east. Once I got clear of the pass I followed the edge of the mountains until I saw a lake on our west side or LH side. I turned in and started descending for a landing and saw it was blowing 25 to 30 knots and steepened my approach. The landing was bumpy, but we started taxing to a small beach on our left. I sailed sideways to the beach, but a gust of wind pulled the floats off of the beach just as we touched. I tried to start the engine but the battery would not turn the propeller, I ran through the cabin and picked up a 100 foot coil of rope and jumped into the water up to my chest. I did get the rope tied to the aircraft floats and wrapped around a tree until I got it pulled to shore. Then I want back to the battery problem, but it would still not move the propeller. I knew it was almost five miles to the nearest road and another six to eight miles to the town of Browning. The battery weight 70 pounds and even when I found a trail running towards the road the amount of bear tracks on the trail discouraged me. I am pretty familiar with bears and these seemed to be Grizzly tracks. The wind was still pretty strong, so we decided we would wait until the wind laid down and then we would hand prop and go. l had never hand propped a Otter, but it is all we could do. About 4:00 p.m. the wind laid down considerably, so I hand primed the engine, got all the controls inside set up and had Tom (who was a pilot) sit in the cockpit to handle the throttle. I climbed down on the RH float, gave it a hard pull and it started first pull. We quickly untied, took off and headed back to Marias Pass. It was nice and smooth now so I decided we would go to Coeur d' Alene and Bill Brook's seaplane base. He had a fairly large dock, fuel, a motel/restaurant right next door and a 24 volt battery charger. Two hours later we landed there, got set up and our battery on a all night charge. l had known Bill Brooks for quite a few years, sold he and his wife several new Cessna 180's – Cessna 185's. a Cessna 206 and a used Cessna 172 on floats, so we did have a couple of drinks before calling it a day. We left the next morning with a two hour flight to Kenmore Air in Seattle. Refueled, cleared Canadian Customs in Nanaimo, BC. Got up along the coast almost to Kelsey Bay, but bad weather made us return to Campbell River for the night. Next day we made Ketchikan, dropped Tom and on I went to Cordova which would not have happened without a hand prop of the Otter.

In later years in Honolulu we had a pilot flying for us part time and also working across the street at a flight school. He was flying for us one day and the flight school called him and said their other instructor was stuck on the Island of Molakai with a bad starter. They wanted him to take a mechanic and starter over there so they would get their Cessna 172 back. I asked how come they do not hand prop and fly it home, but the instructor on Molakai hand never done it and thought it was too dangerous.

CHAPTER 18

AVIATION AND GOVERNMENT

Quite a few times in my career I wondered about the wisdom of choosing Aviation to invest in. It seems like every government agency in existence was determined to restrict aviation companies – especially the FAA. One of the founding statements of the FAA was to promote aviation but that was actually removed from their agenda 30 or 40 years ago. President Harry Truman in December, 1948 signed a bill that established a no – fly Wilderness Area in Northern Minnesota which would go into effect in June, 1953. I was not flying yet at that time, but I remember the U.S. Marshals coming to town and they arrested quite a few pilots who wanted to test the validity of the law. There were four seaplane operators working off Shagawa Lake on the north side of Ely then. Bill Liethold had a Noorduyn Norseman, a Fairchild 51, a Curtis Robin, a Piper J-3 and an Aeronca Champ and was a G-I Bill training school as well as a charter operator. This is where Chick Beel, my flight instructor, learned to fly when he got out of the service after WWII. Going west down Shagawa Lake was Ernie Hautala who had two Stinson 108's, then Elwyn West with a Norseman, two cabin Waco's and a Piper PA-11 and just past West's was a one man operation with a Gullwing Stinson SR-9F whose name I cannot remember. At that time there were 15 to 20 fly in resorts in Lac La Croix, Crooked Lake, Basswood, and Knife Lake, Thomas Lake, Kekekabic Lake, Gun Lake and Horse Lake. Of course these lodges were also forced out of business.

In 1962 I applied for a Canadian 9-4 non – scheduled flight permit – their version of the U.S. Part 135. This did bring on quit a few new regulations, such as the Canadian government controlled the flight rates. This I liked because they were a bit higher and there was no competition in rates. The charges were so much per mile — 80 cents per mile for the Twin Beech, 55 cents per mile for the Beaver, etc.

These were for each mile flown. Sometimes you got lucky and flew passengers from point A to point B going back to point A. Often you picked up another group at point B and get paid double. The first year we were only allowed 20 flights per month and then that limit was dropped. During December 1970 the Canadian government changed the law and permits to allow U.S. 9-4 carriers to only carry passengers to the base of the nearest Canadian air carrier who then would fly the passengers to their destination from there. Our next closest Canadian competition was on Lac La Croix 60 miles away and he had a brother who was on the Parliament in Ottawa. This ruling only took in the territory starting at Lake of the Woods east to Sault Ste Marie. Thus it basically only affected U.S. operators in Minnesota, Wisconsin and Michigan and basically affected only seaplanes as the wheel plane operators were going to airports anyway and that was where most of the Canadian operators were. I think we had seven Minnesota operators affected and only three that were seaplane only. Of those three, I was the largest with nine aircraft at that time, Frank Bohman at International Falls with two aircraft and one fellow on Lake of the Woods with one aircraft who did not do much transborder flying. The second week of January 1971 the seven of us flew to Washington, D.C. to meet with our Congressman — both Senators, Hubert Humphrey and Walter Mondale plus our NE Minnesota Representative John Grahek. I personally knew all three of the gentlemen. Hubert Humphry knew both of my parents and would often stop by their house for a meal or a drink. I had flown Walter Mondale out fishing in Canada a couple of times and I graduated from high school in Hibbing, Minnesota just six miles from John Grahek's town of Chisholm, Minnesota.

Tom Halverson, a friend and aviation operator at Duluth and Grand Rapids provided a Cessna 421 and a pilot, Gordy Newstrom, who handled the LH front seat and I covered the RH front to assist Gordy if he needed it. We spent three days including a stop at FAA on Independence Avenue. We really pushed the fact that everything in aviation is supposed to be reciprocal between the U.S. and Canada. The congressmen all agreed with us but did nothing. Sadly that is the way of politics. The FAA did not seem to know much about seaplanes, but left us with the idea that if we were to purchase several Boing 707's they might be able to assist. We did a second trip there in late February, but nothing had happened yet.

Usually I worked several sport shows in Chicago, Milwaukee, Minneapolis, Des Moines and Omaha advertising our services, but had to drop most of those because we still did not know what we would be allowed to do. We did hire a Canadian lawyer then and in just over three months we got a modification of the last ruling. We would be allowed to land at any licensed tourist operation in Ontario, but not on any lake with no one on it. A good share of our business came from people who wanted to be alone, but we did transport quite a few passengers into Canadian fishing lodges and camps who appreciated the business as we usually had recommended them as a good spot. We had several of these resorts write our Canadian attorney that they wanted the business that we brought in. During late March I did get a phone call from Shaver Strand. We had enlisted in the Marine Corps together in 1950 and he was very political and entertained a lot of politicians at his island on Pelican Lake, Minnesota. He had talked with Senator——— that day about my problem with the Canadians. He told me that Senator ———- could have me flying again in two months for a $60,000 investment — no checks! I told Shaver that it being winter and a good share of the business shut down that I could not come up with that much money. We did get flying trans – border in June thanks to the Canadian Attorney and quickly made a deal with several lodge operators to allow us to drop off canoe parties at their dock for a $5.00 per person charge. You will never convince me that you cannot buy our government — in fact you cannot get much done unless you pay for it.

During the mid 1970's the FAA started what they called The Swap Team annual inspections for Part 135 ops. I think it was the first week of June we had a crew of four FAA persons arrive from Chicago about mid – day. They had flown airlines to Duluth, Minnesota and rented a car to come to Ely. They did stop by our base and said they were going to have lunch and check in their hotel, but wanted to see the pilot and aircraft list when they got back. Two hours later they showed up and were very surprised when they saw that we had ten aircraft and everyone was a seaplane. None of the four had a seaplane rating and could not do our annual pilot check rides per Part 135. I pointed out that including several part time pilots we needed five multi – engine seaplane and thirteen single – engine sea check rides.

They told me that I would have to call Minneapolis GADO and request the check rides. I had done this the first few days of May because we usually did our annual inspection and the check rides either the last week of May or the first week of June. When I had called that spring they said that I would be getting a Swap Team inspection, but they did not know who. The group from Chicago said they could check the aircraft though and so they did. Friday morning they stopped by the office before driving back to Duluth for their airline flight home. One of my pilots, Mark Kortkamp asked the leader of the group what he thought about the operation. He replied that the only thing he did not like was the fact that we did not file flight plans per Part 135. I overheard that and told him that the FAA would not accept flight plans from us. He shook his head and they all left headed for Duluth. Six weeks later I got a letter from Minneapolis GADO that they were informed that we were not filing flight plans. They said they know how busy we were, but we would have a meeting later to cover this. In September I got another letter saying there would be a formal hearing during the first week of November. My attorney, Ron Walls, and I flew his Cessna on wheels, that I had sold him, to Minneapolis the morning of the hearing and were taken to a room with five of the higher FAA personnel. I had brought our large daily flight schedule and after the preliminaries I put it on the table to be examined. I picked a day with the first flight of our DeHavilland Beaver, DHC-2 N11015, departing at 0800 with 3 U.S. passengers, 1 canoe and camping gear. We called U.S. customs at 0730 told him of the departure, that it was going to the Canadian side and we would call him to do the check-in about 1100 and the outward manifest would be on our counter. Then I explained to the FAA the Beaver would take-off, fly to the Canadian Customs call our office on 122.8 mc when he started to descend 20 miles into the flight and land at an island that the Canadian Customs officer lived on with his family. After clearing customs and paying the duty on food stuffs, the aircraft will taxi 150 yards to another island where the Ontario Ranger and his family live and the passengers would get a travel permit and purchase fishing licenses. After all of this the Beaver will call our base and notify our office that it is leaving Basswood for Beaverhouse Lake — a 20 minute flight and then call descending at Beaverhouse Lake. Our base might not be able to receive the message but 90% of the time one of our aircraft would be in the air and pass it on. He will then unload, take off, call in and proceed to another Canadian Ranger for a fish check — even though he is empty. Flight Service does not like the 0800 departure with two hours of fuel aboard including the reserve but not going to be back for three hours. They say that they are required to initiate a search at time of fuel exhaustion. The Canadian government is more understanding and you can file a flight notification for up to seven days. I made out a flight plan for our proposed flight and gave it to the leader along with the 800 number for Hibbing Flight Service and asked him to file the flight plan. He called, talked for a few minutes, hung up and said "He is right"! They will not accept the flight plan." I kind of poked Ron Walls with my elbow thinking that we had proved a point. Then we were asked to leave the room for five minutes. When we came back in a gavel was produced, pounded on the table with the announcement that I was being fined $1,000.00 each for six flights or $6,000.00 and if we want to fight this they would fine me $1,000.00 for each flight for the year. I knew that if they checked U.S. Customs that we had over 200 flights into Canada that summer which would be $200,000.00 and there would be more than that after adding U.S. flights, so I caved in. I did say that is was winter coming up and money would be scarce until spring, so they gave me until the end of May to pay it. I did not pay it by June so they refused to re-issue our Part 141 Flight school permit that was coming up for renewal. Now I know I should have gone to the press, media, AOPA and other organizations to bring up the fact that I was being fined for the failure of another FAA branch. We had gone along this way for 15 years at that time with no problems. Within the next year the FAA made a rule change that operators could bypass the flight plan if they kept the info of the flight plan available while the flight was happening. We had done that for years knowing the loads and fuel carried. We even went as far as stashing 55 gallon drums of fuel in some remote spots.

We used to have annual inspections for FAA Part 135 and Part 141 (flight school). These would usually take place in June because some years we might have ice on the lake until mid – May. Both of these inspections involved an aerial check ride of each chief flight instructor, assistant chief flight instructor or charter pilot. In the early 1970's the FAA had a rule that the chief flight instructor must be on the premises while training is going on one of his courses. I had leased Bob Munroe of Kenmore Air in Seattle a Twin Beech on floats to do multi-engine seaplane training (MES) during the winter. His Chief Flight Instructor, Bill Fisk, made a trip to Wichita, Kansas for a couple of days to pick up a new airplane at the Cessna plant and the FAA saw the Twin Beech out for flight training without his chief flight instructor available. Bob Munro ended up paying a pretty fair sized penalty having Part 141 training going on. He told me about that when I picked up the Twin Beech in the spring. I had 15 pilots flying for me at that time, so I made everybody either a Chief Flight Instructor or an Assistant Chief flight Instructor – that way we would have someone there while training was going on. We had five Part 141 courses – Private Pilot, Commercial Pilot, Instrument Rating, Single Engine Seaplane and Multi Engine Seaplane and Five Chief Flight Instructors and ten Assistant Chief Flight Instructors. I was Chief Flight Instructor for MES rating and Instrument rating. I went up with a young FAA inspector on the Instrument check ride in a Cessna 185 on straight floats. With the blessing of the FAA we had made a NDB approach to the Ely airport utilizing the local broadcast station (WELY-1450) and worked up a good approach plate. Otherwise we had to fly about 95 miles to either Duluth or International Falls to fly an NDB approach. We went out and did that and it went well in spite of south 20/25K, gusting 30K crosswind.

When we returned to our base at Sandy Point he told me he wanted to see a glassy water landing. With the strong south wind we had to come over a 300 foot hill on the north shore and then land across the lake with just under ½ mile of space and a 200 foot hill on the south shore. I told him that I thought that was unsafe and I would do a rough water landing with a steep approach. This is what I did, and he said that his rulebook said that if the check ride was in a seaplane a glassy water landing was required and he could not sign me off as passed on the check ride. I asked how many hours he had on floats and he replied "about 80 hours". I then told him that at that time I had 10,000 hours on floats and when we got docked, we would go in my office. Then I would call his supervisor and tell him that you will not pass me on my check ride unless I do something that I think is very unsafe. After we tied up and started into the office he changed his mind and made the sign -off.

In 1978 President Jimmy Carter put us out of business! I had 16 aircraft on the Part 135 certificate and about 45 people working for me. He passed a bill that extended the boundaries of the Boundary Water Canoe Area and took away about 80% of our winter business and 80% of our American side of our summer business. A bunch of the U.S. resorts and lodges were affected also, so we all banded together and chartered a Boeing 727 to take us to Washington, D.C. to meet with Congress. We spent three days there and everyone got to express their views to Congress. I put in my views explaining all the med-a- vac flights, assisting the Forest Service doing fire patrols and hauling forest fire crews and supplies during fires. We also helped distribute canoe parties and fly a lot of game surveys for different government agencies. We delivered quite a few death messages concerning family happenings or notification of serious accidents with children hospitalized to persons on a canoe trips. We had a good working arrangement with the Sheriff's Department and picked up drowning victims around the area which was almost entirely roadless. The Sheriff Department tried to keep a body bag in our hanger all the time and the U.S. Forest Service would keep one or two of their radio pack sets complete with strap - on antenna there. I remember picking up a fellow at 0600 on Shell Lake one morning on Memorial Day weekend. I found their campsite, quickly landed and taxied in. There were four people on shore, but one was standing there with a duffel bag. I shut the engine down, drifted to shore and told them the name of the fellow I was looking for whose mother had passed away the day before. It was the fellow with the duffel bag and he said he was ready to go. I told him the bad news and he asked if I remembered him because a year before to the day I had picked him up at the same spot to tell him that his father had passed away. He said he heard the aircraft coming and he knew what had happened.

One year we had seven med-a-vac flights in one day in July. This followed by over a dozen phone calls from the USFS offices in Duluth and Milwaukee, Wisconsin questioning our flight into the wilderness area and saying that a couple of these did not report to the Ely hospital. I could only tell them that I was a pretty good pilot, but not qualified to do medical assessment of people. The Sheriff's Department notified us of the need of the flight and we tried to do it immediately. A couple of times the office would call me on 122.8 mc while I was en-route to Canadian Customs with passengers and I would get informed of a broken leg, axe cut or even a heart attack, so I would leave my passengers with Roy Forsythe, the Customs Officer and his wife who would come up with coffee and cookies while I would go make the emergency pick up. An hour or so later I would be back at customs to finish my first trip. One afternoon I was 25 miles east of Ely hopping sightseeing rides at a couple of lodges on Snowbank Lake when I got a radio call from the office asking if I had enough fuel to go to Isabella and pick up a logger who cut his arm off. I said it would take ten minutes to return my passengers and I would be on my way. I also told her to pinpoint the lake and where for the pickup. Just over a half hour later I landed on a lake Northwest of Isabella that had a blue pickup blinking his headlights next to a boat ramp. I landed, heeled back up on the ramp and loaded the injured passenger in the RH front seat. They had a large belt set up as a tourniquet but I could see that it would take two hands to work it, so I took a short piece of rope, a short stick and set it up on his LH upper arm. This way I could loosen or tighten it with my right hand as I flew. I tossed the lower half of his LH arm in the backseat and away we went. Twenty five minutes later he was in an ambulance headed to the hospital. I thought that my business was an asset to the area, but that evening my friend and lawyer Ron Walls came to my hotel room and said I was the scape goat. He said that the Sierra Club had negotiated that they would allow outboard motors on Basswood Lake and some of the other lakes forming the Canadian border — probably because they could not shut the motors off in a foreign country. They also said they would allow snowmobile use on quite a few lakes during the winter — both of these permissions would come if the seaplane (me) operation was shut down. Legally they could not shut me down, but they could and did take away enough business that we could not make a profit. I immediately started selling off my 16 aircraft — mostly at a loss. I finally sold the business (Wilderness Wings Airways) its licenses and permits, six aircraft, all of the dock, office, shop, a van and a bunch of tools. I got $10,000 up front to pay the current short term debt and a contract for $375,000 to be paid over a five year period with six monthly payments of $12,500 during the summer months of May through October. I had known the people who were buying the business for several years and considered them friends, but learned an expensive lesson. l never did get paid one cent of the $375,000 note and those people did not even last the first summer. The Clagget brothers came up from Florida and they hired a couple of so called bush pilots from Florida. Usually pilots from Florida do not fly in a lot of bad weather. They sold the Twin Beech N44573 and kept the money. They left Ely and went back to Florida taking the Beaver N11015 with them. I ended up buying that back through an airline pilot I knew. He bought the Beaver from them (I did not see any of that money either) and I immediately bought it back from him and took it to Alaska. I did talk to some of my old customers in Ely later and they all said that if it was rainy the new owners shut down and had ground school. I had even paid the attorney for the Ely Bank $4,000.00 to draw up the contract. All of this came about because the U.S. government and it's rule. Several of the drive in local resorts were also bought out by the government. One of those was Sunny Dene Resort on Fall Lake that was converted to a Federal resort spot for government employees. I had kept one DeHavilland DHC-3 Otter and took that to Cordova, Alaska and started all over again — hauling fish and fuel at first but then got back into tourism and grew to six aircraft with our own fishing lodges, camps and outpost cabins.

I spent 20 years in Alaska and absolutely loved it. The last 10 years I wintered in Northern California.

Not because of the weather, but it was good for business. My oldest daughter Katie and her husband Tom came into the business so we worked a lot of sport and travel shows during the winter selling our services. At one of these shows we had worked out a trade of the use of a houseboat for the winter, based on the river in Stockton, California for one of our state wide tours for two persons. We had the Twin Beech there and I wanted to get an annual inspection on it. I asked around and someone said there was a fellow up in Clear Lake, California that did some work on seaplanes and I did track him down. Tom Wasson, based at the Lakeport Airport. I told him that I needed an annual on the Beech and would like to trade it out for a multi - engine seaplane rating. He said that he had thought he would never get a MES rating and would really like to do it. I ferried the Beech to Clear Lake and got along very well with Tom and his wife Tina, so every fall we would bring all of our aircraft down there from Alaska for maintenance and we would do single and multi - engine seaplane training.

Our Beaver dropping guests at our Hanigita Lake Cabin

We operated Part 91 in Alaska and I think it was either 1995 or 1996 the FAA tried to make everyone become a Part 135 operator. There were probably 40 to 50 fishing lodges who owned aircraft and flew their customers out for a day of fishing in local waters. They did not charge a defined price for the flight, but built it into their single price. We did the same with our business, Alaskan Wilderness Outfitting Company, but none of us dealt with anyone but our customers. Alaska rules said that if you provided food and lodging and did not charge for flying you did not have to be a charter operator. This saved us almost 50% on our aviation insurance charges and a lot of FAA paperwork and inspections. There was a large scheduled meeting about this in late March or early April in Anchorage, so I went to town for it. There were almost 200 people there and lots of discussion. The general consensus was that the Part 91 operators had a better safety record than the Part 135 operators. Finally Alaska's favorite senator, Ted Stevens, stood up and stated that a lot of good discussion was made by both sides, but then he advised the FAA group that if you do this you have to understand there would be no more money – NO MORE MONEY. The discussion ended there and everyone left. The FAA naturally thought their budget would go up and allow more personnel and pay.

Sunrise at Island Seaplane Service, Honolulu

I was astonished a year later when I was starting a sight seeing operation — Part 91 — in Honolulu, Hawaii that the FAA got their way and everyone had to go Part 135 in Alaska. This lasted a year and then the "No More Money" caught up and the FAA had to allow the affected operators to give up the Part 135 and return to Part 91. I guess that most of them did just that. My daughter and son-in-law were located in a serious fishing area and they did pick up quite a lot of fisherman charters, so they kept their Part 135. About five years later the FAA made another effort to make everyone a Part 135 operator. This time they published a list of twelve aircraft accidents. It was pretty interesting if you studied it. Nine were Part 135 operators, one was a Canadian sight - seeing operator in Niagara Falls, one was an aerobatic thrill flight and one was a bona fide Part 91 operator in Hawaii with a wooden prop failure on a Waco YMF-5 plane. The woman flying did make a safe smooth landing on a golf course with no injuries. So that effort did not go far.

One of the main reasons for Part 91 is to have some control over operators that are transporting passengers from Point A back to Point A and not going over 25 miles from their departure point with no landings en-route. My wife and I had operated on Oahu Island in Hawaii for several years and had no problem with that ruling. Then one day a short, heavy IRS agent walked into our office and told us that we were not paying our 8% transportation tax. I immediately said that we do not transport people from point A to point B and do not have a FAA Part 135 certificate that would allow us to do that. We had a lively discussion for a bit and he said he would be back. We told him to call ahead otherwise I might be flying and gone. We did call our attorney, Chris Ferrara and tipped him off on what the IRS wanted. He agreed with us 100% and said to let him know when the IRS shows up again. We had several more meetings and things were getting heated. I finally was banned from the meeting by my wife Debbie and our lawyer Chris to prevent any incidents that might bring the police in. We had several conversations with the FAA who did agree with us, but would not take any official action. The IRS was also after the helicopter tour operators — although most of them did hold Part 135 certificates. Seeing as we were seaplanes there basically were not places to land and drop off passengers except the open ocean which was too rough. This dragged on for some months till the IRS filed a bank lien against our business account and then we made payments of 8% of our flight income for a few months so we could keep flying. It was either that or they would go back for our entire years of operation and file a claim for that plus interest. It is hard to fight City Hall and even harder to fight Federal Government. Then we received a letter from the IRS saying that it was an unjust tax and we were excused from making the monthly payments. We had paid them just over $46,000 including the bank lien and never got one cent back!

One of the largest helicopter operators had a couple of lawyers working on the matter and he said that he lost about $200,000.00.

One Monday late afternoon I was on the phone talking to someone in America while a fellow walked down our entrance way ramp and was talking to my wife Debbie at the front counter. I overheard his words as he walked out saying they were shutting off our water at 10:30 on Wednesday. I finished my call and walked out into the front office asking Debbie what that was about. She replied that was the new Fire Marshall for Airports Division saying that our water hookup was illegal and would be shut off.

I called Chris Ferrara, our Attorney and passed this on. He said it was too late in the day, but he would find out what was going on the next morning. Years before while I was still in Alaska, I had a Twin Beech in Northern California for a double engine change. I called one day to ask how the project was going and was told that they should be done over the weekend. I said that I would fly down to San Francisco Friday night, pick up a rental car in the morning and drive up north to Lakeport and start back to Alaska when the plane was ready. I got up there mid - morning Saturday and found out the propeller governors were held up and would not be shipped until the end of the week. It was the middle of April so there was nothing going on in Alaska yet and I did not feel like just sitting there for a week with nothing to do.

I then decided to go to Hawaii for a few days, returned to San Francisco, turned in the rental and jumped a bus to the airport. A few hours later I was in Honolulu with a car and a hotel. I spent three days looking around and was amazed at the amount of helicopter tours going on. I made a call to both the FAA and the Airports Property Manager, explained my seaplane experience and that I might be interested in starting a seaplane tour operation. I got the same reply from both agencies "You cannot fly seaplanes in Hawaii"! I brought up to both parties the fact that aviation in Hawaii started with Pan American's Clippers flying boats. Then during WWII there were hundreds of Consolidated PBY's based and flying through Hawaii. In 1929 Inter Island Airlines brought three Sikorsky flying boats to Hawaii and started servicing the outlying islands. They are now Hawaiian Airlines. I kept after then and it took eight years to start a seaplane base. A major part of the negotiation was having fresh water to keep the salt off the aircraft. I was told that there was potable water on the property but when we tapped in we found that it was brackish and could not be used to wash aircraft. The only potable water along the shoreline was to the fire hydrants. This was turned over to Martinez Jacobs of the Airports Engineering staff. In a couple of days he had a drawing of how to accomplish the project. We paid a plumber $3,800.00 to tap into the hydrant, add a meter, shut-off valve (so fire dept could use it for emergency) and a back flow preventer — presto we had fresh water. When Chris Ferrera called the next morning Martinez Jacobs said the system was legal — planned, inspected and approved by the state and could not be shut down by one persons whim. Glen Mitchell the new fire marshal was on our case then and was usually in our office a couple times a month telling us he was going to shut us down. One day he was on our dock carrying on about shutting us down and five times I asked him to leave our private vessel (our office and dock and floating wedding chapel were registered as

Hawaiian vessels with an annual $20.00 boat tag for each structure and no taxes), but he would not leave. Finally I put my hand on his shoulder and mentioned that I could help him into the water if he wanted. Ten minutes later I was under arrest and on my way to jail. Our attorney was in France for a month visiting family, so I hired another lawyer, He and I showed up in court three times and never saw Mr. Mitchell. Normally the case is dismissed on the second time of a no show by the plaintiff, but the third trip they said Mr. Mitchell was in the back room (we never saw him) and they fined me $1,000.00 for harassment. Really who was harassing who?

The early fall of 2017 we got a certified letter from Airport Division of the Department of Transportation of Hawaii giving us a 20 day notice of annual rent increase from $28,000.00 to $91,000.00. Part of our lease was land which had a 400% increase and most of it was water area which stayed the same rate. We had been leasing a 50 foot wide by 300 foot long piece of man made property consisting of rocks and cement fill. We had to put up a standard airport fence, hook up the water and electricity, build a 20 foot by 40 foot cedar floating office, a 30 foot by 225 long dock with two pneumatic ramps to get the aircraft out of the water when not being used and two floating bathrooms, a shower and holding tank that got pumped out every week. Two large ramps of 20 feet by 30 feet were hinged and attached to the shoreline to allow the building and dock to rise up and down according to the tides. We were not allowed to pave the driveway, so we put down crushed coral and built a wooden sidewalk. An interesting fact was that the permit for the floating dock, office and installation was issued by the Army Corps of Engineers at no charge — not the State of Hawaii.

We also built a floating 20 foot by 24 foot Wedding Chapel that we leased out to a Japanese Wedding company that in one year did over 700 weddings. Each bride and groom got a 20 minute flight down to Diamondhead and back to Pearl Harbor. We also did evening dinner parties serving Salmon and Halibut, BBQ chicken or shishkebabs with great side dishes and a 20 minute flight. This went over pretty well with some of the local businesses for their employee parties. We got going on fighting this huge rent increases, but the Airports Division had made several increased rent charges to all of the operators on the land airports and were doing it every few months. This had caused a couple of flight schools and smaller tour operators to go out of business and we felt that if we went along with the increase there would be more down the road. After just over a year of new rent and some previous billings we were told that we owned them $144,000.00 including interest. Interest was 1% per month so it grew pretty fast. We had put the business up for sale, but airports did not seem to want a new operator even if they got paid in full. We had two offers from Jimmy Buffett who had a great net worth.

Another young Canadian couple really wanted it also. He was an airline pilot and hated it. Both his father and his wife's father had been bush pilots in Canada flying seaplanes. We did reduce our asking price and they came up with a ten year loan, but the lender did ask for a ten year lease on the property instead of the current 30 day revocable lease. That only makes sense! He also agreed to make twelve months rent up front when he took over - almost $100,000.00 plus we would have paid off the $144,000.00. Another plus would have been to have a very nice young fellow to replace us as operator who was in his late 80's. We had operated there in Hawaii for 23 years without an accident or incident while the helicopters were routinely having accidents. Supposedly Blue Hawaiian Helicopters was the Cadillac of the helicopter industry, but they had twelve fatalities in ten years. One thing I am proud of is over 60 years in commercial aviation, owned 488 aircraft and had 300 plus pilots, flew over one million passengers and never had a customer so much as cut a finger. Some of my pilots did have a very few accidents during the early years, but no injuries — and we did a lot of our flying in tough places — a lot of it north of the Arctic Circle. Yet the Airports Division and its manager, Roy Sakata, wanted the Seaplane Operation gone and it was more personality than thinking of safe operations. One month we got a bill for 57,000 gallons of water supposedly used in one month. I quickly questioned that and said it had to be a transposing error because over the years we seldom hit 5,000 gallons a month. After a week or two of talking about this we finally got our lawyer and four people from airports and showed them there were not wet spots or depressions that a water leak of that size would cause. Then we opened up the water meter and they stood there for almost an hour with absolutely no movement of the meter needle. 57,000 gallons per month would equate to 1,900 gallons per day and that basically would come in a twelve hour period which would make a usage of almost 160 gallons per hour - which would have definitely showed up on the meter. Everyone agreed that the charge was a mistake, but it took a couple of months to correct that and of course we were charged interest at 12% meanwhile.

We left Hawaii early in December, 2018 and it is wonderful. We are not writing letters to correct some state mistakes or spending a day or two trying to reach some bureaucrat by phone. Since we left there have been another dozen or so operations that have been shut down — and even some airports closed. It is not a place for General Aviation.

Pat getting ready for a morning tour

ISLAND SEAPLANE SERVICE

HISTORY

1989 1ST week of May I visited Hawaii and made a inquiry of airports property manager and the FAA re starting a seaplane operation. They both said that you cannot fly seaplanes in Hawaii. I spent 8 years trying to get a permit. Aviation started in Hawaii in 1929 when Interisland Airways purchased 3 Sikorsky S-38 flying boats and starts serving out lying islands. Now they are Hawaiian Airlines.

1996 October. Debbie and I (Pat) sold our business in Alaska and moved to Oahu to pursue the permitting process for Island Seaplane Service Inc. This allowed us to meet with airports people at least weekly.

1997 July 1, 1997. I sent a $10,243.80 check to Barry Fukunaga the airport manager at that time as deposit. Mid – August I called him to see what was going on and he thought it was all done and the permit issued. I told him that I had never gotten anything – including a receipt.

August 18, 1997. Had meeting with Barry Fukunaga, AP Manager and Stanford Miyamoto, General Aviation Officer and signed the lease agreement. We only had Sealane 8 and they promised to open up Sealane 4/22 and Sealane 26 so we could fly in all winds. This did not happen for 3 years and we lost $345,000 the first 3 years because we were not allowed to fly when the wind went westerly which was about 35% of the time.

Rent was $2,439.00 monthly but because Ben Schlapak Airports Manager contended the two areas Space # 425-003 and # 435-004 should not have been charged and changed to $2,389.00 It took many years to make up for this $345,000 loss.

2001 Airports filed suit for eviction for rent arrears. ISS filed a counter suit and won with Federal mediation. ISS owed $124,000 and this was reduced to $62,000 because airports never did open the other sealanes and we were not allowed to fly when the winds went westerly. A contract was made to pay that off monthly with interest and was completed 5 years later. Rent became $2,389.00 monthly 9/11 ISS was shut down after the attack, but ended up being the longest shut down operation in the U.S. – 100 days! At 4:00 p.m. on December 19 the local FAA FSDO office called and said we could fly again. We negotiated with Patsy Mink and Daniel Inouye and could prove $107,000 of cancellations and Congress passed a bill to re-imburse all operators that lost money during the shutdown, but never did fund the bill. Everyone else was shut down a max of 2 ½ weeks.

2003 April. Roy Sakata sent a letter saying we did not pay two $500 payments for our tour permit for 2002 and 2003. We sent copies of two cashiers checks for those payments, but did not get an answer when we asked if we were charged interest for those years.

2004 Letter from Davis Yogi Airport manager asking us to take two cashiers checks totaling almost $3,000 back to the bank to be replaced. Some how they sat on someone's desk and did not get cashed for almost a year. They were only good for 180 days – this was done, but we did not get an answer if we were charged interest.

During 2004 we had a visit from the IRS who said we were not paying our Transportation Tax. I immediately replied that we operated under Part 91 not Part 135 and thus we were not required to pay a transportation tax as we simply do not transport passengers from "A" to "B", but simply fly a circle form "A" to "A". After several months the IRS filed a lien against our bank account and simply took $46,000 from us up to mid 2005 when they said it was an UNJUST TAX and we were not required to file anymore. Absolutely no restitution of the $46,000 was ever made to us. We have files going back over the years of airports applying funds that we paid for one account applied to another account. It is hard to keep up on everything that way.

2008 ISS made a deal with Ben Schlapak, Airports Manager to have him apply for a transformer and electric hook up and we would pay for it. This allowed us to cease operation of generators. Hawaiian Electric said they could not hook us up because we were floating.

November. I spoke to Ben Schlapak airport manager about a 5 year lease on our site, but he said to send him a letter requesting a ten year lease and he would take care of it. Not too long after he passed away and I assume the application sat on someone's desk until it went away. A copy enclosed.

2009 ISS found out they had been charged sewer charges for 13 years even though they had a holding tank and paid for pump out every week. Sued the State and got most of that back along with a promise to send us a check for the balance due. Still waiting for the check and never did get a written record of the payments applied.

2013 September. We received a check as deposit on sale of business by Mr. Aaron Singer of San Francisco, but Abby Larue, property manager, told him that we owed airports a lot of money and they would come after him to repay it. The repay was actually paid off in 2006 and upon checking we found out that we only owed the current months rent and water. Mr. Singer meanwhile backed out and bought San Francisco Seaplanes and we lost a $1.6 Million sale.

November. We got a bill of $5,000 for 10 years of $500 tour permit that we had not been billed yearly for. We did send a copy of the 2004 pmt. cashiers check and sent airports a check for $4,500. No reply on question if we were charged interest for 10 years when they forgot to bill us.

2015 Monday August, 3 at 4:30 p.m. Airports Fire Marshal Glen

Mitchell stopped by our floating office and home and said they were going to shut off our water at 10:00 a.m. Wednesday, August, 5 and shut us down saying our water source was to be shut off because it was illegal. Tuesday August, 4 our attorney pointed out that the water system was designed and permitted by airports when our plumber made the installation, that cost us over $4,000.00. This stopped the shut down, but Mr. Mitchell came around many times "insisting he was going to shut us down" until we ended up in court. This is hardly a landlord procedure any where else.

2017 We fell behind on our rent early in the year and agreed to make a repay program and sent the Attorney Generals Office a check for $8,000.00 on July 9, 2017 which was finally cashed on 7/31 with the same for the two months following. To this day we cannot find credit on our account for the $8,000.00. I wonder about the interest of 1%per month. Of course then we were not much for making our August and September payment. No one will explain this why we are receiving no credit so why would we of agreement. To this day the credit has never showed up. We have been charged for rent of December 2018 though and we already left our business in Hawaii as ordered.

On September 9th at 4:00p.m. we were informed that our rent would increase on our fast land by 370% on October 1st, 2017. This would make a rental increase from $2,389.00 monthly to $7,553.60 per-month or from $28,000 per year to over $90,000.00 per year. We did not feel that we get any benefits from this because airports has never provided one cent of help to us – including security, electricity or water.

We filed a Section 13 and Section 16 complaint with the FAA as the law allows. Our main response was from Mr. Kevin Willis of the FAA Washington DC who wanted to know why we sent the complaint to him.

2018 February 29. My oldest son Patrick, age 56 died riding as a passenger in a Kodiak Quest aircraft in Florida. He was a 27,000 hour pilot with 22,000 hours on floats. I started him flying from the right seat as soon as he could see over the instrument panel. I soled him on floats on his 16 birthday, he took his private pilots check ride on floats on his 17 birthday, but his birthday was on Halloween and we froze up early on his 18 birthday. We had to wait about 10 days until the ice would safely hold an aircraft and he took his commercial check ride in a Cessna 180 on skiis. He was the only pilot I have known that has flown a seaplane on every continent on this planet except Antartica where they are not used. This of course hurt us tremendously and our business slipped for a few months – in fact we really wanted to return to Alaska and start a small fishing lodge.

April 21. We accepted an offer of a well known and wealthy celebrity – Jimmy Buffet. When he found out the rent increase, he just said that "No one will ever purchase that operation" and backed away. Since than we have had several buyers get very interested in buying the business and we have greatly reduced the price, but with the absurd rent and the archaic 30 day revocable lease no one gets serious. We had a young Canadian airline pilot and wife that were here in mid-August 2018 with a ten year loan set up and reasonable down pay. He hated airline flying and wanted to be home at night with his wife. Myself, my wife and the prospective buyers for several days tried to talk with Roy Sakata, but could not get a response to calls, e-mails or faxes. We had greatly reduced our selling price, were to pay off our debt in full to the airports ($145,000.00) at that time and the buyer was prepared to pay one years rent in advance of the closing. He needed a 10 year lease to satisfy his lender who wanted a ten year lease to cover his ten year loan – which only makes sense. No one is going to make a ten year loan with a 30 day revocable lease. It was a win win deal for Airports – paid in full by us and paid one year in advance by a new younger customer who would be around for many more years. But Mr. Roy Sakata thinks it is right to auction off the facility to the highest bidder instead of being very selective of aviation operators in having a background and safety minded experience, not how much money they have. I have been flying for 62 years, logged over 40,000 hours, hold the worlds record of seaplane time with over 33,000 hours, and owned over

488 aircraft and had 300 some pilots flying for me and never have had a passenger so much as cut a finger and have operated over quite a bit of the world. Hawaii has aviation accidents very commonly with 17 Helicopter fatalities in 2016 and another 7 in 2017. Island Seaplane service operated 22 years in Hawaii and never filed an insurance claim.

In November 2017 we filed a Section 13 and Section 16 complaint with the FAA opposing the high rental increase, but they seem not to care much how much people have to pay for their freedoms. Can you imagine some one paying $2,500.00 monthly for an apartment that has a rent rise to $9,250.00 per month and keep the apartment. If all of the tour operators in Hawaii would raise their fees accordingly, they would be out of business in a few days with a $1,106.30 per person one hour air tour. Recently three Hawaiian flight schools have gone out of business, maintenance facilities are scaling back and there was a waiting list for "T" Hangers four years ago but many are available now, fuel prices have been raised sharply and people are selling off their aircraft back on the mainland. Three flight schools have closed down within the past few months. The State of Hawaii does not do anything to promote business.

In 62 years I have sold several aviation business, but have never had the state tell me who I can or cannot sell my business to. I have a corporation for sale and who ever purchases the corporation becomes the owner. Anything else is a form of discrimination. Many private boat owners and aircraft owners have sold their investments and shipped them back to the mainland because they cannot afford to indulge themselves in Hawaii. A couple of months ago we spend a couple of weeks at a Marina in Keehi Lagoon packing up our aircraft and goods to escape before everything was confiscated by the State. The owners of the Marina with a multi – million dollar investment and a large payroll told us they were not sure if they can stay much longer – after 20 some years there. We also saw and heard another marine operator packing up and very vocally telling everyone within hearing that he moved here from California 12 years earlier to start a new business and it was the biggest mistake of his life. We also say the same thing, but we came from Alaska 23 years earlier and lost a million dollars in the shut down. We were forced to sell one classic seaplane that I had owned since 1972 that was worth $400,000 plus for $80,000 at the time just to get enough cash to ship out everything back to the mainland and not loose it all. We are now broke and trying to get funded to start a fishing lodge back in Alaska. We are very interested in finding a aggressive attorney to try to get and economic settlement. We cannot believe that any landlord should be allowed to treat their customers in this manner, especially a governmental one. We are proposing a 50% split on any funds obtained - OBO William (Pat) Magie Owner Island Seaplane Service Inc.

Nationwide the states are all generally programmed to increase business in their own state but in Hawaii taxes and rents are raised indiscriminately and raise their charges several times a year. Bus fares recently jumped 300% which really affects some of those people who can least afford the increase.

CHAPTER 19

HUDSON LAKE

One late October evening about 8:00 p.m. someone knocked at our door which was answered by my oldest daughter Katie. A minute later she told me that there were three young fellows there that wanted to return a rental canoe to Canoe Country Outfitters next door but they are locked up. I called the owner Bob Olson, and he said he would be right over. Meanwhile Katie came back and said that I had better come talk to these people because they had pulled a body out of one of the lakes. They told me that they were paddling through Hudson Lake that morning and found a body wearing a life jacket but he was dead. They said that they pulled him out of the water and stretched him out on a granite ledge. I told them I would call the sheriff that he would want to talk to them. I got hold of Martin Carlson, Lake County Sheriff who said he would be there in five minutes. I got the information that the body was on the very western end of the lake and the south side of the river. Martin talked to the people for a few minutes, got their names and addresses, then told me that he would need an airplane in the morning to go to Hudson Lake for recovery. I told him that it was forecast to drop to 25 degrees that night, then rising to the low 40's during the day. That would make it hard to taxi with freezing water rudders, but I would be fueled, warmed and ready at 0900. I did ask him what he wanted for an aircraft — a Cessna 180 or a Beaver. He replied that the Cessna would do because Lake County was short of money right then. I took all of the seats out in the morning except the two front seats and when Martin showed up we immediately took off. It was about 30 minutes until we landed in Hudson Lake spotting our passenger as we came in for a landing. He was stretched out on a large and smooth granite ledge. We tied off and checked the fellow still wearing his life jacket, but now frozen stiff. There was a tent about 200 yards down the shore on our side, so we walked over there first to see if we could put a name to the remains. We found two sleeping bags — in fact two of almost everything, so we knew that someone else was missing also. Then we went back to the rock, took out the RH front seat, removed the RH door and turned the Cessna around so that the RH side was against the rock. The passenger was over six feet, and 200 pounds and as stiff as you could get. We started putting him in feet first and stuck his legs out the LH baggage door, then we could get his head in against the rudder pedals. It quickly showed us we could not put the RH front seat back in place and we would have to leave some of his legs sticking out on the way back to town, but Martin said he would just sit on him on the way back. We had found that he had a wallet in his back pocket, but he would have to be thawed out some to get it out.

During the flight back to Ely I could not help thinking about some stories I have heard about Don Sheldon of Talkeetna, Alaska when he was alive and flying out of there. He had found a very small patch of snow that was barely workable at the 14,200 foot level where he could land a Super Cub. He did a lot of flying servicing the mountain climbers of Mt. McKinley — it required landing uphill on a pretty steep slope and taking off downhill. One story I remember was a State Trooper called Don and told him that some climbers had a fellow pass away and they took the body down to his landing area and left it.

When Don got up there he found a six foot plus body that weighed over 200 pounds frozen stiff and there was no way that he could fit him inside a two place Piper PA-18 Super Cub. The story goes that he flew back to Talkeetna to call the trooper to ask if he could saw the corpse in half. I was told that the trooper replied "don't tell me how to do my job and I won't tell you how to do yours". It was a great story and there was not much else he could do. Though it was documented that he faced that problem once more and flew a two inch by twelve inch by six feet long piece of lumber and tied the body to the board and then tied this to the wing struts. Don did fly some Cessna's on floats, but made his fame flying off McKinley and other mountains and glaciers in his Super Cub. This was before there were any high performance helicopters.

When the sheriff and I landed back at our dock at Sandy Point we unloaded the cargo and laid him out next to the road. The Sheriff said he would get another deputy, pack up a tent and camping gear along with a boat and motor and dragging equipment. He said that he would be back in about three hours and would need a Beaver to go back to Hudson Lake. We were certain there was another drowning victim in the water and they wanted it out before freeze up. Our first victim was not a drowning victim but evidently died of hypothermia while floating in the cold water. We could not find a second life jacket when we checked the camp, but the second person evidently was not wearing one or we would have him already. When the sheriff left to regroup, I called Jimmy Kerntz, our local undertaker and a good friend, and told him he had some business on our dock that he needed to pick up. He replied that he had two funerals going on right then back to back and could not make the pickup for about three hours. We went about our business, but a half hour later a couple drove into the parking lot, got out and walked down to the dock to look at the airplanes. We remembered what we had there when we saw them stop, start talking excitedly and pointing at the body. When they came in the office and asked us if we knew there was a dead person on our dock, I backed my station wagon up and put him inside, opened the hanger door and parked inside. Jimmy Kerntz showed up with his hearse just as I was tying a 15 foot Grumman boat on the Beaver, then I delivered the dragging crew back to Hudson Lake. The next day it started to rain which turned into snow the day after. I finally got a call from the sheriff's office asking if I could make a pickup of the two fellows doing the dragging. I said that I would go right away and to advise the crew so they would be ready and I would not get snow covered while they tore the camp down. When I arrived we decided to leave the boat there as they would have to come back again to finish up to find the second person. The sheriff department had gotten hold of the wife of the first person we brought in, advised her she was a widow, and they had picked up some information about the missing person, Gary Mitchell. The next day or so it snowed fairly hard and we did not do much flying. Then I got a call from Martin Carlson asking if I could haul the rescue squad of six men, their diving gear and an inflatable boat from Silver Bay on Lake Superior to Hudson Lake on Saturday. It was supposed to be a nice day and with six divers we should be able to finish this up. We established a pickup point and I said that I would leave in the dark at 0600 to arrive at Silver Bay at 0645 just as it was getting daylight with a Twin Beech. It worked as advertised and I had the rescue squad onsite at Hudson Lake shortly after 0730. I left them saying I would be back at 4:00 p.m. to return them to Lake Superior and I should be back in Ely about dark. It was a beautiful Indian summer day until I got a call from the Ely Hospital. The woman asked if I was looking for Gary Mitchell. When I said we had divers looking for him in Hudson Lake she replied that he was in a room at the hospital. She said that his cousin had driven up from Minneapolis to look for him and found him hiking on the Fernberg Road not far from Lake One. He had walked out all the way by following the shoreline for almost a week. I called the Sheriffs Office and passed on the message and climbed in the Twin Beech which was already fueled for the afternoon return to Lake Superior. When I landed to tell the rescue squad what transpired, they said that they had found a heavy sweater and life jacked hidden behind a large log on the shoreline and had discussed the chance he was not in the lake. We did quickly load up and got them back to Silver Bay and I stopped in Hudson Lake on my way back to Ely and collected the boat that we had left there earlier in the week. I thought that was it for that project until a year later.

The following spring I hired a fellow from Minneapolis as an aircraft mechanic. He was also a pilot so I told him that if he liked the job we would get him seaplane rated and might use him later on. Late that fall the days were getting shorter and three or four of us were having a drink before heading home and our pilot/mechanic said to me "you don't remember me do you? I was the guy you were looking for during that Hudson Lake episode". All I could say was "Oh my god, you will never know how much I thought about that last winter and what I would say if I ever met you". He then told us what happened.

They had a 15 foot square stern canoe and a 3 h.p. motor. They had caught a large fish and somehow dumped the canoe over. They both were wearing life jackets but it was late fall and the water was cold. Gary said his partner was panicking and Gary did not want to get to close where he could be grabbed.

Gary did empty a 2 gallon gas can and pushed it over to the partner as extra floatation. Finally his buddy said he could not make it and put his head down. Then Gary got out of the water took off his life jacket and sweater and hid them behind a log and started walking to the nearest road. No map — just follow the shoreline — Lake Four, Lake Three, Lake Two, Lake One. Probably 25 miles by air, but it had to be over 75 miles by shoreline. The first thing I asked him is why he did not walk a few hundred yards to his tent — dry clothes, dry sleeping bag, food and people paddled by the next day. Number two question was why he hid the life jacket and sweater. We would not have placed him in the lake if we had seen them. Number three question is why not go back to the tent, start a large fire with green boughs to make a lot of smoke which would have drawn a fire patrol aircraft. He said he must have been in shock.

Gary stuck around for awhile and became an excellent pilot. I had him flying into tight lakes like Fourtown Lake, making trips to Hudson Bay for goose hunting. Then he went on to flying corporate jets and gave up on adventure.

CHAPTER 20

BANK ROBBERS

Just after 11:00 a.m. one morning, I got a phone call from Jesse Swanson telling me that Warren Kregness's bank in Tower just got robbed. The guy left in a white van and headed on the south road to Biwabik. Can we follow him? I told him that I would have an airplane ready in five minutes, bring a radio. Jesse was some kind of a honorary sheriff. He would usually come down to the base and we would look for lost deer hunters or missing boaters. There was a Cessna 206 at the end of my dock, so I went out fueled it and started a warm up of the engine. Jesse showed up and we took off and headed southwest climbing to 1000 feet above ground level. State Bank of Tower is 20 miles from Ely and it took about seven or eight minutes which now put us only 20 minutes or so from the time of the hold up.

Jesse was on the radio with the Sheriff's office in Ely who told him that the Minnesota Highway Patrol in Virginia had dispatched a patrol car that was coming up the road towards us. A few minutes south of Tower we spotted the getaway van speeding down the highway and we quickly descended and came up behind him about 20 feet above him and showing about 70 mph. Our idea was to distract him and possibly slow him up some what. We did this several times with Jesse telling Ely what we were doing and they would pass it on to the Highway Patrol in Virginia who were communicating with the two cars they had out now. After three or four passes the Sheriffs passed on the information that the hold up weapon was a 30 - 30 caliber rifle. This really got my attention and I decided that low and slow might not be the thing to do. A hand gun was not too much of a worry, but a rifle is definitely a more serious matter. We flew off to the side and slightly behind him for several miles while keeping everyone posted on his speed and location. I noticed a fairly steep hill coming up ahead with a good drop off on the far side and thought I could really get close to the vehicle if I could catch him right at the top. We stayed higher and wider until he started up the ridge, then we made a tight descending turn and it could not have been more perfect! He was west bound and probably doing 45 to 50 mph at the top of the climb and I was showing 170 mph at the bottom of the dive eastbound, my left float was centered on the van and about five feet over it. As we passed over him I thought I saw that he started to move to his right.

Sure enough, as we climbed in a steep turn back to the road we saw that the van had made a right turn, passed through a ditch and stopped about 60 yards into a field that was covered with some pretty large rocks. He was not going anywhere without help. We climbed to 2000 feet and made a wide circle while informing the Sheriffs. It was only minutes until the flashing lights of the first patrol car showed up and when the second one arrived we started back to Sandy Point at Ely. There was a local sheriff there to thank us and pick up the radio.

A year later I went to Seattle to pick up Twin Beech N44573. I had dropped it off at Kenmore Air the fall before on a lease so that they could use it that winter for multi engine seaplane training. We had a late ice out the following spring so I could not pick it up until just after the middle of May. I got to Kenmore in the late afternoon to start prepping the aircraft for an early departure in the morning — fuel, oil and load the beaching gear. 0730 in the morning Bob Munro and I were standing in the rain.

Weather was calling in five miles visibility and nine hundred feet so Snoqualmie Pass was closed.

Portland was calling it 1,400 feet and ten miles visibility improving to

Pat Magie

2,000 feet and unlimited visibility at Tri Cities, Washington, so I told Bob that I was going south and then up the Columbia River. I really needed this airplane back in Ely. It went as advertised and I made a quick fuel stop at Bill Brook's base in Couer d' Alene, than locked on to Interstate 90 to Missoula, Montana. Seventy five miles later I turned off on Montana # 12 for Helena with the ceiling leveling about 1,500 feet with 20 miles visibility. As I got closer to Helena I could see the "V" notch of MacDonald Pass which had a very black colored rain or snow shower moving north to the Pass. The Pass has an elevation of 6,320 feet with a steep drop to 4,000 feet. As I got closer I could see it was going to be a race between the Twin Beech and the shower — which went right to the ground. Helena shortly before was calling their weather 4,000 and 20 miles.

Five miles from the Pass and the snow shower won the race and I was in heavy snow. l had dropped to 25 feet above the highway with 15 degrees of flaps and 90 miles per hour. It would only be about three minutes and I could start my descent to better weather. Right then a pair of headlights showed up coming right at me. As I went over him I watched him (or Her) make a sharp turn to the right and hit the snow bank. His speed was very slow — maybe 20 to 30 miles per hour — but I am sure he was stuck. A minute later I could start a steep descent with the highway still under me. I did not talk to anyone, but l turned NE to Fort Peck for fuel. I did make Ely just after dark that night, but it was a long day. I did start thinking that I should stop running cars off the road or I might get on the AAA's hit list!

CHAPTER 21

DOLLIES

In quite a few places around the country airplanes can be installed on seaplane floats, but there is no water available for take - off. This is handled in some of these places by constructing a dolly which is merely a low built three wheeled trailer that the aircraft can taxi on and then make a takeoff run down the runway to lift off. They are usually made with a brake system that is activated when the aircraft is airborne which should stop a runaway trailer moving at 50 or 60 mph. The three wheels will quite often come off of a Cessna 185 with the two main wheels being attached to the front of the dolly and a swiveling tail wheel to the rear. Most light aircraft dollies are made out of 2 ½ or 3 inch galvanized pipe and are 10 to 12 feet wide by 12 feet long. You do need to have some means of steerage for the first 5 - 8 mph. when the air rudder has enough authority to steer the aircraft. Usually one or two persons can handle this by running behind steering with a rope.

The first time I took off on a dolly was at Zahn's Aviation on Long Island, New York. I had sold a new Cessna 180 on floats to a fellow from Northern New York and he wanted it as soon as possible as he was a FAA Part 135 operator. I had talked to J.J. Frey at Edo Floats about it and he suggested that we should have the floats installed there locally instead of shipping the floats to Ely, and then assembled and installed. He said that he would get the floats delivered to the operator who would have them assembled when I got there and I would be on my way the next day. Then I went to Wichita picked up the new Cessna 180 and flew to New York. Two days later I flew up the Hudson River on floats and dropped it off to my customer. We found this worked well and did it several times after that. We later hooked up with an operator in Minneapolis and would have them install the floats during the winter months, then we could take-off on a dolly to make a delivery of them to Louisiana or other warmer spots.

It was not long after that I bought my first DHC-3 single Otter, but our hanger was barely wider than the wingspan. We talked to other operators, but none had ever floated an Otter and did not want to try it. I had bought a nice set of Edo 7170 floats from Ed Rinas in Fort Francis, Ontario. These had Noorduyn Norseman gear, but I had ordered a new set of struts, wires and fittings from Canadian Aircraft Parts, so when I talked to Matt Reid from Bristol Aviation, he suggested a maintenance facility on the Winnipeg International Airport. I talked to them and their price was right, so I made an appointment.

They even said that had a dolly to use for take- off from the airport. I sent a truck and trailer to Fort Francis to move the floats to Winnipeg. I followed that up by flying the Otter on wheels to Winnipeg.

They were surprised to see how nice the airframe was. We had spent almost eight months going through it then topped it off with a new paint job and interior. They said that they should call me in about five days for pickup — but I did not look at their dolly.

The next week they called and said it was finished. I had worked out a ride from Ely to Winnipeg (425 miles) and I told them I would be there shortly after noon the next day. We landed, parked in front of the shop, I went in and did all of the paperwork including payment. Then we went out the back door to where the Otter was already loaded on the dolly. Oh My God! I had never seen a dolly like this one. It was constructed with 4 inch x 12inch x 20 foot long beams with four large truck tires that were five feet high, nothing steerable. The wooden frame was painted white but definitely showed signs of being in a fire. The timbered top was six feet high and the Otter was sitting on top with two ropes tied to the front cleats. Two mechanics and one of the office personnel had come out on the ramp with me and he told me to never have those two bow ropes untied until the engine is running. They said that this dolly was primarily used for Beavers, but the Otter is much larger and untying the ropes would allow it to tip off the back with a lot of damage to the tail end. They gave me the feeling that they personally knew this to be true — so I put rule #1 in my mind — Do Not Untie Bow Ropes If Engine Is not Running. It was now almost 3:00 p.m. on a Friday afternoon and we had a south wind of 15 knots. We had a truck hooked up to tow me to the runway, but the tower declined the request for Runway 18 and said it would have to be Runway 24. I was towed to Runway 24 and lined up on the center line but had to wait another 15 minutes before the tower told me "Cleared for immediate take - off". As I started rolling and picking up speed "P factor" (prop started pulling me left helped by a LH cross wind) and before I got the throttle fully forward I was off the runway and in the grass. I throttled back, but kept the engine running. I then noticed a fire truck on my RH side and one of the crew ran behind the Otter, he jumped up on the float to stand by my cockpit window. He also reminded me not to shut down the engine while I got towed back to Runway 24. When we got there I told them to position me to the downwind side of the runway so that I would have the entire width of the runway to accelerate on before going on the grass. The fireman on the float also came up with Rule # 2 "Make Sure You Have Enough Airspeed Before Coming Off The Dolly". He said that a couple of months earlier a Beaver pilot came off the dolly without enough speed to fly, his RH wing and float hit the runway, split the belly tank which cremated the pilot and aircraft and scorched the dolly. Ok - Rule #2 is enough airspeed. I had another ten minutes wait before the control tower passed on the "go" word. This time I opened up the throttle little more slowly and I was moving faster before I went onto the grass knocking out a runway light that did not move out of the way fast enough. Within a couple of seconds I fixated on a two story brick control tower that was probably built during WWII. This was growing pretty large in my windshield when I glanced at the airspeed indicator and realized that I was concentrating on Rule # 2 a little too much. Just a slight back pressure on the control wheel and I took to the air while remembering that no one had mentioned anything about a brake system on the dolly. The dolly had to weigh a ton and was aimed right at the control tower. I immediately rolled into a 90 degree turn to the right — almost catching a wing tip on the ground — then turned off the radio and headed south to North Dakota. I had filed a flight plan to Kenora, Ontario before I got into the take off procedure because I knew I could be there by dark. Once I was back in the U.S.A. I advised flight service to cancel that flight plan which might not even got activated. I continued my flight to Ely, Minnesota arriving about 8:30 p.m. in the dark. Of course I did not have a flight plan for that because I would have arrived after their 6:00 p.m. cut off for U.S. Customs.

For many years I had to pay the U.S. Customs Department an overtime call out fee for Sundays and holidays which came to almost $250.00 if we kept it to an eight hour day — which we usually made it from 10:00 a.m. to 6:00 p.m. We had to have a bond with customs to do this, but then we were allowed to charge other private aircraft flights for part of the fee. We usually charged them $10.00 to $12.00 per flight and that would cushion our fee somewhat. We always seemed to be battling the Customs Bureau quite a bit. I remember one year when I got a letter from the Duluth, Minnesota Customs Office during the first of January listing five aircraft that had cleared Canadian Customs, but did not report in on their return to Ely. This did not take too long to clear up and I replied that they should check the U.S. Customs at Crane Lake for two of the aircraft, one at Ranier, MN and two at Ketchikan, AK. They were sold to people in Alaska and we had cleared Canadian Customs for a trans Canada flight to Ketchikan. That had to be before the computer was too common. We did not hear of that activity again.

No matter what, when you hear about Dollies in aviation, do not think of music and the sound of ice tinkling in a glass — some of them are hard working tools of seaplane flying.

CHAPTER 22

ENSIGN LAKE

It was Labor Day and we had a busy day just finishing up at 4:15 p.m. The weather had been miserable all day and I had just come in on my last pick up for the day with a Twin Beech with five passengers, two canoes, all their camping gear along with several large coolers of fish from Four Town Lake. It was raining, about a 400 foot ceiling and three miles visibility. We only had one Beaver left coming in from the Canadian side. A minute later the Unicom spoke up " Sandy Point, Beaver, 11015,

U.S. Customs in 15, 3 U.S. citizens (USC), canoe and gear". Our gal behind the desk called U.S. customs and advised him and the outfitting company up town to come pick up their party. I told everyone else "Lets shut her down, tie everything down and we will get out of here before someone else calls and wants to go flying in this weather". By 5:00 p.m. I was walking the hill up to the house ready for a drink and dinner.

About 7:30 p.m. the phone rang and it was a local sheriff saying that there was a fellow on Ensign Lake with a heart attack. We discussed where he was and I was very familiar with the campsite I told him that I would try to get up there. I went back down to the base. Beech N44573 was tied up at the end of the dock looking east so I fueled it up to one inch over the baffles on each side. Leaving it tied up, I started the engines and let it warm up while I went back in the office to get a stretcher and flashlight. I also called a friend, Jim Kobe, to ask if he would come down and monitor the radio. It was only a 35 to 40 mile flight to mid-Ensign Lake and I would call him on the return if I got the fellow out and would need an ambulance. It did seem that the weather had gotten worse than it was a couple hours earlier.

After a few minutes of warmup I got back into the Beech and checked oil temp. Both were over 40 degrees C, so I shut the RH engine off and full carb heat and throttled to 350 RPMs on the left. Then I got back on the dock, untied the bow rope, then the rear rope and quickly climbed aboard as the aircraft slowly moved away from the dock. One of our major concerns with maintenance is getting a low RPM at slow idle. You do not have brakes, so docking is mostly a matter of steering. If you can back up in a 10 knot wind you have it made. Slow idle on one magneto, full flaps and you can usually go sideways and can easily park between two aircraft at a long dock. Busy seaplane bases can be confusing—there are no taxiways – everyone seems to be going all directions. Rivers with a strong current also take some adjusting in your thinking. If the current is stronger than the wind, you usually land up stream and take- off down stream and always dock upstream. I have seen a lot of 20K currents and some of 30K.

Naturally a sharp eye is needed for spotting debris—especially right after the ice goes out in the spring.

The wind was out of the east at 15 or so. So I just took off for the end of the lake and the lights of the village of Spaulding. I quickly found that I could get only 400 feet altitude, so I stayed level at 300 feet above terrain (AGL) by that time I was by the upper end of Moose Lake. I was down to two miles visibility but I only had a few more miles more to go. When I did get to Ensign Lake I just turned down the channel to the east and set up for the landing –no circling in this weather! The campsite was in a small bay with a sand beach, so I landed, did a step turn into the bay and pulled the power back and fell off the step. Then mixtures off and I went out the hatch, ran down the wing and jumped to the beach as the airplane weather cocked into the wind. I caught one of the wing ropes and tailed the aircraft onto the beach and waded out in the water up to my waist to hold it in place. Several people were there by that time and I told one of the fellows to grab the stretcher and get the patient back to me within five minutes or that I was going to have to stay the night. It was 200 feet, two miles visibility, heavy rain and blowing 20 knots out of the east. This meant it was going to get worse with the weather being blown in from Lake Superior.

They brought the stretcher and patient back to the aircraft very quickly and I told one of the fellows to jump in and hold the stretcher from sliding around as I did not want to take the time to tie it down.

We taxied out and pointed westerly and towards town. This is where the Beech excelled—up wind or down wind – it just went. This way I did not have to make a steep turn in this weather. With this tailwind I knew it would be a quick trip to town, but because the weather was absolutely miserable I kept on 15 degrees of flap and the airspeed at 95 to slow it up a bit and compensate for the poor visibility. I could not get back to Moose Lake, but kept a westerly heading. I had thought that if nothing else worked I could land on Moose Lake at one of the fishing lodges and call to get the ambulance to drive out there to the end of the road and telephone lines. I started to drift a little more northwesterly to hit Basswood Lake thinking I could follow the shoreline down to the Four Mile Truck Portage. This would bring me down Fall Lake and only three or four miles to my base. It started raining even harder and I lost almost100 feet and decided that was not going to work. I then swung to a SW heading hoping that I would be able to pick up some traffic on the Fernberg Road between Moose Lake and Ely. I was still too far out to communicate with my base because of my low altitude.

After another 15 minutes or so I picked up a light about at 11 O'clock from me and turned left to get to it. In another minute I recognized it as the dock at Garden Lake Resort and started a 90 degree turn to the right. Very quickly I came upon Fall Lake with the power dam on the right and the small town of Winton on the left. I immediately called my seaplane base at Sandy Point," Beech N44573, coming up on Winton at 200 feet. What is your weather". I got an answer that "it is blowing East at 20, pretty heavy rain and I can see the lights of Spaulding (1 mile). I've got an ambulance and a cop car here. The top of the hill on the north side is in the clouds". I replied that I would come down the north shore flying over water just past the point and make a 180 degree left turn and land to the east. I also asked that send one of the cops down to the end of Sandy Point and have him shine a flashlight on the edge of the water there and I would touch down there. From there on it went down just as advertised – I touched down right at the end of the point, made a 180 degree step turn to the right, cut the power and tied up at the dock. A few minutes later the ambulance and my stretcher holder left for the hospital with the police car leading the way.

The next afternoon I had a call from Dr. Ed Ciriacy telling me that the patient I had flown in the night before was OK, but then really chewed me out for going out in that weather. He complimented me on all the parties I had flown in – night and day, but he did say this last one was not worth the risk. I guess the fellow had a 10 year heart problem including a couple fairly serious heart attacks and had no business being out on this trip. He also said that he would not be alive in another six months. The doctor had flown with me on several med-a-vac flights and felt it was a great service to the area, but he felt that the trip the night before was not worth an accident and the possibility of deaths. That did get my attention and I started getting a little more attentive to really bad weather. Not a month later I got a call from Ronnie Massaro that he had a guest there with a Strep throat and could I bring a doctor in to his lodge at Powell Lake on the Canadian side. 1:00 a.m. I found Dr. Horgan and I was about half way to Powell Lake when a bolt of lightning right in front of our propeller and quickly followed by several more and a quick turn around for Ely. I did not realize it at that time that I did not have much more time in Ely so I never came up with that again. A few months later President Jimmy Carter signed the Wilderness Act of 1978 which shortly after forced me out of the flying business. 16 aircraft and over 40 people put out of work. I often wondered in the ongoing years what happened to the seriously ill and injured people, were they just left to die with no way to get medical help. I sold off what I could, kept a Single Otter and moved on to Alaska.

CHAPTER 23

SALES AND MISC.

I bought my first airplane in 1956 paying $850.00 for the plane, $1,200.00 for a set of Edo 1320 floats, $380.00 to a mechanic for an annual inspection and float install plans plus $79.00 for a new metal propeller. I soloed and flew that plane for a few months and sold it for $2,850.00. This started a train of thought for me that I should always make some kind of profit when I sold each unit. I replaced the J4Cub with a Stinson 108-3 for $5,500.00 with Edo 2425 floats, wheels and skis, flew it two years, then sold it for $6,000.00. A 1955 Cessna 180 replaced the Stinson for $12,500.00 and I flew the Cessna for four years before trading it in on a Twin Beech for $13,500.00 credit against a $27,500.00 sales price. I collected $32,900.00 when the Twin Beech was sold after six years. Of course, many many thousands of dollars were spent for fuel, oil, maintenance and parts after that, but I considered those costs training expenses because I had a lot to learn. After I became a Cessna dealer I might buy six to eight aircraft in the spring for my own use, put them on floats, fly them all summer and spend the winter selling them off with at least $1.00 profit per my rule. The big thing was that I was flying brand new aircraft on the line with no large drop in valuation from new. This was fairly easy to do on the Cessnas, but took a little more scrambling on some of the older ones. The first Cessna 180 that I bought in 1960 was a low time 1955 model that first came out in 1953 and was registered as N4636B. I was surprised to see this aircraft in 2019 in Kalispell Montana — still flying and still looking good. I had a lot of memories of that aircraft — I flew it the first time I went out at night and saved a life. This was the first plane I flew fish houses out to remote fishing holes on skis during the winter. It also was the first airplane I tied a Christmas tree on and flew it to town. This was on the morning of Christmas Eve and I had not gotten out yet to cut a tree, but I had a friend who went out with me that morning to fly in and set up a fish house. When we finished that we got in the air and I spotted a neat looking tree right along the shore of a small lake.

WOW — power back, flaps 40 degrees and landed right next to the tree. In less than ten minutes the tree was cut down and tied on the RH side. I suppose it was about seven feet high and four feet wide. It was securely tied blunt end forwards and secured to the landing gear leg and the rear fuselage fitting — that was a rule of external loads to have the blunt end forward on boats, square stern canoes or similar objects because the whole airplane was built that way. It also reduced vibration of the tail plane and the elevators. That morning we taxied back to get all the room we could get for take - off, set 20 degrees of flap, pushed the throttle forward and we were flying. We just cleared the trees on climb out while Bernie Carlson held his hands up to signify the tree had blown to a two foot circumference and was not sliding back. OKAY! Flaps up and the whole airplane started shaking pretty badly. Right then another lake showed up right in front of us — power off, flaps 40 degrees, land! We got out, walked around the airplane checking the fastenings of the tree. Everything looked good, but I did not want to go through that shaking again. I did notice the twenty foot rope tied onto our tail ski that someone would pull sideways while you added power in deep snow so you could turn around some days. That rope went on at the beginning of ski season and stayed there all winter. In those good old days many northern airports kept a snow packed runway on the infield near the terminal and I remember quite a few calls from tower on departure that "you forgot to undo your tail tie down". Anyway I untied the Christmas tree from the landing gear and tied the tail rope to it. The take - off went fine and we never felt a bump in cruise. When we were about 10 minutes out I called our office on Unicom and asked them to call my house to tell a couple of the kids to come down and pick up the tree. It was a westerly wind, so I swung over town to turn into the wind and land as close to the office as possible to avoid scraping the needles off. It went well, but we got a laugh when a couple dozen cars quickly came down to the base to see what was going on. It is not often you see a airplane towing a tree. The tree came through this pretty well with some needles missing, but we stuck it in a corner so that it would not be noticed. If anyone did ask, we said that Santa Claus brought it on his sleigh.

I used to buy a lot of airplanes over the telephone sight unseen and do not remember one that I got stuck with. I bought quite a few sets of floats new and got some healthy discounts on some damaged floats that we could rebuild. I would watch Trade-A-Plane and if I saw a used aircraft that was approved on floats I would make an offer with the condition that they faxed me a copy of the log books for the last annual inspection and I would Fed-Ex a cashier's check that day with pick up within the next week. I even bought a set of Wollam plywood floats with Cub gear for $200.00 one day and found a cheap 85 h.p. J-3 Cub to install them on. I made a quick $2,000.00 profit on that — which is not much today, but this was 50 years ago or so in the past when a dollar was worth more — and I can say that I once owned a set of plywood floats which most people have never seen. Those years I was looking for Aeronca Champs and Sedans, Stinson's, Cessna's and even some Fairchild 24's. I even bought a Fairchild 's F11 - Husky with a R-985 450 h.p. engine which was a power deficiency when considering the size of the cabin. Because of this only 12 units were built starting in 1946 and ending not long after. I think the owner's name was Peter Lazarenko and he would not sell the plane until the second week of December because of a contract on floats that he had, but he would have it installed on skis before mid — December. I primarily wanted it to haul two canoes and four passengers which made it perform pretty well. This aircraft had a huge cabin with a double belly door that opened so that you could slide two 18 foot canoes inside. I think the Canadian Registration was CF-REI and I agreed that I would give him a $10,000.00 deposit with the balance due when I picked it up. We would bring a trailer and take the floats then also. December came and a couple of days before the scheduled pick up several of us were sitting in the office talking about it when someone mentioned they had never seen one in the U.S. Wow!

That got me thinking - Vern Jones of Rainy Lake Airways in Fort Frances, Ontario had one which we saw around quite a bit. He hauled quite a few canoes in the summer, and it would carry 30 bales of hay to some of the logging camps for their horses during the winter. First thing in the morning I called the FAA to see if there was a Certificate for the Husky, but they could not find it. Then I called Fairchild Aircraft Company in Hagerstown, Maryland asking if they had done a U.S. certification on the aircraft. Surprise, Surprise! They told me that they had never heard of a Fairchild F-11 Husky much less built one! Back to the FAA asking what I would have to do to get a U.S. Certification (STC). They said it would not be to difficult if the aircraft was in the same condition that it was when it left the factory. That I knew was going to be a problem as most people in the bush business will make some changes to meet their jobs. I knew that the Husky came with a control stick, but several had been changed to a control wheel by installing a 2 inch by 4 inch board mounted on a hinge installed on the floorboards and some kind of a wheel on the top that was hooked up to the elevators and ailerons. So I called the owner and told him about this and he said he would return my $10,000.00 deposit — and he did. I was sorry that I did not get to own and operate a Fairchild Husky. I did get a call from the president of Fairchild the next day saying that they had said a janitor that had been with the company for over 30 years that remembered the airplane had been built in Canada by a company under license from Fairchild.

Early in the days in Ely I bought a Waco cabin biplane YKS-6 on 3430 floats because I had need for an airplane that would carry a pilot and four passengers. We were flying almost daily trips to Kettle Falls on the end of Namakan Lake for lunch at a neat old restaurant that offered a great chicken meal for $3.00.

That probably was the most fun airplane I ever owned. It had a cabin door on the left rear side, but a large window on the left up front with a hand crank to open and close. The pilot always loaded his passengers first, then climbed up on the lower wing to the window which made easy entry and exit. The Waco had a Jacobs 225 h.p. engine, but with all of those wings it loved to get up and go. It had a quirk with one magneto and one distributor. On skis during the winter months the engine started so easy by hand propping that often we could not bother putting the battery back in if we only had one or two trips — which were usually short during the winter. Then one day it dawned on me that when we had no battery we had no juice to the distributor, we were running on one magneto only. I had that airplane for a couple of years until the Cessna 185's and 206's caught on, but I will never forget the Waco!

I also got signed up to purchase surplus goods at military auctions for aircraft and parts. As far as parts went I was mostly bidding on Beech and DeHavilland parts plus some floats and skis. One day I bid on a large assortment of Twin Beech exhaust parts brand new for $750.00 with a 10% deposit and balance with removal of the goods within 30 days. I went and drove a 15 passenger van to the bid site with seats out and made a crate to go on top to get them all. A lot of these would work on a Beaver or other aircraft using P&W 985's Wind shields, control surfaces, seats, doors plus other parts would show up. I bid on a unit of three DeHavilland DHC-3 Otters brand new Rudders for $1,500.00, sold one for $1,500.00, put one on an aircraft of ours that needed a rudder, leaving one for spare. I even made bids on airplanes. I got a Beaver needing work for $16,000.00 plus bought a conversion kit from DeHavilland for $3,300.00 to cover the four windows on top of the cabins and replace the cabin door hardware. An exchange engine, propeller overhaul, fresh paint and clean up the interior would allow us to fly the aircraft for a year or two and sell it for around $100,000.00 while putting in a bid for another. I did win a bid on a DHC-3 Otter one year. It was short the RH cabin door and was located in Norfolk Virginia. I found out that I had won the bid when I received a call from Harold Hanson of Boeing Field in Seattle. He was giving me a hard time about driving up the bid pricing. I had bid $32,000.00 and when I asked him about his bid he said it was $31,000.00. I did trade him a brand new Otter rudder for a Otter RH cabin door though. We had built a heavy duty 40 foot flatbed trailer which went to Norfolk to pick up the Otter. I also found a market in Cessna L-19's. I think I paid $2,000.00 for my first one and a new set of Edo 2425 floats for $3,500.00 from Frank Bohman of Rainer, Minnesota. He had won a bid on those a while before. We would do new paint and interior ourselves then add an overhauled engine and propeller. I found out that I could usually sell one for $15,000.00 within a day or two after I advertised it. This was a better rate of return on the dollar than selling a new Cessna. We usually kept one Cessna L-19 on the line for game surveys. We would install the rear seat backwards so that the observer could get a good look at the animal we were tracking.

I got to fly a lot of different older aircraft also that I did not own. Some of these were a Bellanca Sr. Skyrocket with a Partt & Whitney 600 h.p. R-1340 mounted on Edo 7170 floats, Cessna T-50 Bamboo Bomber on Edo 5870 floats, Cessna 195 on Edo 3430's, Beech Craft D-17 Stagerwing on Edo 4665 floats, Artic Tern on Edo 2000 floats, Fairchild 51 on Edo 4580 floats, Piper Aztec on Edo 4930 floats, Found Brothers 100 on Edo 3430 floats, Piper Cherokee 6 on Edo 3430 floats, a Stinson Gullwing SR10 on Edo 5250 floats, Waco UPF7 on Edo 2425 floats (open cockpit), DeHavilland Turbo Beaver DHC-2MK3 on Edo 4930 floats, all of the

Gruman Amphibs, Widegon, Goose and Mallard. A couple that I really wanted to fly but never got the chance even though I did get to spend some time sitting in them were the Barkley Grow on Edo 9225 floats and the Bellanca Airbus on the same 9225 floats.

During my early days in Ely I ran across a Grumman Goose for sale in a crate in Japan for $50,000.00. It supposedly was a very low time aircraft in great shape, but I realized that most of our flights involved carrying canoes which would not happen with the Goose. The Goose is a nice flying aircraft, but would not work for me. Very shortly after that I saw a picture of a Twin Beech on floats that Joe Marrs had for sale and tracked down a Beech 18 to measure the cabin. I was sure I could get two canoes in there — and I did. I think back now remembering that for quite a few years we had a Scout Troop from Rockford, Illinois that booked the first flight of the day (0600) on the first Saturday of June — with 54 passengers, 18 canoes and all of their camping gear for a week. So every Friday on the evening before I would make two trips to their drop off point in the Twin Beech and leave the canoes there for the morning flights.

Without passengers (except for one helper) we could put 2 ½ canoes inside leaving the cargo door off and 2 ½ canoes tied on outside. It did not climb very fast, but flew fine. We would probably take 2 Cessna's with 2 canoes each night before also. Then we could get the group out in the morning and be able to fly other groups by 8:30 or 9:00 a.m. It was a great revenue and great fun!

CHAPTER 24

HIGHLIGHTS

I had an Aero Commander 500 for a couple of years. We got into that for mainly flight training at first. For three or four years I offered a "Bush Pilot Course" during the winter months. We accepted three or four applicants each Fall starting September 15th. They would all be recent veterans of the military and qualified for the GI Bill flight training. The VA requires that each person receiving flight benefits had to have a Private Pilots License or better before they could apply to train for the higher ratings. We charged a $10,000.00 deposit with their Private Pilot's License accomplished on floats by the middle of November and freeze-up. Then they would switch to wheels as well as skis once there was enough ice to hold an airplane. The day after their Private Pilots check ride they would be starting their Commercial Pilot training as well as take a single engine land plane rating within the first few days. We guaranteed each of them about 400 hours of flying time with a Commercial Pilot's license, with single engine and multi engine land and sea ratings, an instrument rating plus a Certified Flight Instructor rating. At least 100 hours of this would be on floats, 100 hours on skis, the balance on wheels — but most importantly a fulltime job starting Memorial Day weekend until mid — September again. By then they would be an experienced pilot with all of the ratings and about 1.000 hours flying time — very employable. The VA paid for 90% of the flying after the Private Pilot check ride. We also had a couple of house trailers they could live in and do their own cooking. We usually would pick one of them to stay on and work the second year. During the winter training they would usually get trips to Florida where we kept one or two seaplanes working all winter as well as a trip or two to Wichita, Kansas during the spring to help with ferrying new Cessna's back to Ely for float installation. This program worked well until the Wilderness Act passed in 1978 and we had to make the move to Alaska. I do feel good that almost everyone I got working stayed in aviation for their working life. Many of them ended up as airline pilots which I always thought as too boring — but it was flying.

I did enjoy flying the Commander so I promoted trips to different places. I promoted a fishing trip for six fellows from Ely to a fishing lodge on Reindeer Lake — about 600 miles north of the border. I flew them up there to find a 4,000 foot landing strip that was cut across the island with water on each end.

It was not gravel — more sandy — but had an eye catching wrecked Douglas DC-3 at either end of the strip. No sweat — I landed and let the passengers off. A week later I came back for the pick-up with a landing at Lynn Lake Airport for some fuel, then flew 50 miles west to the Reindeer Lake strip. Now I had six full sized, plus a little extra, men. Six coolers of fish, six duffle bags and six tackle boxes. I stood there for a few minutes looking at the load and finally decided that I would take four men with their bags to Lynn Lake, drop them off and come back for two passengers and most of the gear and fish.

When I had landed at Lynn Lake I had noticed a DeHavilland Single Otter belonging to the Royal Canadian Mounted Police on amphib floats parked on the ramp and thus hated to leave people there for an hour or so while I made a second trip. We loaded up the first trip and took off. It went so well that I swung around, landed and loaded everything. The next take off was no problem, so we headed south. We did land for fuel at Dauphin, Manitoba then on to Ely.

1976 was a hot dry summer with a lot of forest fires. We were very busy doing quite a bit of flying for the Forest Service. I had just bought a new 1976 Cessna Cardinal RG and we started flying it 14 hours a day. Federal Forest Service Regulations put a maximum of seven hours of pilot time in one day, so we would dispatch the aircraft with a pilot plus one USFS person with a USFS radio set at 6:00 a.m. to proceed to the fire site, orbit for seven hours at reduced power to return by 1:00 p.m. They were there as an aerial control tower that was directing the air activity over the fire. There were two Twin Beeches on floats hauling all of the freight and personnel into a designated spot and temporary dock on the fringe of the fire. This would be water pumps, generator, food supplies, many barrels of fuel, fire hose, tents, sleeping bags, boats, canoes, medical goods and other things that would be needed by 100 or so men on the fire that might encompass thirty or so lakes. Then we had two Beavers delivering these goods around the fire. There would be three or four helicopters, two B-17 fire bombers, two B-26 fire bombers and three USFS DeHavilland Beaver water bombers. That made a lot of traffic in a smoke filled environment. Meanwhile we would have three Cessna's on floats that would be flying several 1 ½ hour fire patrols all day. I think we had three of these large project fires that summer plus several smaller ones that got caught and under control quickly. At one time we had just finished a fire that lasted almost three weeks when a charter came up for the Aero Commander hauling four passengers to Chicago and another party of five persons flying Chicago/Ely the next night. We had a stack of several hundred USFS flight sheets that needed to be completed and priced out. These were made for each flight departing our base giving times for every take off and landing and signed by the pilot. These each had to be converted to flying times, then, dollars and cents. My landing was at Palwaukee Airport in Chicago — just north of O'Hare International. I unloaded the passengers and got them on their way, checked in at the hotel on the field, had dinner and started several hours of paperwork. I worked all the next day and by my 6:00 p.m. departure I had finished the stack for over $52,000.00 worth of flying to be billed. No one ever brought up the fact that a pilot might fly a seven hour surveillance flight in the morning and then another 2 or 3 hours of fire patrol during the afternoon — or sometimes they would fly several of our tourist flights in the morning followed by seven hours of USFS flights that afternoon. The important thing was that it all got done and safely. I used to get a lot of grief from the USFS from the Duluth and Milwaukee offices for our excursions into the Boundary Waters Canoe Area Wilderness for med-a-vacs, delivering death messages and other flights of mercy, but the local Service Center was very happy to have a dozen or so more aircraft and pilots available when needed. Early in June of 1976 I got a personal call from the USFS asking if I could fly over to Seagull Lake to run the top cover over a fire that just started earlier in the day water plus 2 B-17 bombers and needed an aircraft above to keep everybody separated. I told them " No problem" and 15 minutes later I had a USFS radio hooked up, fueled and in the air. It was a forty minute flight to the fire site, but it did not take long to pick up the smoke. As I neared the fire I checked out with the Service Center and told them I was switching to the fire frequency and they told me that I should have two B-26 fire bombers there in the next hour also. When I checked in on the fire frequency I talked with Chick Beel who taught me how to fly twenty years before. He was flying one of the Beaver water bombers and told me that Walt Newman had just left the fire with another Beaver to return to Ely for fuel. He had found the fire and would not be able to fly much longer, so he would probably cover the afternoon 1 ½ hour West Patrol. He also said that the wind had just picked up to 30 knots which crowned the fire and was running through the tops of the trees very fast.

This caused one four man ground crew to jump in a small pond with their water pump to save themselves. He told me where the pond was so that I could keep the heavier tankers from hitting them with a load. A full load of retardant from a B-17 bomber could actually turn a small bulldozer or truck over on its side, so we wanted to keep their drops away from the ground troops. The Beaver only dropped 125 gallons of water and the helicopters 90 gallons from their bucket, so they were not really dangerous. We quickly decided we would have one Beaver and one helicopter working each side trying to contain the width of the fire, the last helicopter dropping on hot spots along the upwind side and the heavies working the downwind side. The B-17's could haul about 1,800 gallons of water and 1,000 gallons or so for the B-26. One of the B-17 pilots complained that the smoke made it tough to stay on course, so I told him that I would stay a thousand feet higher while behind him and coach him. This worked pretty good. I could keep track of him through the smoke and then tell him when to drop just before he came out in the clear and keep his load in the flames. They had to go back to the Ely airport to pick up a load of water and fuel, so they only made a drop every hour. When the two B-26's arrived they had to return to Ely each run also, so we staggered them so we had a few minutes to maneuver between drops. The two Beavers and the helicopters were picking up their water off of several lakes right there, so they were making a drop every few minutes. The USFS had parked a fuel truck at the Seagull Lake landing a few miles away, so we were covered for fuel. About 8:00 p.m. we got a radio message from Ely to go over to Gunflint Lodge on Gunflint Lake which was about 15 minutes away for food and shelter for the night. I knew Bruce Kerfoot, the lodge owner and it was a nice break. Then we got going again about 10:00 a.m. Everybody took some down time during the day so we did not exceed our seven hours flight time, then back to the Lodge to stay for the night. I had my toilet articles and some clothes dropped off at the Lodge by one of my aircraft that was on fire patrol for the USFS. This went on for a week, but the seventh day just before noon I landed at the fuel truck and was told to fuel and return to Ely without talking on the radio. They had just realized that I was flying for my seventh day when only six days were allowed without a day off. I went back to my base and did some flying there so that my pilots could have some break time. The fire was starting to come under control after a day of light rain, so I was just sent over to site and spend the day — flying for 1 ½ hour, then land and rest for an hour. That way I could fly throughout the day until the fire was secured and shut down. Little did we know that in two weeks we would have an even larger fire.

CHAPTER 25

ODDS AND ENDS

My operation in Ely was not liked very well by many of my Canadian competitors. We were flying a lot of new aircraft — all of our Cessna's — and kept our larger aircraft well maintained and looking good.

And we really worked at keeping our schedules even if we had to push some weather. Tony Massaro of Powell Lake Resort on the Canadian side always said that he could set his clocks by our arrivals — if we had a 10:00 a.m. pickup that is when we landed there. Some of our competitors might wait until afternoon because they had a flight going near there at 2:00 p.m. and they got paid for two trips while only flying one. Our rates per mile or hour were controlled by Canadian Transport Board. Mike O'Brien was the Canadian Ranger at the station on the west end of Lac La Croix where we dropped off quite a few canoe parties. When all of the stations checked in on their weather to reports in the morning, he would often call it "Magie Weather" if the weather was not too nice. That usually meant that the Canadian operation 25 miles from him was not flying whereas our aircraft were flying in and out although we were 60 some miles away.

One day one of my pilots flew a Twin Beech trip 140 miles north with eight passengers to a lodge on Shikag Lake. When he landed two Canadian Mounties met him at the dock complete with a scale. They weighed each person along with each piece of luggage. Then they checked his fuel gauges, and gave him a written notice of a over gross weight of 128 pounds when he took off from Canadian Customs on Basswood Lake. This was followed up by mail with a notice to appear in Court at Ignace, Ontario for trial.

I had already heard on the grapevine that the prosecutor from Thunder Bay, Ontario was going to ask for a $5,000.00 fine. My good friend and lawyer, Ron Walls and I flew 120 miles to Ignace and got a cab to the courthouse. It was a surprise that the judge did not ask either attorney to speak. He made the observation that often he and several others would be at his cabin on the lake just outside of Ignace having a Friday night cook out. Then they decided that four of them were going to fly out with Jerry Jorgenson's charter operation the next day for a day's fishing on Metionga Lake with a 8:00 a.m. pick up at his cabin. Then two more friends showed up for cocktails and stated that they would like to go also.

The next morning a young fellow showed up in a DeHavilland Beaver who was not happy about having six passengers. He suggested that he make two trips, but that was turned down as the cost per person went up quite a bit plus they would loose a lot of fishing time. So he finally took all six and went —it worked fine. The judge then said "Then we have this Twin Beech, even though a little over gross, which has a legal gross weight of 10,200 pounds on wheels, 8,725 pounds on a Canadian registered Beech on floats and 8,180 pounds on a U.S. registered Beech on floats." He then pounded with his gavel saying "$50.00 fine, case dismissed".

Northern Minnesota and southern Ontario very rarely see tornados, but twice I brushed up against one. The first time we had one was in mid summer when we had a wild morning with very heavy rain, low ceilings, gusty winds and no urge to fly. A little after noon the wind and rain let up with the ceiling rising to almost 1,000 feet. I had a Beech pick up at 1:00 p.m. on Powell Lake, so I said that I would go out and take a look at it and give the office a radio call before I landed at Canadian Customs on Basswood Lake. Between our base and customs there was a 12 mile stretch with a no fly zone with a tops of 4,000 feet. We had approached the FAA a few years earlier to create an open route following a road between Fall Lake and Basswood Lake to make a safer route for international traffic between the two countries. There were docks on both ends of a road with trucks hauling people, boats, motors and equipment between the lakes. The FAA proposed a ¼ mile wide passage, but we all turned it down as dangerous putting all of the two way traffic into a narrow stretch in bad weather. We suggested a section with a five mile width of a normal airway for that four mile stretch. It did not happen. There was a huge fine if you were caught below that 4,000 foot restricted area. In low ceilings that caused us to fly straight east of town until we hit Wood Lake, a 90 degree turn to the north, climb slightly into the clouds where we could not be identified and hold that heading for 12 miles, then descending on the Canadian side with no ceiling limits and land at customs. Just the reverse for traffic headed for Ely. This particular day I held my heading for five minutes, reduced power and put my nose down and started a descent.

This got very confusing — everything was done for the descent, but my altimeter was showing a climb.

Very quickly I added power with my nose still down, but still showing a gain in altitude. Suddenly that reversed and I was going down quickly — I added power while slightly raising my nose. I broke out about 900 feet above the terrain in moderate rain and four or five miles visibility. I sorted out where I was and turned back to the Customs station. Roy Forsythe, the agent ran out on the dock to catch me as he was yelling "Why are you flying — we just had a tornado go through here". We got the airplane tied down, then ran to the cabin where his wife made coffee and a batch of cookies. I had radioed my office while I was struggling in the air and passed on the word to keep the others there. An hour later it cleared off pretty nice. I went on my way while radioing the office to have everyone start their day. When I taxied out of the Customs station I saw where the tornado had passed about 300 yards north of their cabin and I must have been right on the edge of it.

Three years later I was flying a trip from Ely to Lac La Croix ranger station in heavy rain and a 600 foot ceiling and crossing Argo Lake. I was going from lake to lake — Argo was just north of Crooked Lake and the U.S. border, then to Roland Lake, McAree Lake north to the rapids on the left, followed by Lac La Crox and the ranger station. As I was halfway across Argo Lake my left wing abruptly dropped 90 degrees with a major bump. I had to adjust differential power to quickly recover without much altitude loss — I had five passengers and two canoes back in the cabin and everyone was throwing up. I had the aircraft under control very quickly so I kept on going in spite of the odor. A few minutes later we touched down at the ranger station with Mike O'Brian coming to the dock saying "What are you doing flying, we just had a tornado pass just north of us going east". I told him that I had taken notice of something odd, unloaded the sick passengers and gear then borrowed a bucket and rinsed out the inside of the cabin. I was up there a couple of days later (on a nice day) got a good view of the path of the storm while realizing I was about two miles south of it when I was over Argo Lake.

Back in the late 1970's I almost bought the beginnings of a fly-in fishing resort in Northern Manitoba.

This was located right between North Henik and South Henik Lakes and was the site of a closed down Hudson Bay Company trading post. The original store was there, a large storage shed, a cabin for living quarters and, a 4,000 foot gravel landing strip complete with a Caterpillar D-6 bulldozer. This was all located on the north end of South Henik Lake where a short river flowed in from North Henik Lake. This provided some very nice lake trout fishing of 20 to 30 pounders plus fishing for Artic Grayling in the river. A fellow had bought all of this with the idea of fixing up the trading post to a lodge, kitchen and dining room while building several cabins for guest quarters. He was asking $31,000.00 Canadian which then was about $29,500.00 U.S. funds. He had developed a medical problem that made him decide that the project might be too much for him. I thought that I would buy a Mitsubishi MU2 and make a flight up there with six passengers up and six back every other day. But then the Wilderness Act of 1978 popped up and I held off — and soon went on to Alaska.

CHAPTER 26

NAMES, FACES
AND PLACES

The thing I have really liked about Aviation that I have liked is the travel that is involved and the people you meet. I have spent a lot of time in the Artic along with the sub Artic and love it — other than the black flies. Most of the time the wind will blow 10 to 20 miles per hour, but when it quits, get in somewhere sheltered. At times I have seen people with streams of blood pouring down their faces, but the wind cures the problem along with a liberal dose of a good bug retardant which is 100% Deets. After WWII there was a lot of mineral exploration going on all over northern Canada utilizing DC3's on skis, PBY's, Norseman's on floats and some Twin Otters on floats. An entire camp would be flown in with large tents erected with wood floors and walls — some for sleeping, a dining tent, kitchen tent, shower and toilet facilities and a shop to maintain the core drills. Later the camps were abandoned with everything left standing and we noticed there was quite a supply of leftover barrels of aviation fuel — mostly 80/87 octane and a bit of Jet A. These were stashed where it was a fairly long distance from the normal outlets of aviation fuel. For several years I kept a notebook of these different locations and the gallonage concerned. These camps would usually be operated one summer and after not striking it rich they would be shutdown. A lot of spots that concerned a lengthy flight, they simply left everything there except the core drills and shop tools. Aviation fuel was then selling for $1.00 per gallon or less which made it cheaper to leave it there rather than fly it out. This all changed in 1973 when the mid-east fuel producers tripled their prices and cut production. A Noordyn Norseman could carry six to eight drums of fuel while burning the same amount but creating a minus on the engine and crew time. For a very few of us it was fantastic. We could fly a group of fishermen to the site, set up camp — or even use the old camp in some places — and then use the fuel stash to fly out fishing other lakes and rivers in the area. The drums of fuel left sitting so long that it would make a lot of moisture inside, but we simply carried several empty five gallon fuel cans, some hose or a brass pump and a Chamois cloth to strain the water out. When we got the amount of water to equal the amount of fuel we would move on thinking the fuel got stale. I had talked to several of the fuel manufactures about this when the Cessna 185's started getting common and they told me that we could use some 80/87 octane fuel in the engine, but do not take off or climb on the stored fuel. They suggested keeping one tank for 100 octane all of the time and the other side for low power cruise settings. We used those stored fuels for several years and found a lot of good fishing. While on one trip from a fuel stop in Uranium City, Saskatchewan I headed to Lynn Lake, Manitoba and Lake Winnepeg I noticed a old mining camp set up on Black Lake, Saskatchewan then proceeded to land and check it out. There were four large tents with wood floors and walls — two sleeping, one Kitchen/dinning plus a toilet shower set up, two 23' Chestnut square stern freighter canoes besides almost 40 drums of 80/87 Avgas. We used this as a destination several times in the next couple of years. We would fly in with a party of fishermen, then fly into surrounding lakes and found some excellent fishing. Another spot we liked was Mountain Lake which was 245 miles northwest of Churchill, Manitoba. This area had some pretty hills around it instead of just flat tundra as well as some good lake trout fishing. We had a pretty good little campsite set up on a sandy beach and a river flowing in. You could stand on the shoreline and catch 20 to 25 pound lake trout. We used that spot occasionally for three summers and never saw another person, but it was about 25 years later while we were operating in Hawaii when a fellow walked into our office and identified himself as an Air Canada pilot. He said that he had flown seaplanes out of Landing Lake in Churchill, Manitoba for awhile. I used to stop in there for fuel many times giving us a lot to talk about. It turned out that both he and his brother had considered Mountain Lake to be on of their favorites, so he stopped in to visit whenever he overnighted in Honolulu.

There were many camps started for the purpose of mineral exploration, but there was one camp that I could never find out about it's original purpose. This was on Thompson Lake way up in the northwest corner of Hudson Bay. When I heard about this I did have to go check it out. There was a DC3 on skis sunk along the shore of the lake, but I had been told there was 18,000 gallons of 80/87 fuel there in barrels — that would be close to 400 drums, but the black flies were to thick that day to stick around very long to count. I am sure that with the volume of fuel that it came in by Caterpiller chain over the ice after unloading from a barge. The only thing I could figure is someone wanted to start a gas station with no competition. Later on someone did start a lodge there.

Chantrey Inlet was another Artic coastal area that we did an occasional trip to in July for large lake trout. This would be a 10 to 12 hour flight in a long day, but it would be almost 24 hours of daylight on the northern portion. We would have a stop for Canadian Customs, a fuel stop at Pickle Lake, Ontario, Landing Lake at Churchill, Manitoba and Baker Lake in the North West Territories. Baker Lake was interesting in that it was a Hudson Bay Trading Post which required ordering and paying for so many drums of fuel you wanted there in August the year before. It would be $7.00 to $8.00 per gallon at Baker Lake, but some times was $1.00 per gallon in Churchill where it came into port on a ship. Baker Lake's fuel would be off loaded on shore at Chesterfield Inlet the first week of

September, stacked up on shore to be Cat trained to Baker Lake during the winter after freeze-up. These trails would show up on aeronautical charts as winter roads which many, many tons of freight would be moved during the winter. The larger trains could have 20 large Caterpillars towing large sleighs of freight plus living quarters for the crews. Of course day or night did not matter much as much of the north might be dark for several months. I think that Vern Jones started the first fishing camp on Chantry Inlet by barging in a Caterpillar in to carve out a runway of 3,500 feet or so that was serviced by a Piper Chieftan and a DC-3.

Pooch Lisenfield, who was well known in Arctic flying was running and supplying the camp with its customers from Churchill with his wife being the camp cook. She did have a two burner gas stove explode one day which blinded her. In the mid 1970's we would probably run two trips a year up there.

We would land the Twin Beech in the freshwater lake right above the rapids of the Inlet. There was a small island with a sand beach and a water falls about 100 yards in front of it. I once had a photo of six lake trout laying on the beach with the smallest at 51 pounds and the largest at 61 pounds. One summer I had a pilot, Alan Bjorhus, who was en route to Chantry with five guests when he lost an engine just north of Baker Lake. We always carried IFR route charts with us so that we had center frequencies available if we had a problem. The next morning he tried calling in blind which allowed him to talk to a British Overseas Air Carrier (BOAC) en-route from London, England to Winnipeg, Manitoba over the North Pole. BOAC relayed the message to center and they called our office on the phone. I had just landed and pulled up to the dock when one of the office girls came out telling me that Winnipeg Center wanted to talk to me. I ran in the office, picked up the phone and was asked if I owned Twin Beech N44573. I replied yes and that it should be just about at the Arctic Ocean in the Northwest Territories.

He then told me the aircraft had an engine problem the day before making him land. I wanted to know where he had landed and the fellow from Winnipeg said he was still talking to the BOAC plane, so he asked him to check. My pilot said that he did not know his exact position, but he was about 100 miles north of Baker Lake. I had him describe the lake to which he said was four to five miles long running NE and SW with a fair sized sand beach on the NE side with a river running out of it to the NE. I told Winnipeg Center to pass on to our pilot that I thought I knew that lake and we would have a plane there the next morning so have a fire going with a lot of white smoke while clicking his microphone. I then I went out in the hanger and told one of our pilot mechanics to grab one of the other guys, a spare magneto, cylinder and the tools needed to change them. Then they should run home and pack enough clothes for a few days while I packed up a tent, camping gear plus food. When they came back I went over the maps with them and told them to stay as high as possible when they got up there while watching for smoke and clicking their microphone. They were flying a Cessna 172 XP on PK floats powered by a 213 h.p. engine which was a nice machine, but they would not get there that night. What an adventure for a couple of young fellows.

Late the next afternoon I received a phone call from the two mechanics who were back in Churchill again. They broke the news to me that a magneto or cylinder was not going to get N44573 flying again.

A master rod had failed so we needed a whole new engine. I told them to come on back to Ely to regroup while I try to get a new engine here. I did catch Paul Abbott at Covington Engine in Oklahoma who I bought two fresh engines from that spring and installed them in Beech N44573. I told him that we had not put 200 hours on those yet and I had a airplane stuck in the Artic. He called me back in less than an hour saying that he would have one ready for pick up mid morning the next day. I told him that we would have a van there before noon and would appreciate a quick turn-around. Then I got two of the dock hands and told them to quickly pack and hit the road for Oklahoma, drive to midnight get a room for six hours sleep. On the way back they should drive to seven or eight p.m., get a room again for a six hour sleep then go, go, go. They did get back to Ely mid afternoon. We had two Beeches on floats at that time with N6561D in Ely at the moment. The van showed up during the afternoon so we loaded the engine up in the Beech as well as tools and a chain hoist plus rope. We also prepared a Cessna 206 and a Cessna 185 to go along to fly the guests the last leg to the ocean for a day or two of fishing while everyone else changed the engine. The two pilot mechanics that just flew in from the Sub Artic were telling everyone about the trip and seeing a lot of Beluga whales (white whales) around the Churchill area. We finally got everything loaded and the aircraft topped off with fuel. We planned on taking off at 0730 so that we would arrive at Canadian Customs by 0800.

It was late afternoon four days later when the Artic fleet landed back in Ely. The only hitch was that we had to fly over 200 miles south to find three trees long enough to make a tripod to move the bad engine off and the good one back on.

Talking about Beluga Whales brings back memories of one Friday in Alaska when I was on our seven day tour. We had left Chikuminuk Lake to fly down the chain of lakes to Aleknagik Lake for a fuel stop.

We then left there to proceed to the Kvichak River and northeast to Iliama Lake. It was a beautiful day, with light winds. I glanced back into the cabin of the Beech and saw six people there asleep. A couple of minutes later we were about 20 miles downstream of the village of Igiugig when I noticed a 10 to 12 foot Beluga whale going up stream headed for the 90 mile long lake. The water was clear as well as shallow, so the fish showed up clearly. I immediately rolled the aircraft over into a tight bank while yelling for everyone in back " look at the size of that salmon". Around the campfire that night on Kakhonak Lake I told the guests that every year a few whales would follow the salmon up the river to spend some time feeding.

I remember meeting a fellow, Don Nelson, who with his wife started a small fishing camp on a river almost in the middle of Victoria Island almost

200 miles north west of Cambridge Bay. They had a very short season — four to five weeks — but terrific fishing for Arctic Char.

I also had a booth at the Minneapolis sport show right next to a young couple from Churchill, Manitoba who opened up a camp a little over an hour north of the town (by air) fishing for lake trout and Artic Grayling, a month of Goose hunting in late August and September with some Polar Bear watching.

Ketchikan, Alaska has been a busy tourist spot for many years, but did not have an airport or airline service. The closest airport was about 20 miles away, which was Annette Island, an old military airfield. I think at one time for a few years there were nine Grumman Gooses (Geese) working off the docks in Ketchikan waterfront. They would meet the incoming flights at Annette Island to fly the passengers to the Ketchikan seaplane base as well as the opposite direction for the outgoing flights. In 1973 an airport was built on Gravina Island near Ketchikan. This is a seven minute ferry ride to town across the channel with trips every fifteen minutes plus a $7.00 fare. Ketchikan is usually one of the six busiest airports in Alaska. A bridge was proposed a few years ago, but the $400 million dollar proposed price did not carry.

Our Twin beech 18 parked in Ketchikan

Ketchikan had a large share of seaplane operators along the main street waterfront. Bob Ellis was one of the early ones back in the days of the cabin Waco's. Paul Breed and his wife Helen ran South East Airways for quite a while. She even had her own personal Super Cub on floats that she parked on a twenty foot elevator that they used to get their aircraft out of the water and on the top of the dock above the twenty foot tides. She came in late one night, parked the Cub on the float of the elevator, raised it to the top and went home leaving the float up. The next morning the first arrivals found that the elevator had run up and down all night — twenty feet below water at high tide. This stripped almost all of the fabric off of the airplane. Art Heck who had a single DHC-3 Otter rebuilt in Seattle only to have the engine quit while ferrying it on wheels going home — 600 miles of water en-route. Chuck Slagle had a couple of Twin Otters on floats as well as some of the first Turbinezed Single Otters on floats. Jerry Scadero and his wife Candy spent many years working the waterfront. Jim Vreeland who started flying with me in Ely spent many years in Ketchikan. He crashed a Beaver in the hills of Ward Cove and severely burned his hands getting the five passengers out safely. Lots of seaplane history in that town — I think it was nine Forest Service people died in a Grumman Goose after an engine failure.

During the fall of 1974 I made a trip to Hot Springs, Arkansas to meet with Jessie Kimball who had advertised a seaplane operation for sale. I thought that it might be a decent spot to place several seaplanes during the winter for sightseeing and seaplane training. I had a Part 135 Certificate and a Part 141 Flight School Certificate so we were doing a lot of single seaplane and multi engine seaplane training under the G.I. Bill at that time. I spent a couple of days talking with Jessie. He had a 1973 Cessna 172 on Edo 2000 floats that he had priced pretty high to me considering that I was buying at dealers price — but we were talking. Three days later he called me saying that he had talked to the operators of the Holiday Inn, which I think was on Hamilton Lake, and they would be interested in providing a complimentary seaplane ride for each of their rooms if I would bring more aircraft in. I talked with the owners of the hotel and I followed up by looking for a Twin Otter on floats. I found one that interested me for $650,000.00 then applied for a $500,000.00 Small Business Administration (SBA) loan.

I got a little Congressional help and had approval within a couple of months, but then SBA said that we had to hire one person for every $10,000.00 of revenue borrowed. I could not afford to hire 50 pilots for one airplane and passed on the deal.

While I was a Cessna dealer I picked up Russ Myers, President of Cessna Aircraft as a customer. He and his son would fly one of the company Citation Jets to fly out with us to some good Canadian fishing.

I always made a point of driving them back to the airport so that I could make a couple of touch and go take offs and landings. One evening on one of his returns we went out to dinner with a two hour discussion of the than proposed Cessna 208 Caravan. He did a great thing for me one time when I sold a Single Otter to a doctor in Anchorage and took a nice Beechcraft Queen Air in trade. I had the Queen Air back in Minnesota during the winter, but it did not have boots or hot props so I could not find a buyer.

One day I noticed an add in Trade-A-Plane that a fellow said he was a serious buyer of Beech King Airs and Queen Airs. I called him to explain the lack of de-iceing equipment which he said was not important if it had the long range fuel tanks. I was pretty naïve at that time living in the North, but I told him that I would bring it to him at Opa Locka, Florida that weekend. I did and was back in my office Monday morning where I heard from an aircraft broker in Provo, Utah who had a buyer for the plane. I told him I had left it for some maintenance for the next ten days. We agreed on a price and a meeting in two weeks in Florida. He picked me up when I arrived and then we went to the buyer's house on a canal with his and her Mercedes Convertible's plus a nice thirty some foot boat tied up in front of the house in a canal. We picked up a brief case that showed me a large number of $50.00 and $100.00 bills. I was pretty naïve about the drug trade or I would have been more cautious about this project. Alvin Celsure, the broker said he knew a banker that we could get to open the bank in spite of the late hour. He and I went over there, got let in to meet with one of the vice presidents and the head teller. She counted out the bundles of cash and it was the correct amount. I had a wire transfer for $100,000.00 sent to my bank in Ely, a cashier's check for $4,000.00 made to the maintenance operation that worked on the aircraft and the balance went to the broker for his commission. The broker had me sign an aircraft bill of sale which he would deliver to the buyer. Two weeks later the buyer was arrested in San Juan, Puerto Rico with 1,300 pounds of illegal happy stuff. The aircraft was still registered to me. He gave them my name, posted bail and left. A couple of weeks later the U.S. Marshals had a warrant out for my arrest. A good banker friend called to say that the Marshals were looking for me for drug running. I got my attorney friend whom I had sold a couple of airplanes to call them to see what was wrong. It turned out that I was in Wichita, Kansas picking up a new Cessna 206 that same day of the supposed arrest and having dinner with Russ Myers at the time I was supposed to be in San Juan.

Loren Olsen spent a couple of years flying and wrenching for us in Alaska, then went back to Minnesota and started a maintenance facility called Caravans, Inc. Gary Merrill flew for us in Hawaii, but then succumbed to Southwest Airlines in Dallas, Texas.

We also got to know Richard Schuman of Makani Kai Helicopter pretty well while we were in Honolulu. He was a pretty neat guy who was involved in some of the same battles we were. Both his rotor wing and fixed wing business were shut down during the recent pandemic problem.

CHAPTER 27

BEING A CESSNA SEAPLANE DEALER

Being a Cessna Seaplane dealer I sold quite a few aircraft all over the nation. I remember selling a new Cessna 185 to the Aqua Float guys one day during the winter. They were in a hurry to get a no radio airplane with the factory seaplane kit. I called Cessna to find they had one just like I wanted. I got the price, called the Florida people to tell them what it would cost and that I probably could have it there the next afternoon if they OK'd it quickly. A hour later they called back and said "Go". I went up to the bank, got a cashiers check for Cessna, then packed a bag before one of our pilots flew me to Duluth for a flight to Minneapolis and on to Kansas City, ending up in Wichita about 11:00 p.m. I got a room, up at 0600 for breakfast before a cab ride to the Delivery Center, arriving just before 0730 and paying for the aircraft. After taking my money they told me that they would bring it to the hanger to defrost it. I tried to talk them out of that explaining that all winter I had several airplanes tied down on the ice on the lake and it only took 30 to 40 minutes to sweep the wings off while heating the cabin and engine with a Herman Nelson heater. This would be done at 30 degrees to 40 degrees below zero, but they had several accidents there at the delivery center because of frosted wings making it a firm "Warm them up" rule. This kept me there until 11:30 a.m. when

I got the airplane. One thing I will give them credit for at the Delivery Center is they had an excellent system for checking weather and you could buy a map for almost anywhere in the world. While I was waiting that morning I had noticed a small warm front moving along the Gulf Coast between Tallahassee and New Orleans with rain, fog, and low ceilings and visibility. Seeing as I was a no radio aircraft it made sense to stay inland close to the northern border of Tennessee then turn down the middle of Florida. I had breakfast at 6:30 that morning making me pretty hungry by 1:00 p.m. or so, but not having a radio I could not land at any of the larger airports. I finally found an airport coming up with two paved runways but did not have a control tower, so I landed. No restaurant, not even a candy machine, so I topped off the fuel before heading east again. Another hour and I have a serious hunger problem when I came up on a road project. It was an asphalt covered road that made a 90 degree turn with the pavement torn up and a wide gravel slightly banked turn while right there behind the turn was a building with a large red neon sign saying "Café". No hesitation — throttle back, flaps 40 and touch down, shut down and quickly entered Heaven ordering a "Cheese Burger and coke for here". There were two women there — one in the kitchen cooking and one waitress who kept peeking out the kitchen door watching me. I got nervous about that, so when my order came, I said "Make it to go" and paid her, went back to the C185, fired it up, flaps 20 and started a take-off going around the corner again. Sure enough, when I just came off of the ground a Sheriff's car came down the road with red lights flashing! I aimed right for him, probably 20 feet above him so that he could not get my registration number. This was in the days when there were a lot of light aircraft used to bring drugs into the country — but I was just hungry.

The next time I landed on a paved highway again was in another Cessna 185 on wheels that I was delivering from Ely, Minnesota to Anchorage, Alaska during the winter. I stopped at Dawson Creek, B.C. for fuel and then headed north along the Alcan Highway to Fort Nelson. I got about halfway when I ran into some pretty heavy snow fall. Pretty quickly I was down to less than a mile visibility and I did not feel comfortable about this — in the mountains I had only flown through a few times. I did find a fairly straight stretch of highway, looked it over carefully for wires, power back, flaps 40 degrees, land. There was a side road I had seen from the air so I taxied up to it, shut down and pushed the tail back on that road and got the airplane completely off of the highway. I probably sat in the airplane not more than 15 minutes when the first car pulled up with lights all over it and a Canadian Mountie getting out walking towards me. I really thought I was in trouble, but he just asked if I had anything wrong. I told him the weather was getting bad so I decided it would be wise to sit for awhile until it got better. He did ask if I needed help to get out again, but seemed very agreeable when I told him that I would warm it up again while on the road, then make about a 10 second take-off run on the highway. He did give me a phone number to call if I needed help. He said it was an auxillary station about 15 minutes away and someone would be right there if I wanted help. He went on his way while I waited for another hour until the storm flurry eased up so that I could leave. Another time I was ferrying a Cessna 206 to Anchorage on wheels during the winter and we landed at Fort Nelson for fuel and a weather check. Flight service was in the same building, so he pulled up the weather west bound which was scattered snow over most of the route. He did call an Air Canada 737 that just made an IFR departure out of Watson Lake who said the bases were at 7,000 feet. The flight service person also told us that Fort Nelson now had a VOR which was working but had not been signed off as yet. He gave us the frequency and said to use it if it helped. We left Fort Nelson headed for Watson Lake (one of the prettiest airports you can find during the summer months). An hour later we (I had a passenger George Bertulla who I had sold a couple of airplanes) hit some pretty heavy snow and turned around to return to Fort Nelson. We were just scraping along, but landed back at Fort Nelson just in time to hear someone screaming " Mayday Mayday" on their radio. A fellow,

Rusty Hayes, was flying a Cherokee 6 down to Illinois from Anchorage to trade the Piper to Watcha McCallum (another character) for a Found 100. He had a non pilot friend with him when they ran into some of the same heavy snow we had. He was a VFR pilot and had made an IFR climb out in a narrow valley to where he broke out at 10,000 feet. Somewhere he had gotten the info about the VOR at Fort Nelson and was trying to get there. We stayed there to listen to this — the non-pilot did know that Rusty was not IFR rated, making him very scared. They did get in about 45 minutes later, so one of the men there gave the four of us a ride into town and a hotel. There was a government liquor store down the street and everyone's first stop. We ended up spending three days there — one north bound and one south bound aircraft. Each morning the four of us would have breakfast, check weather and watch heavy snow falling. 2:00 p.m. would be the final weather check and no-go, then another trip to the liquor store. We did get a lot of time to talk and Rusty told me that after three days of bad weather that our destination, Merrill Field, would be swamped with traffic and do not even use your entire registration number on the radio calls, just the last three digits. When we did get there that was exactly what was going on. I listened to the tower starting at 20 miles out, but when we got close I heard the tower clear one aircraft to land on runway 8 and instantly cleared another to land on runway 26 which is head on. This is a thing you just do not hear very often, but I thought the guy in the tower must know these two and where they are based on the runway. Then I called the tower saying "57 Uniform Seven North for landing". His reply was "57 Uniform can you land short?" "Yes sir, very short". "57 Uniform cleared runway 33". Three aircraft cleared to land short with no sequencing and it was non stop talking from the tower. I probably used about 600 feet of runway before I turned off to the right on a cut in the snow bank on the edge of the runway —almost as high as my wings — only to see it was a street with houses on both sides of the street, but cars parked only on one side. Thinking it was my fault, I called Ground Control and explained where I was and got the simple reply "Taxi down the street two blocks, then turn left for one block and transient parking is right below the tower". As soon as we got tied down, I called a local lawyer who was the buyer of the aircraft, thinking I might need legal aid. He just laughed when I told him about it — that's the way it is done and it works.

Five years later I moved to Alaska and saw many quirks in aviation. The village of Iliamna on the North shore of a lake with the same name had a gravel runway which was used as the main street. You could land and taxi up to the post office, grocery store or other businesses as needed. Some of the small runways along the saltwater coastline would be under water at high tide, so you always carried a tide book. Quite a few runways had curves in them. I used to land on a 800 foot runway with a 45 degree bend in the runway. We used to land on a 1,800 foot runway where the bottom end was 400 feet lower than the top — land uphill, take off downhill. Sand beaches were used at low tide for a lot of things including drop offs and pickups plus clamming. There was a 4,000 foot nice grass runway down the coat by Yakataga that had a lot of wild Strawberries growing on it. One day I landed with a Cessna 206 for a mail drop and pick up, then I started to pick a few strawberries for dinner that night. I got totally engrossed in that until I noticed that I was about 2,000 feet from the airplane with a brown bear (Grizzly) picking strawberries between the airplane and me — and my .44 magnum was still in the plane, dummy! I immediately moved thru the trees for about 100 yards to the beach, and then ran to where I thought I could go back to the runway and the airplane. I found the airplane (and the bear still eating) and wasted no time getting back in the air. Another day I was making a mail run down the coast and went into the landing strip at Icy Bay which had a small logging camp. These mail runs were under a Post Office contract and we would get a large green mail sack going in and would pick up the outgoing mail sack. There would be a fair sized wooden box at the end of the gravel runway where we would leave the incoming mail and pick up the outgoing. This day when I picked up the outgoing sack, I noticed a note pinned on it. It said to please bring 100 rolls of duct tape on the next flight. I was standing there pondering this when a man walked out on the trail from the logging camp. He showed me his Stinson 108 tied down on the strip. A bear had ripped off almost all of the fabric covering of the plane, but he needed the duct tape to patch it up to fly it to Anchorages to have it recovered. We were there three times per week, but I did tell him that we might have to order some of the 100 rolls from Anchorage if we could not get that much in Cordova. We did get the tape he needed to him and a couple of weeks later we saw his Stinson flying over going to Anchorage. About three days later he landed in Cordova for fuel on his way back to Icy Bay — with a lot of duct tape still on the airplane. He told us that no one would do the re-cover project during the summer months because they were too busy, so he is going to take it in again in October.

I have asked a lot of people over the years "How do you fly two airplanes at once"? The simple answer is to dismantle one and tie it on the floats of the other airplane. Years ago when I had my first single engine Otter (DHC-3) I got a phone call one evening in the spring. The caller said that he had been fishing in Seven Beavers Lake and his airplane had broken thru the ice and he as wondering if I could help them get the airplane out of there. I asked if it went all the way through and was the engine running when it broke through. He replied that the engine was running when the nose broke through, but the wings were on the ice and kept it from sinking all of the way, but the propeller was bent. His airplane was an Aeronca Champ and there was a Stinson 108 also with a total of five fisherman. They cut trees down, made some poles and got the airplane back on top of the ice. I told him that the ice was breaking up around our dock and hanger and we had moved all our airplanes off the ice to start changing over to floats. This would usually be a week or so until the ice would be completely gone so that we could start flying again. I did tell him to go back there to move the Champ over somewhere they could get it ashore.

Then take the wings, tail group and engine off and I could probably fly it out within the next 10 days. He called back the next night to say that they had accomplished that and would check in when all the lakes opened up.

It was about ten days later and we agreed to meet at the site on Seven Beavers Lake. I had put a few hours on the Otter and they had the Stinson on floats. There would be four of them. A little earlier I had called to make sure everything was broken down. When I got there we loaded the engine, prop, tail surfaces and landing gear inside the cabin. The two wings were tied back to back with a couple of boat cushions in between, then tied down on top of the RH float. Finally the fuselage was tied down on top of the LH float. It looked cumbersome, it but probably only weighed a little over 800 pounds and took just under a hour to Devils Track Lake at Grand Marais, MN.

A few years later I was standing on a dock on Lake Hood in Anchorage when I noticed several people pointing to the west so I turned around to see Dean Carroll in one of his Beavers coming in for a landing with a Cessna 180 dismantled and tied on the floats. One of his Cessna 180's on wheels landed on a sandbar in the Two Lakes area just over 100 miles west of Anchorage. The sand was soft causing the aircraft to flip upside down. The rudder, vertical fin, wings and propeller were in pretty bad shape, so it was a lot simpler to fly the Cessna back to town than to try to make it flyable again from there. This is how you do it if you want to fly two airplanes at one time. I was surprised that he came right into Lake Hood right in front of the FAA, but I guess he did not get harassed too much about the flight.

Flying in the bush in a roadless area puts quite a bit of pressure on the operator. Back in Ely one morning I got a message from Jim Pascoe, a good friend and good customer that there would be a freezer delivered to our dock that day that he needed flown to one of his fishing camps 110 miles north of Ely. Late that afternoon a truck dropped off a large wooden box that was heavy with a note on the box that said it needed to go to Baril Bay. We opened up the crate and it was a propane chest freezer — I seem to remember that it was about two foot by two foot by seven foot long out of the crate. We just had an engine go out on the Otter and were waiting for a OH engine that was supposed to be shipped at the end of that week. The twin Beech was on a week long trip to the Artic Ocean, so I called Jim and told him of our problem saying it might be a week before he could get it flown up. He replied that the camp was full of fishermen that needed some way of keeping their fish. They were many miles from the nearest road, so we were the only answer. I went out on the dock and measured the main cabin door.

Lo and behold — it looked like it would fit in the door with a half inch to spare. Because of its length we could not slide it in the cabin, but we took both doors off and it just barely fit in with about 1 ½ feet sticking out on each side. By simply tying a rope on each side to the float struts, we were ready to go.

And the next morning that was the first flight for the Beaver. When I landed at Canadian Customs, Roy Forsythe, walked down the dock shaking his head and asked "why we did not just tie it on top of the floats like you do with everything else"? I told him that we did not want to get the freezer wet with the water spray from the floats on the takeoff and landing. It stayed dry being higher than the floats. I gave him the invoice so he could make out the bill for duty and we would get a check to him on one of the flights later in the day. He and his family lived on a small island on the Canadian side of Basswood Lake in a cabin with no electricity, no radio, telephone or road access. His customers came by canoe, boat or seaplane. We would fly the family to and from Ely when they needed plus we brought all their food and mail into them, so we got along pretty good. We would work their flights on back hauls so we did not have to charge them. But the freezer got there!

Beside the med-a-vac flights we also did some emergency messages. These quite often involved the death or serious injury to an immediate member of the family. This could be hard to do having to break the news to someone about his or her loved one. Then of course sometimes it would go the other way.

One night I got a call at my home about 10:00 p.m. informing me that a member of a party of archery deer hunters that I had flown into Seven Beavers Lake needed notification that his wife had passed away. I told the caller that I would be in the air right at daylight so that I could catch him in camp before they went hunting for the day. When the daylight started showing up in the east I was fueled and warmed up followed by a quick take-of with a south bound turnout. Breakfast at the camp was just being made when I landed. l told the fellow I was looking for that I need to talk to him alone. We stepped off a bit while I passed on the message I had received concerning his wife then told him to pack up his gear and I would take him back to town. He looked at me and said "I am not going anywhere". I guess he saw the look of surprise on my face, so he added "We were divorced 25 years ago and I have never seen her since. I am staying here to hunt". Oh Well — I never did charge him for that flight. Sometimes it works, while some times it does not.

CHAPTER 28

WHY I FLY

My father got his first pilots license #8 signed by Orville and Wilbur Wright in 1920 issued by the Federation Aeronautique International. This was long before there was a CAA or FAA. His last license was issued as #229 was a Sporting License.

He had a business with a couple of Lockheed Vega's on floats delivering mail around the shores of Lake Superior and went broke at the start of the Depression. This was followed by a stint flying the U.S. Mail based out of Wausau, Wisconsin. His family was growing and the safety record of mail service was not too good, so he gave up flying in the very early 1930's. Then he joined FDR's Civilian Conservation Corps as a civil engineer. This got us started living in log cabins on lake shores which started my love of the woods, fishing and hunting. During the summer of 1955 I made a 2 ½ month canoe trip paddling to Hudson Bay which satisfied an ambition of mine, but only fueled the desire to see more of the far North. During the summer of 1956 I arranged a fly - in fishing trip on a northern river for one of my guided parties. This was that lighted bulb over my head telling me that the seaplane would open up the whole North country to me. Now the flying itself became a new love and headed me to a new career — instead of wanting to own my canoe outfitting company I now wanted to own my own seaplane business moving people around the wilderness. I bought my first airplane in 1956.

Looking back now I am astonished at how little I knew about the difference in cost of operating these two businesses. An aluminum canoe can be bought for a few hundred dollars while an aircraft on floats could easily cost a couple of hundred thousand. A few dollars purchases the paddles to propel the canoe while an exchange engine for the airplane will cost you $30,000.00 to $50,000.00 every year or two — plus freight. It might cost $20.00 per year to maintain the canoe— to touch up the paint and maybe replace a couple rivets. The aircraft requires a pretty thorough inspection every 100 hours of flying time that will probably cost $1,000.00 to $3,000.00 — and of course a fair amount of fuel every hour it's used.

But I am very glad that I did it. It has been a fabulous life with lots of travel, adventure and very happy customers. I have spent a lot of time north of the Artic Circle and I am a member of Screen Actors Guild (SAG) for years — and sometimes taking in as much as $100,000.00 plus expenses for a month or so with one aircraft on movie work. Some of the happiest customers were med-a-vacs that had some very serious ailments that desperately needed to get them to a hospital. For some reason these often came along in some of the most miserable weather and at night. I did pick up a fellow with a heart attack at Basswood Lodge while they were still operating. I only had one Cessna 180 at the time, but I started up there immediately after a call — about a 20 minute flight. Upon docking I loaded his two sons in the back seat while a pickup drove up to the dock with the patient. When he got out and started walking the 100 foot long dock I yelled at him that we would come carry him, but he answered that he was fine. He stepped on the float and moved into the front right seat, groaned and collapsed. His sons both yelled "Go, go — hurry". I was already in the aircraft, started the engine and immediately started a take-off. I climbed to 300 feet, hooked up my seat belt and just slightly reduced power while I radioed my office to have an ambulance there waiting for us. We landed, pulled up to the dock and the ambulance crew unloaded the patient, but it was too late. Over the years I have flown a lot of bodies, but that was the only time I had a person pass away sitting next to me.

Another Memorial Day weekend we were really busy with people sitting all over our dock with their canoes and gear. About noon I was at the dock loading again and refueling when I got called into the office to take a phone call. It was our local undertaker and a good friend named Jimmy Kerntz. There had been a drowning on a local river about three days before when a 22 year old woman — and a new mother — fell overboard and was swept away by the currents. Her body had been found the day before and he wanted to know if we could fly her remains to southern Minnesota that afternoon. I had to tell him that we would not have an airplane available until mid-day the next day. He said he would pass that on to the undertaker at the other end and get back to me. I went out on my flight and got back a couple of hours later, but I had remembered a day or two earlier I had taken a used Cessna 185 in trade and it was sitting up at the airport on wheels. I called Jimmy Kerntz about that and told him that I could fly the trip myself about 8:30 p.m. arriving there shortly after 10:00 p.m. We decided that would work so I finished up my float flying for the day with several other flights while one of the shop people went to the airport to top the fuel tanks, check the oil and remove all of the seats except the pilots. I got there just before the loading time and we removed the passenger from the hearse to the right side of the plane laying on the floor with a seat belt holding her in place. As normally done when the transfer is made to the attending undertaker who provides the casket, the remains are wrapped in a couple of safety pinned sheets. The loading was quickly followed by a takeoff and climb to 4,500 feet then leveled out. A little over a half hour later it started to rain with the sky turning to a very strange purplish hue in the air along with some high rising puffy clouds, so I climbed to 10,500 feet on top of most of this. Just then my passenger started making some noises that sounded like groaning. This really got my attention just as it was getting dark! It even seemed like the passenger was moving a little — this is really spooking me. Shortly after the clouds opened up so that I could start descending to the destination and then get rid of my load — which had settled down again. By midnight I was back home in need of a strong drink as well as a good night's sleep. I flew 13.5 hours that day. Over the years I flew several 12 hour days, but I did hit 13.5 hours several times. The next morning I did call my undertaker friend telling him about the strange noises and movement of the passenger, but he said it had to be gasses still in the remains with the higher altitude causing the happening. He also said that a strong series of thunder storms had just moved off to the east just before us that might have also stirred up some of those gasses.

Over the 20 years operating in Ely, Minnesota my aircraft were involved in many medical evac flight — probably about 40% of those we never got paid for, but we never did hesitate to dispatch a flight. One day during June, 1964 a fellow was driving his pickup along the north shore of Shagawa Lake with a five gallon can of gas in the rear bed. Somehow he ran off the road, crashed and the truck caught fire. They took him to the hospital, but he was severely burned and needed to get to the University of Minnesota Burn Center in Minneapolis. The hospital called our office to ask if we could do the transport. It was a low ceiling and raining and we were flying a relatively new to us airplane — the Twin Beech on floats. I told them that I would call them right back and then called Steve Gheen at the U.S. Forest Service hanger. I explained the problem to him and asked if he could fly himself and David Hangartner to Minneapolis IFR. Steve had been a USMC pilot earlier and had a lot of instrument flying off aircraft carriers. He said that the way the weather was there would be no forest fires that day and he was on his way to our base. I called the hospital to let them know it was a go and then they said they would have a patient there in 20 minutes, I told them that they would need to arrange the transfer from the Mississippi River at Downtown St. Paul Airport. Dave and I fueled and warmed up while Steve filed an instrument flight plan with vectors to the river. The aircraft had a brand new VHF radio with a VOR plus an ADF and NO — Transponder, GPS and other exotic radios of today were not around. The ambulance arrived with the patient followed by a quick take-off. An hour and forty -five minutes later they touched down on the Mississippi River to unload their patient. Then they took on some fuel, filed another flight plan back to Eveleth, Minnesota, shot a VOR approach there, then squeaked in six miles over to Bill Martilla's seaplane dock, He lent them a car to go get a motel room for the night. Ely at that time had a grass strip and no instrument approach. Midday the next day the weather improved enough to get back to Ely. I sent the family a billing for $500.00 which did not begin to cover four hours of Twin Beech time, 200 gallons of fuel, motel room and meals. Meanwhile the patient died at the University Hospital and our local City Attorney, Keith Brownell, told the widow she did not have to pay us — and we never did get paid.

Later on the FAA created "Ambulance Flight Rules" which also took a large dent in our med-a-vac flights as far as getting paid for them. We usually sent in our billings as "Ambulance Flights" for several years and had a fairly high ratio of paid for flights by the insurance companies of the various injured or sick passengers. But when the FAA started the labeling of ambulance flights, we were usually informed that we were not a licensed "Ambulance Operator". The FAA rules required you to wear white shoes white clothes and have oxygen in the aircraft. Of course, we usually were in hip boots on med-evacs, a light rain jacket and water resistant pants which disqualified us, but we still provided the service because we were the only ones there. I can remember one day in July when we had seven med-a -vacs.

Of course, most of these were happening in the Boundary Water Canoe Wilderness Area and the Canadian Quetico Park and could generate a lot of paperwork afterwards. The Canadians were very practical — "Get the sick and lame out of there". The US Forest Service really wanted us to get prior permission, for the flight but that did not work after 5:00 p.m., weekends or holidays, so we finally made a deal with the Sheriff's Department and referred any phone calls or messages to them — then they would call us and authorize the flight.

With the wilderness area being used by thousands of people in canoes there always were accidental drownings. One I remember was a 17 year old boy who was in a canoe that rolled over near the bottom of Upper Basswood River Falls while shooting a rapids. His body evidently got trapped by the current and did not rise to the surface while someone was there to spot it. The body moved slowly downstream through another small rapids followed by going over Wheelbarrow Falls where it got snagged in some bushes at the bottom. This is where a USFS two man portage crew noticed a strong odor and located the remains. They had a battery pack radio so called the Service Center in Ely concerning their discovery while saying they did not want to go back there. They were camped on the top side of Lower Basswood Falls about a half mile away. A sheriff came in our office that morning saying he was there when the message came in making it into the third week in the water. Because the Forest Service crew wanted nothing to do with the project, I asked the deputy if he wanted to come along and he said yes. I knew that stretch of river was pretty short so I decided we would take the single Otter that was tied at the end of the dock. I grabbed a few tools, filled the nose tank and 15 gallons of fuel in the center tank.

We found the portage crew camped on a smooth granite ledge where we tied up. They pointed upstream to where our passenger was while telling us that we could not get the airplane in there due to trees and brush, so we asked them to take their canoe down there and bring him back. They said NO, but we could borrow their canoe. It was just over a third of a mile to the site when we got a small rope attached to the drowning victim to tow him back to the aircraft. Then I removed both rear cabin doors, for air flow, wrapped the passenger in a couple of tarps and loaded him in the rear of the plane.

We taxied back to Wheelbarrow Falls, manually turned the aircraft downstream and took off. This way we only had to clear the top of Lower Basswood Falls by a couple of feet instead of looking at trees 40 feet high at the other end. It all worked and I radioed ahead to have Jim Kerntz on the dock when we landed. Jim had gotten wind of this activity and located a copper casket which sealed the odor very well.

He had also talked with the family and their mortician who wanted the casket flown to Rockford, Illinois that day if possible. I told Jim that we had a brand new Cessna 206 on floats which would land on Rock River at a marina on the north side of Rockford three hours after we receive the casket. Jim said that he would be back in less than two hours and the people would have a check there for both flights. I told our pilot to call from there when landing so I can tell him that there will be fuel at Madison, Wisconsin.

Another Jimmy Kerntz event!

When I started flying, the flying fever hit several of my friends also.

Jim Pascoe got interested and bought a Luscombe 8A with floats, wheels and skiis for $2,500.00 from Joe Perko, a Chevrolet dealer.

Jim Kerntz was another who got the flying bug and bought a Aeronca Chief. I found him a set of floats and skis and he was on his way. I ended up selling them brand new Cessna's later after owning several airplanes and working their way up. Jim Pascoe ended up owning Wilderness Outfitters in Ely and had several outpost camps on the Canadian side that we transported his customers to and from. We loved Tommyhow Lake where he had his northern outpost — 180 miles out and great fishing — everyone was really happy coming out of there.

Jim Kerntz was the manager of Basswood Lake Lodge until the government closed down the operation. Then he went with a hardware store which had a mortician business added. Later on as he became more proficient as a pilot he bought a small fishing camp and hideaway about 125 miles NW of Ely on Stormy Lake which had the main cabin, two smaller sleeping cabins, generator, a radio phone, a good dock and lake trout. One weekend he and wife Mary snuck off a little early on Saturday and took the Cessna 185 to Stormy Lake for a couple of days. Jim had a serious ulcer and woke up in pain on Sunday. It got worse as the morning went on, but Mary was unable to reach our base on the radio phone. She did call a couple of local Canadian operators, but they said they were too busy to make a pickup. Finally she reached our office about 1:00 p.m. She said that Jim had asked for the .30-30 rifle a couple of times because of the pain, but she took it outside to hide it in the woods. I told her that I would be there in a hour telling one of the dock hands to fuel the Twin Beech that was at the dock. I got hold of Dr. Ed Ciriacy at his cabin on Burnside Lake with his bag, so I told him that I would be there in ten minutes. Just then Kenny Lobe and wife Liza walked in the office. Both were pilots, so I asked if they would go along to fly Jim's Cessna 185 back to Ely so that it would be there when he was better. They answered "Sure" as we walked to the plane. Following a two minute stop for the doctor, we landed at

Canadian Customs at Sandpoint Lake and quickly left again only to land at Stormy Lake when the hour was up. Dr. Ciriacy actually started his inspection as we carried Jim Kerntz out to the plane and stretched him out on one of the bench seats. Liza Lobe went with the doctor to assist while we strapped Mary in one of the front seats. I told Kenny that both of my radios — the VHF and the ADF — had been sent out for maintenance a couple of days before so I had no communication or navigation and he should climb high enough to notify our base to have an ambulance there for our arrival.

I leveled off at 2,500 feet, but with a 25 knot wind and broken clouds it was very bumpy. In fact after a few minutes the doctor came forward asking if I could make it smoother for the patient. I then found a sunlit hole in the clouds, observed how the shadow of the cabin roof showed up on the left hand cowling right between two rivets. Then I climbed to 7,500 feet and put that shadow between the same two rivets heading for Ely. A few minutes later the doctor stuck his head in the cockpit and said that was much better. Then I guess he noticed my missing radios and asked what I was navigating with. When I showed him the shadow he said "you just sold me a new airplane with $20,000.00 worth of radios while you run around looking at shadows". All I could say is that it gave him a great advantage at night. Not much later I recognized part of a lake below us and started a descent to the base and a waiting ambulance. An hour later I got a call from the hospital asking if we could transport Jim Kerntz to Duluth for emergency surgery for a perforated ulcer. I told them that we would be ready by the time that they got him to us. We were fueled, warmed up and ready to go when the ambulance with Jim and Peg Likar who was one of the head nurses there to monitor the patient. Our other Twin Beech, N44573, was in now so we had radios. Just north of the Duluth Airport I asked for a ground speed check and was told 174 — pretty good for a seaplane. I also asked them to call the aerial bridge in the harbor so they do not raise the bridge and stop the ambulance to Park Point and the seaplane base. It all worked and Jim came back to fly some more.

I just drifted into flying so that I could see more of the North and Artic. I did raise four children that grew up in an aviation environment. My oldest daughter Katie did go through one of our ground school courses and passed her Private Pilot's exam, but did not follow through on the flight portion. She did utilize and own several airplanes though. My oldest son Patrick did have quite a life in aviation flying 27,000 hours, but got cut short when he took a ride with someone else. The youngest daughter Kelly married a fellow that I groomed and gave him his first job in aviation. He went on with a career as a Delta Airlines captain. Scott was the youngest son who needed a boat cushion to see over the panel when he first took over the controls. He went on to building his empire in Park City, Utah plus having a home on an island in a Lake out of Ely, Minnesota — his birthplace. For traveling over the years he has owned a Cessna 206, Cessna 210, DeHavilland Beaver on floats and even a Turbine Aero Commander.

He also worked in the commercial fishing business in Alaska for awhile.

CHAPTER 29

OFFERS

I first met Jeno Palucci at my base at Sandy Point of Shagawa Lake in Ely, Minnesota when he and his pilot Donny Anderson landed for U.S. Customs clearance and fuel. They were flying a very unusual twin engine amphib of Italian manufacture — a Piaggio P.136 called the Royal Gull in the U.S. It had five seats and two Lycoming 340 h.p. pusher engines. I think there were only about 75 or so produced and even though it had a good cruise speed it was hard to handle around docks with the wing -tip floats. We had a very good looking polished aluminum Cessna 185 with Edo 2870A floats on a side dock cleaning it up. I had just taken it in trade on a Cessna 206 and it had very low time and a simple auto pilot. Donny Anderson wandered over looking at the airplane and when I told him that it was for sale at $18,000.00 he called Jeno over to look at it. They then took off and headed back to Duluth, but Donny called the next day saying that Jeno wanted the Cessna and gave me a fax number for the accounting office. This billing was for $18,000.00 with a sales tax of $900.00 which quickly brought a phone call from Jeno saying he would not pay the sales tax. We negotiated a couple of days finally agreeing that I would pay half of the sales tax — a fair sum of revenue. Also this engine was a 260 h.p. IO-470 Continental and one of the early fuel injected engines that had a tendency to catch fire on a hot start with a three foot flame coming up from the cowling. This was pretty hard on the nerves of the passengers, but you let the engine run for a couple of seconds and the fire is gone. I did not want to pay interest and insurance through the winter and I did make the money back from Jeno in a Cessna 206 sale a couple of years later. Jeno got out of the military in 1945 and went back to Hibbing, Minnesota and started planting and canning vegetables under the name "Chung King Foods" which he sold for 92 million dollars in a few years. Then he went into "Jeno's Pizza and Pizza Rolls" and did even better. We became friendly and for a while he was pumping me about the Twin Beech. I had bought N6799C and it was the first Twin Beech on floats registered in the U.S. Jeno was intrigued by the Beech, but at that time only the C-18s were approved on floats by the FAA. I think his pilot Donny Anderson, did not like the idea of not being able to feather a propeller on a failed engine — or the single fuel selector which shut down both engines if you let a fuel tank run dry. The D18's was approved in Canada with all the safety features plus a higher gross weight. A couple of years later I bought a D-18 and made a deal with Bristol Aerospace in Manitoba who had the STC for the D-18s in Canada. Bristol manufactured the 7850 float and made me a good price on a new set of floats for buying an aircraft to do the certification with. Jeno ended up floating two D18s aircraft which were very handsomely furnished with four reclining chairs in the cabin of each airplane and murals on the walls. I used to help him out occasionally by flying some of his customers when he needed help — quite different than our Beeches with working interiors — plywood walls, metal headliner and folding benches in the cabins. Jeno also became a large invester in Disney World when they started in Florida. He called me one day to tell me to buy six brand new DeHavilland DHC-6 Twin Otters on floats. His idea was to put these on the small lake alongside the entry road of Disney World. Three of these would be flying all day, but there would always be a spare right there if there was a malfunction of any kind. I told him that there was no way I could ever afford to buy six Twin Otters on floats — to which he said not to think about the money as that was his department! He just wanted me there every day flying and running the business. I thought about it for a day and then told him that I liked flying the Bush. I did not think that I could live in Florida year around because it is so flat and hot. I think at that time 337 feet was the highest spot of ground in the state — and that was a garbage dump just outside of Tallahassee. That was undoubtedly a great deal financially, but I knew that I would not see moose, caribou or bears — or catch a fresh fish for dinner.

I did get a phone call from the Bill Bailey, the hand propping man of the year, who was a banker in Minneapolis. He wanted to know if I would be interested in taking over Mesaba Airlines. This had originally been started by Gordy Newstrom of Grand Rapids, Minnesota and used primarily to transport employees of the locally owned Blandin Paper Mill. Later on he got a Cessna 310 twin engine aircraft and started scheduled flights to Minneapolis - St. Paul. Gordy ended up selling his Grand Rapids operation to Tom Halvorson who had an operation in Duluth, Minnesota — Halvair. I lost track of the owners then for a while, but Rob Swenson came in there somewhere and evidently got tied in with Northwest Airlines and using DeHavilland Dash 8's. His father built snowmobiles on the northern border of Minnesota. I had sold the father a couple of Cessna 185's with floats and skis. Under Rob the business became Mesaba Airlines and was connected with both Northwest and Delta Airlines as feeder operations while ending in bankruptcy in 2012 with over 180 aircraft owned over the years including many jets. I could never have spent my life sitting at a desk as a cog in a large wheel and was happy later that I had turned it down.

In 1966 I started to look to buy my first DeHavilland Beaver — and probably made one of the largest mistakes of my life. This was still before DeHavilland ceased production of the DHC-2 so the U.S. military was not allowed to sell off surplus aircraft. I found a civil Beaver for sale in Panama for $25,000.00 on wheels, foreign registry without ever being in the U.S. and had not been flown for a couple of years. I called the owner and he agreed to mail me photos and a copy of the log books. I got these a few days later along with photos of five Vought 4FU Corsairs for which he was asking $5,000.00 each or an offer on the group. I passed on all, but it was only a few years later a flying aircraft of that type was bringing over ½ million dollars on the market.

I did end up purchasing a Beaver from a fellow in Miami who had one in Chile. He offered me package of the Beaver, fresh engine and prop, new paint, unit inspection, a set of 4580 floats and a set of straight skis for $42,500.00. I quickly airmailed a $20,000.00 deposit and he had someone start ferrying the aircraft up to Miami Aviation for the maintenance. Meanwhile he drove the floats and skis to my base in Ely. Several weeks later the seller called to say the aircraft would be finished, but the FAA would not be available for the inspection to issue the original U.S. Certificate of Airworthiness for three weeks or so because of the Christmas holidays. I told him that I would get back to him that day, then called the FAA in Minneapolis and got the inspection arranged there. I called the seller and told him to get a ferry permit and hire someone to bring it to Minneapolis as quickly as possible. The winter fishing season was just starting so we would have some flying for the aircraft. This all happened pretty quickly. I had made arrangements with a friend to get plane in his hanger in Minneapolis as well as a mechanic to open it up and close it up for the FAA. I did get a call the day of the inspection saying the aircraft could be picked up about 6:00 p.m. to which I said there will be someone there to get it.

I told my pilot/mechanic Wiley Hautala to take one of the Cessna 206's that needed some radio work fly it to Minneapolis, leave the 206 and bring the Beaver back. He was eager to fly the Beaver and was very quickly on his way. We planned on getting it in our hanger that night to install the skis for a $900.00 flight the next mid morning. About 7:30 p.m. we heard him talking to Bill Martilla 40 miles south saying he was flying over in our new Beaver. It was just before Christmas and we had our ice runway plowed out and some oil cans filled with sand and Kerosene lighting up the runway along with some of our students doing night take-offs and landings. We had a light easterly wind, so Wiley made a low pass over the runway, added power to climb then the engine quit as he turned downwind. The RH wing struck a tree along the shoreline which caused him to stall and fall on his LH wing which struck the ice while in a fairly steep bank. His brother Jack and I jumped in a four wheel drive pickup driving across the snow covered ice to the wreckage. One of our students, Dave Jallen and his girlfriend (later wife) made the trip with Wiley that afternoon, but there were no injuries.

I called the FAA in the morning to report the accident and seeing that it happened less than three hours after their inspection we had a couple of days of several FAA people on the premises. We ended up replacing the main landing gear bulkhead, the LH wing, two lift struts and repaired the RH wing and cowling. The ice was going out in the spring when we reassembled and found an interesting problem in that during the engine change in Miami someone had transposed the hook up between the carb heat and the oil temperature. Thus when Wiley made a prolonged descent in a plus 10 degree temperature thinking he had high carb temp and low oil temperature which he attributed to reduced power — but they were reversed. I flew that plane two years and then replaced it with another.

CHAPTER 30

ICY ADVENTURES

Late one Friday afternoon I had a pickup of one person on Seagull Lake near the end of the Gunflint Trail. Bruce Skubic was my passenger who wanted to get dropped off at his house on Lake Vermillion.

He owned a road paving operation out of Virginia, Minnesota. Earlier he had won a contract to repave a large share of the Gun Flint Trail out of Grand Marais, but it was over a 200 mile drive from Virginia to Seagull Lake versus an 80 mile flight. We had the Otter for 10 passengers, the Twin Beech for 8, Beaver for 6, Cessna 206 for 4, Cessna 180 for 3 and the Cessna 172 for 1 or 2 passengers and had picked up a fair amount of flying transporting his crews and supervisors back and forth.

When I dropped him off he commented that was pretty nice 40 minutes compared to half a days drive. He also said he used to be a private pilot and owned a Super Cub on floats, but sold the airplane as his business grew to buy more trucks. I told him to start flying again he only needed a current medical and a checkout. Sure enough he called in a few days saying he got the medical and asked if I could fly with him that weekend. Within two weeks I had him not only comfortable to go, but also sold him a brand new Cessna 206 N6994M with a seaplane kit. It was September so he would buy the floats in the spring.

In November we had decided to take the Beaver and the Otter down to Florida for the winter to find some flying to do. When Bruce heard about that he asked to come along with the Cessna to get some long cross-country time.

The night before we were scheduled to leave Ely for Florida the temperature dropped to 5 below zero, so we moved the Beaver and the Otter over to Burntside Lake before dark as it was a much deeper lake and probably would not freeze overnight. The next morning we had to take a couple of Herman Nelson gas heaters to start the two aircraft which finally got into the air in the early afternoon. We made it a short distance SE of St. Paul later that afternoon. We flew over a small narrow bay that had a nice looking beach to tie the planes up with a motel about one block away.

The next morning we found the bay covered with skim ice but we carefully broke it up by taxing very slow until we reached the open water of the river. This slowed us up quite a bit, but we finally started down the Mississippi River. The weather was up and down all afternoon, but we did pull into a small marina at Oquawka, Illinois in a heavy snow flurry. There was a small motel in town, but it was completely filled with a road construction crew. The operator of the marina gave us his truck and told us to drive 15 miles to Burlington, Iowa where we would find several motels. We awoke in the morning to find the river covered by a bank of fog, so we had a leisurely breakfast and then returned to the marina.

This brought a large shock — we could stand on the dock while watching the water inside the marina freezing and making ice. We got both aircraft started and again taxied out to open water of the river, but now we only had about ½ mile of visibility in the fog. We had just driven down the river from Burlington and Oquawka which showed us there were not bridges or power lines until reaching Burlington. I took off first, climbed 50 feet with 20 degrees of flaps showing just over 50 mph and my head halfway out my side window. It took about 20 minutes with only one surprise — an island that came up pretty close on my right side. I landed, taxied into the marina with the Beaver showing up a few minutes later. It was now early afternoon the day before Thanksgiving, so I called our office in Ely to see about a ride home for the four of us for a couple of days. I got Mark Heizler and he said that he had just flown a Cessna 185 off the ice to the airport after its float removal. He said he could be there in Burlington, Iowa in less than three hours to get all of us. I told him to come and we would be waiting at the airport. Thus we did get a three day break from fighting freezing ice every day.

Now Bruce Skubic wanted to get involved by taking the four of us back to Burlington in his Cessna 206 and then continue on to Florida with us. This put us back in Burlington mid-morning Saturday. When we left there a couple of days earlier I had asked the marina operator about when they normally froze up to which he replied "about Christmas time and occasionally early January". But we now found the entire marina and the river itself frozen. Bruce had rented a car that he drove downstream until he found a tug operator that agreed to run up and down the river to open a channel, but he would not enter the private marina. I went to the marina office to rent a boat and outboard motor. I paid for that in cash without the operator asking what we were going to do about the ice. We got the boat out on the ice and four of us jumping up and down until we opened a channel, then started the engine and kept jumping until we had a taxi way to the river itself to meet with the channel that the tug had opened. By then we had both aircraft warmed up. Dick Mahl was flying the Beaver and I followed him out in the Otter. Once we got upstream a bit we could see the channel was starting to freeze-up again, so we decided to get out of there. There was a large and high bridge between Iowa and Illinois downstream ahead of us, so I asked Dick on the radio if he was going over it or under it. He very quietly said "under" and away he went. I waited a minute, then followed him. I went over the top of the bridge by 50 feet or so which gave me a great view of cars stopped and the toll collector and motorists standing there. About three hours later we were in the center of St. Louis, Missouri planning on a landing on the Mississippi River. I had made prior arrangements for fuel with a helicopter operator working from a barge anchored right uptown on the Mississippi River. He told me that they were on the western (Iowa) shore just north of the Arch. We would see one bridge crossing the river, then two bridges two miles later and they were parked just north of the next bridge. We had talked to Bruce a little earlier as he landed at St. Louis Downtown Airport (which is actually in Illinois). He said he would get a car and meet us at the barge. We found the spot, landed and heeled back on a wood covered levee to tie down just as Bruce drove up. I had talked to the operator on the barge to set up a refuel time for the next morning. We could see a Holiday Inn one block away so we settled in for the night.

We were in for a big shock when we arrived at our planes the following morning to find them 20 feet from the water — high and dry. On top of that, they were sitting in a rock pile with quite a few large holes punched in the float bottoms. I tracked down the Harbor Master to tell him of our problem and he said "get those airplanes out of here". I finally got him to walk over to take a look. He said that they had closed up several of the locks upstream to stop ice movement down the river to prevent damage. Once he looked at what happened he agreed that we were stuck there for a few days to repair the damages. I had him call a wrecker when he returned to his office. Then we lifted each float one at a time so that we could remove the rocks that were stuck underneath. The next step was to wet down the wooden levee so we could tow each airplane a little higher just in case the water was to rise again. Bruce and I went across the river to the airport to hire a mechanic with his riveting gear. The temperatures were running 25 to 30 degrees at night and about 40 degrees during the day with a wind, so we picked up a couple tarps with 2"x4"s to make some shelter. Luckily we got that done because a day later it started snowing which lasted for three days. Our hired mechanic would not even work during this, but let us use his tools. We had Jay Carlson with us who was a pretty good riveter. Every day one of the local TV stations would be there filming our progress which usually was shown during the opening of the 6:00 evening news.

The Beaver took three patches on each float and the Otter needed two large ones on the RH float.

Finally we were done, but now we were about 40 feet from the water. Bruce and I worked our way along the channel finding a barge operator that said he had never picked up an airplane before and he would do it for $150.00 next morning. This went off very well with a flight under the Interstate 70 bridge — all though I really wanted to fly through the famous arch. I knew we were to well known then in the neighborhood for that. It was miserable working where we had to for the past week, but I did get to spend some time with my sister Sally and her brood who lived in Webster Groves — part of St. Louis. I also got to meet and have a couple of drinks with a fellow I had heard about that spring. He was a veteran helicopter pilot from Vietnam days but was currently flying the helicopter off the barge we had been next to for a week. One day eight months earlier he had a charter flight to take a woman south to Cape Girardeau, Missouri for a property inspection. Before they got to their destination she pulled out a .44 caliber pistol and told him to fly east to Marion, Illinois with a landing in the yard of the Federal prison there to pick up her boyfriend and two other prisoners. Just before they were about to land the woman got distracted and the pilot let go of the controls to get his hand on the pistol. A wild struggle followed with the helicopter pitching and rolling. Five shots were fired with the fourth on striking and killing the woman. The pilot recovered control of the helicopter and landed in the prison yard leaving three prisoners standing on the roofs of one of the cell blocks. Believe it or not, he was then charged with murder, but this did go away later. Allen Barklage was his name and he died in a helicopter crash twenty years later.

After our welcome departure from St. Louis we headed south east to Guntersville, Alabama on the lake of the same name. Bruce landed at an airport about five miles away and found someone to bring us some fuel for the two seaplanes. We did get refueled and both aircraft cleaned up after our two weeks of snow and ice. We got an early start the next morning to make a two hour flight to Panama City, Florida where we could taxi up to a ramp to have a fuel truck top us off. After that we flew down the west coast of Florida until just north of Tampa where we turned towards Winter Haven. As we passed over Lake Parker at Lakeland I noticed a motel on the south shore with a long narrow dock and an interstate highway passing by. We talked to Bruce on the radio, swung into the wind, landed and tied up to the dock. We got three rooms and then walked down the road two blocks to a tire shop to get some used tires to use as fenders on the dock. A woman driving by stopped when she saw us on the dock. She wanted to know if we did sightseeing rides, then went on to say that they were having a Strawberry Festival this coming Saturday at Leesburg that should draw about 4,000 people and they would be happy to have a unique activity. Leesburg was 50 miles north of us so we had a discussion about rates, etc. and after which I said I would fly up there the next day to look at the site.

I had a new experience in life the next morning when I walked out on the dock and bent over to untie a rope on the Otter. Right in from of me about 6 inches away was a water moccasin sticking his head and white mouth moving. I yelled and jumped back to see a snake coming out of each tire. I assume the black tire got somewhat warmer water inside over night which attracted the snakes. We learned when we come out on the dock in the morning to jump up and down on the dock a few times and each tire would discharge a reptile.

As soon as I returned to Lake Parker I went to the motel office to make an offer to the owner — if he would make us an attractive offer for two rooms we would winter there and pay him a 10% commission on all on site sales. He had already seen a lot of traffic pull over and stop to look at the planes. He had even picked up rental on two rooms through that. I also agreed to build a small platform with two benches so that people could sit there watching the seaplanes come and go. It only took a few minutes to make a deal.

Bruce had left for a few days visiting a friend in Sarasota on Longboat

Key. I talked to him almost every day and told him now that we were set up for the winter here on Lake Parker but that we could fly him back to Ely Monday after the Strawberry Festival — which turned out to be a busy day. The woman that I had worked this deal out with said that practically every weekend there would be some large function on the beach at Leesburg, so I told her that we would hold Saturdays for that. The next step was to find a few restaurants that were located either on a beach or with a dock in front to schedule them for a whole afternoon of rides that they could promote and advertise. We would give them a 10% commission on each ride. The first one to sign up was a nice restaurant on the east end of the Campbell Courtney Causway. They got Wednesdays from noon to dark. They also agreed to sell the tickets over their counter and just write us a check for 90% of the income. This made it easier for my crew doing just flying instead of running back and forth to make change.

Monday morning saw us in Bruce Skubic's Cessna 206 headed back to Ely, Minnesota. We left one man there to watch the aircraft and move them if the weather got bad enough. I had it worked out that two of our regular pilots and two of our bush pilot students would pack up to drive one of our vans down there to work by the weekend. Then we would trade them out every two or three weeks so that everyone would get some Florida time during the winter.

On the flight home to Minnesota Bruce mentioned that he liked Sarasota and might buy a condo to winter there — there is no road construction during the winter in Minnesota! Sure enough a week later he called saying that he purchased the condo which made a faster airplane necessary. I did sell him a turbo Cessna 210 and took the Cessna 206 N6994M back in trade. I floor planned this as a trade-in and we now had a airplane for our Florida transfers for the winter.

Another problem arose though. After a few trips hauling his family to and from Florida, he decided he needed and instrument rating. I agreed and we started training in the Cessna 210. He did very well on the flying, but could not pass the written exam. He had flunked it three times when he and I flew to Minneapolis, checked into a hotel on the airport to spend two long days studying for the written.

Monday morning he went to the FAA across the field and took the fourth written. It was another three weeks before we heard back on the exam which was another failure. I told him to get his pilot's license to me as I was going to Atlanta for a day that week and I would take the exam under his name. When I did walk into the FAA testing site, there was a FAA person that I knew very well sitting there — so I passed. A week later I had to take a customer's Cessna 310 down to NW Chicago for some auto pilot work. This was an all day deal and there was a FAA testing site, so I signed and wrote that test as Bruce Skubic — and he passed. I was surprised when I came down the stairs from the testing area to run into Jim Peterson, who used to be the head of the FAA office in Minneapolis and I knew him very well — but no questions asked. I never felt bad about what I did because Bruce was a great pilot. Over the years I sold him three Cessna 206's on floats, one 210, one 172 on floats for the kids, a Cessna 402 as well as a Cessna 310. He flew all over the U.S. and during the winter months kept a runway plowed out on the ice at his home so he could come home late or leave early. His wife Gladys said she could never thank me enough for getting him into flying again. She said he had gotten to be a very overweight, surly guy with a drinking problem. Now he had turned everything around so that he could stay in aviation.

CHAPTER 31

NORTH TO ALASKA

Earlier I had talked about the sale of Wilderness Wings Airways in Ely, Minnesota. When I signed the contract of sale I had said that I would stick around to assist the first summer to aid in the transfer. Mid May saw the beginning of fishing season and a couple of weeks of bad weather. I did quite a bit of flying myself seeing as the owners and pilots were not familiar with the area. It did not take too long for me to figure out that these people did not like flying in rain or low ceilings. I tried to explain to them that we were practically over water everywhere we went, so we always had a place to land if it became necessary. Also that our customers plan these trips for a long time and do not appreciate just sitting on the dock for a few days — especially while other seaplane operators are coming and going — stopping only to clear U.S. Customs. Of course the U.S. Forest Service was a mile down the lake with their aircraft flying all day. Finally the new owners said I did not have to stay and they were turning me loose to leave.

I had one DHC-3 single Otter, N90627, that had just been rebuilt, so I started going to the coast of Lake Superior to do sight seeing rides all day, but well clear of their area. This got old pretty fast, so I started calling everybody I knew in Alaska trying to find someone who would lease an Otter and pilot for the summer. It was nearing the end of June and everyone was pretty well staffed for the season. I did call for Mudhole Smith (He was one of the founders of Alaska Airlines) at Cordova, Alaska, but the gal on the phone said that her father, Jim Foode, had bought out Mudhole's Chitina Air Service two months earlier. He had two Cessna 185's of which one was on floats and a Cessna 206 on floats plus one on wheels, but he was out flying. I left my name and phone number and was very surprised when she called me the next day saying her father wanted to talk to me.

We talked for a few minutes. I told him I was a 15,000 hour pilot with most of it in seaplanes, operated my business for 20 years, but the government put me out of business with the wilderness extension. I also told him that I was one of three Cessna seaplane only dealers and had delivered airplanes all over Alaska. He then told me he had just won a contract to deliver 400 55gallon drums of fuel to a Korean test coal mine 70 miles away. He thought it would be hard to move with two barrels at a time, but he did not want to have his competitor get the contract with his two Beavers. I brought up the fact that I had hauled many drums of fuel over the years and he wanted to know how soon I could be there. We negotiated for a few minutes, but when I asked him what would be his commission he replied "Nothing". I told him that I would not come on that basis. I felt he would promote some more business for the Otter if he made a clear 10% off each flight I got. After all I would be operating on his certificate. We agreed to that, so I told him that I needed two days to arrange things there in Ely, but I would be in Cordova in five days. The fifth day at 4:00 p.m. July 4th I pulled up to the last dock on the west end of Eyak Lake in Cordova — just as his girlfriend Terry took a roasted turkey out of the oven.

After a sumptuous meal Jim Foode drove me to a friend's house where he had arranged a room for me to rent with kitchen privileges. I was scheduled for Part 135 check ride the next morning with Terry who was also his chief pilot.

The next morning we took off on a 1,800 foot gravel strip that was just a road pushed out another 25 feet into the lake. We had three persons headed 40 miles away to the native village of Tatitlek with a 2,000 foot gravel runway at 25 feet above sea level and less than 100 people living there. We were flying a Cessna 206 on wheels, so we traded seats after dropping the passengers so that I could fly the trip back. We climbed up a little to do some slow flight, stalls and steep turns and ended up with a short field landing back at Eyak Lake landing strip. This strip was interesting — there was no fence or separation of the terrain between the runway and the road. Occasionally you could be rolling with your wing tips just 20 feet or so from a moving vehicle. The lake was 12 feet above sea level while being about five feet below the runway.

The next morning I loaded up six barrels of fuel and started for Kushtaka Lake. There I landed and taxied up a narrow river for almost 200 yards. I had to pass through a small rapids and then several of the crew there would grab my ropes while pulling me sideways along the shoreline. Then we would place a reinforced 2" x 12" x 20' plank on the top rung of the ladder and slide the barrels down to shore.

They we would walk the airplane down the river to the lake with ropes. It was too narrow and too much current to manually turn the Otter around. This trip was about four hours all told, but after a few trips I got it down to a little over three hours per trip with a hour and a half of that flight time. The local native corporation, Chugach Corporation, had invested a lot of money into a Korean test coal mine.

There was a short lived history of coal mining in that area many years before — even with a short railroad spur running to the coastline where it could be loaded on ships. When Alaska first became a state thirteen Native Corporations were formed with healthy financing and huge amounts of property so that they could support their indigenous peoples. Most of these corporations lost money, but retained their properties. Chugach Corp probably would have done better investing in the fishing industry. That was the primary industry of the region.

At the time I arrived in Cordova the seining season was underway

— mainly for pink salmon. There would be a couple of hundred boats scattered around Prince William Sound with a three to five man crew on each. The season closed at 9:00 p.m. Friday night and re-opened Monday at 6:00 a.m. At this time of year it would be daylight at 3:00 a.m. to 4:00 a.m. and last until 11:00 p.m. or so. These fisherman only had five months to make a living, so they did not sleep much during the summer. On Wednesday we would start getting radio messages booking seats to town for the weekend. Thus these guys could get some sleep, see the wives and kids, buy the next weeks groceries and restock the alcohol.

Friday nights pickups would start at 6:00 p.m. with the last one coming in just after dark and start the next morning about 5:00 a.m. I had ten passenger seats in the Otter plus mine. I would place a plastic fish box in the center aisle filled with ice and a case of free beer. It did not take long before the Otter was the first choice and booked early.

As August got close to the end, everyone got ready for silver salmon and gill netting. A very serious fishermen, Jerry Thorne came in and talked to Jim Foode about hiring the Otter to fly fish to town.

Theirs was a fishing family — all the sons and father would have four gill netters and a seine boat out on the Copper River flats and tender their own fish. All the wives and daughters would pick up the fish at our dock, take them home, clean them, ice and pack them and deliver about 10,000 pounds to Alaska Airlines for the late afternoon flight # 66 to Seattle. If they did have a few thousand extra pounds Alaska would have a later flight between Anchorage/Seattle make a quick stop in Cordova and pick it up. This family had set up their own market in Seattle and had put it all together. We negotiated the haul from the flats planning on a nine or ten minute run each way making it possible to fly about 3,000 pounds of fresh fish on each trip at 17 cents per pound. This worked out to over $500.00 for each 20 minutes of flight — and a lot of muscle loading and unloading. They would simply radio their women at home and then they would call me with the pickup time. Several times I made ten trips a day for them plus some other flying for other people. We finished this in early October, but they definitely wanted to do it again in May with the Red salmon.

I had finished off the 400 barrel fuel haul to the coal mine, but I did pick up quite a few fuel runs down the coast to Barney's Hole between Kayak and Winghan Island. This was usually to a 120 foot whale back tender which of course was anchored so that it was pointed into the wind and current all of he time. I would use flaps full, one magneto, water rudders down taxiing sideways until my left wing goes right over the deck just in front of the deckhouse where the deck hands can reach my wing rope to pull me in and tie off. Then the cargo door opens so we can place a plank from the ship deck to the aircraft cabin and roll the barrels out. I really wish I had a dollar for every 55 gallon barrel of fuel I have hauled in my life.

CHAPTER 32

24 HOUR TAXI

In the middle 1980's after my oldest daughter Katie and her husband Tom had come into the business we were expanding and we started talking about adding one more aircraft. We had several floating cabins on Prince William Sound, a small fishing lodge on the Sound plus two outpost cabins, another small lodge on Tebay Lake 85 miles out of Cordova, another outpost cabin on Hanigita Lake just past the Tebay camp, a large tent camp on the Tsiu River 100 miles east of town on the coast plus our seven day tour of the State of Alaska almost every week. Lo and behold — the next day Trade A - Plane showed up and a Twin Beech on floats was listed for sale by Dick Folsom of Greenville, Maine. I had known Dick for a few years and called him the next morning. I had been trying to sell him a Twin Beech D-18S a couple of years earlier for $42,500, but he bought one from Orville Weiben in Fort William, Ontario for $32,000.

Dick had been to my base in Minnesota a couple of times and was excited about carrying two canoes and passengers inside the Beech. He was very disappointed when he got the aircraft back to Maine and could not fit a canoe inside. He had been carrying two canoes, four passengers and gear with his Beaver.

I told him that if he ever had a bad accident with the second canoe tied on the Beaver he might get cleaned out in a lawsuit. He did not realize that we had to make quite a few modifications on the aircraft after the cargo door was installed. We removed the baggage compartment entirely, put a folding plywood ramp to the back end of the cabin, then widened the entry access to the cockpit and lowered part of the instrument panel so that a 17 foot canoe could slide up to a ½ inch clearance of the windshield. Then we could slide the canoe back in the cabin, put the second canoe in and then slide that one back upside down to sit on top of the first one. He did not get the use of the Beech that he planned on and sold it a few months earlier to a man from England who was going to take it to Bermuda. Dick had painted the aircraft in white and navy blue for the fellow. It had a 200 hour RH engine and a 1,400 LH engine (1,600 TBO) and would be sold with a fresh annual inspection for $28,000.00. I told him that we would mail him a 10% ($2,800.00) deposit that same day and make a similar payment each month until I picked it up in the spring. It was still in U.S. registry (N1042H) so that was not a problem. As it got closer to May and ice out I kept in touch with Dick who thought it was going to be a late spring. We used to have that same problem in Minnesota. Some years the ice might go out the last few days of April, but usually just before mid May and occasionally we prayed that it would be gone before Memorial Day weekend. Finally he said that it should be in the next few days, so I grabbed a flight to Seattle with an overnight there. Seattle, Minneapolis, New York in the morning and a commuter flight to Bangor, Maine. I had advised Dick of my arrival time in Bangor and he said that one of his office girls with a van would pick me up to give me a ride to Greenville. The day was pretty well done when we arrived at his base, so Dick and I went out for a couple of drinks, dinner and a lot of storytelling. He also said that the temperatures were supposed to drop for the next three days and then warm up, so it would probably be another five days at least before the ice goes out. We were both pretty anxious to see that. He had people that wanted to get flown out to different lakes — some were fishermen, some were loggers and some were lodge operators — but everyone wanted to make some money and needed the ice to go out. We spent a couple of days going around the area meeting people and getting a little more familiar with the area. I had been in Greenville before, but was always trying to keep a schedule.

No rush this time. Dick did show me a Douglas DC-3 he had on wheels at the airport. He had started a Part 121 Commuter operation, but with the amount of paperwork involved he gave up fairly quickly because it interfered with his established seaplane business. Time was passing by slowly, but finally a nice warm day with a fair wind came up and started moving the ice. We all agreed that it should all be gone by morning — and it was.

The next morning we got the Beech in the water, removed the beaching gear and Dick's son, Max took it for a check flight. When Max taxied back into the dock, Dick Folsom said "I am not selling that airplane, It sounds so good that I will just keep it to listen to". I thought he was kidding, but I quickly realized that he was serious. He avoided me the rest of the day, but we did go out for dinner late that evening — and many drinks! I kept telling him that we had just about paid for the aircraft the past few months, that I had come all the way down from Alaska and we were counting on having the use of the plane for the summer. I finally told him that I knew where the only set of DC-3 floats were — brand new, amphibians for $10,000.00 in Texas. There were no struts, but I had gotten a quote of $100,000.00 from Jay Frey of Edo Floats to manufacture a set of the ten struts required. Two years before I had thought about buying the floats in South America for $5,000.00 and make a water bomber out of a DC-3 with an 800 gallon fiber glass tank attached to the belly between the floats. Two tubes hanging down would allow filling the tank while step taxiing on the run with a manual operated camshaft to open the doors for a water drop. I had talked to the USFS about using the aircraft if it was available, but could not get a letter of intent, so I forgot about it. Meanwhile the owner shipped the floats from South America to Love Field in Dallas Texas with a price increase to $10,000.00. I told Dick that if he would honor our deal I would tell him how to get hold of the owner. He did show a interest in that and he would talk to a couple of his friends to see if they would invest in the project he said he would let me know by noon. A little before noon he said " Okay" and we started the paperwork on the sale. He asked me to drop off one of his office girls at her parents home on a lake in Vermont and I said that I want the opportunity to fly the DC3 once after it got on floats. Shortly after 2:00p.m. I was on my way, made the stop in Vermont and found out that the battery was almost dead. I got started again and flew to Jamestown, New York with the master switch off. I landed at a marina there, asked about docking for the night and asked if they had a 24 volt battery charger. The parking was good, but the fellow tending the shop said he would take me to the airport with my battery and then drop me at a hotel. The battery was on the RH side, so I climbed out on the RH wing to take the battery out. I was surprised to find two smaller batteries there — both 12 volt hooked up in series to make 24 volts. They had several 12 volt battery chargers and got a couple plugged in. Then the operator drove me to a motel saying he would pick me up at 0800 on his way in. I really like the Pratt & Whitney R985 (450h.p.) engine. It is a low compression engine which makes it easy to hand prop and it will run on almost any kind of gasoline - 80/87 — 100LL — 100/130 and almost any marine gasoline except for the pre-mixed with oil. I got the batteries hooked up again, bought a couple hundred gallons of fuel and got started on the next leg west bound. I flew across Lake Erie, Lower Michigan, Lake Michigan and a fuel stop at Shawano, Wisconsin for fuel. From there it was an hour to my mother's log cabin on Middle Eau Claire Lake just north of Hayward, Wisconsin. Patrick, my oldest, son had been there for a few days waiting for me and a ride to Alaska. We spent a very nice night and left in the morning to clear Canadian Customs at Sandpoint Lake — just north of Crane Lake, Minnesota. Then we flew to Pine Falls, Manitoba for fuel followed by a few hours to Lac La Ronge, Saskatchewan for more fuel and our overnight stop. The next morning saw a four and ½ hour flight to Charley Lake just west of Fort St. John. I noticed a fair amount of oil dripping under the LH engine. I called my daughter Katie in Cordova, Alaska and told her where we were. She said to hurry up, that the dock at the base was sinking with all of the freight piled up for different camps. I told her that we would be out of there in a few minutes and would be in Ketchikan, Alaska that night. An early departure would put us in Cordova just about noon so have a sandwich ready at the dock for me so that I could start hauling freight. A few minutes later we were in the air headed directly to Williston Lake. Less that a hour later, I was napping in the LH seat while Patrick was doing the honors from the RH side. A pretty loud "Bang" and the Beechcraft started shaking pretty bad. Both of our hands met at the fuel selectors.

I told him that "I've got it" and decided that we were going to land. We had about 500 feet and a light a tailwind, so I reduced power on the right side, carb heat, flaps and made a pretty smooth landing without making a steep 180 degree turn at low altitude. Once we fell off the step and shut down, I went out the roof hatch on the LH wing, looked in the cowling and saw nine cylinders hanging by a bolt or two which indicated a crankshaft failure. We sat there for a few minutes — we were on a lake 150 miles long with a VHF radio in the aircraft, but it was a cheapie that did not work plus we were not on a flight plan.

The flight plan would have been all but useless anyway seeing as we were on a 600 mile leg of wilderness with no roads and probably not a dozen cabins scattered along the route. The Canadian rules make a flight plan required, but seeing that we usually do go to places without communications made it almost impossible to filter down where you are. On this flight our plan was to file with Prince Rupert, B.C. to Ketchikan, AK with a call out for U.S. Customs. I told Patrick that I had flown this route a couple of years earlier when I saw two cabins at the junction of the lake that had a radiophone tower there. I put that into to a back corner of my mind just in case I should ever have the need — which was now. It did not take much time to start taxing on the live engine towards the antenna.

It was 4:30 when I fired up the RH engine, water rudders down and started downwind. Some times it is nice to have to travel downwind, but not when you are taxing a multi-engine plane on water with one engine. The airplane naturally wants to weathercock into the wind like a windsock and of course the live engine is trying to turn the airplane. About 8:00 p.m. the wind picked up to 20 knots or so and we had a hard time to keep pointed downwind. Several times we had to shut down the live engine, retract the water rudders, extend the flaps and sail backwards. If the wind laid down enough we would start the RH engine, put down water rudders and raise the flaps while steering again. We each had a sleeping bag so all night we would trade off every other hour — one sleeping in the aisle and one working up front. Midmorning Patrick caught an eleven pound Dolly Varden while trolling from the LH float. So we sailed into a small cove, tied off, got a fire going and had roasted fish for lunch. All the years flying in the bush I made it a point to have a sleeping bag, small tarp, matches and an axe — plus a 30 inch bow saw on the larger aircraft — and a small packet of fishing tackle. Winter would probably see snowshoes and a bit more fire starter than just matches. Of course we could always get a cup or two of av gas to help with the fire. We kept taxing or sailing at times all day and arrived at two cabins next to a radio phone tower just after 5:00 p.m. A man and his wife and teenaged daughter lived there. The first thing I did was to call my daughter Katie in Cordova to explain why we were not there. I was worried that she might have initiated a search, but after growing up in a bush flying environment she held off. I did tell her to start looking for a replacement engine the next day with no exchange. Patrick and I got moved into the second cabin which was used as a rental for fishermen. Daughter Katie called late in the afternoon the next day to say it was hard to buy an engine without an exchange, but she had found one in Oklahoma. I told her to wire transfer the engine funds and get my youngest son Scott to go pick up the engine. He had just gotten out of school and was driving my Ford pickup to Alaska and then going out commercial fishing for the summer. Katie called the next day saying that Scott was on his way and was going back to Ely to pick up his gear before delivering the engine to us. I started thinking about that and him getting through Canadian Customs. The next morning I flagged down a south bound barge, got to the end of Lake Williston, hitch hiked a few miles to the highway and caught a bus to Prince George, B.C. The next morning I caught a flight to Winnipeg, Manitoba, then a bus to Ft. Francis, Ontario arriving at midnight. I checked into a motel and slept until 0600, had breakfast and walked across the bridge to International Falls, Minnesota. I knew that Scott would be crossing here sometime that day so I found a spot to sit right next to the approach to the international bridge. It was late afternoon when I spotted my pickup coming up to the bridge and I waved Scott down. He was very surprised to see me, but I jumped in and we started across the bridge. We stopped at the Canadian Customs office on the north side and a young girl who was summer help came up to the truck. We handed over our ID's and then she lifted the tarp in back covering a nice overhauled engine worth $40,000. She then said that we could not bring that into Canada without a documentation from a U.S. Customs Broker. This being late on Friday of Memorial Day weekend I could not even talk to a broker until Tuesday and the paperwork would cost $300.00 to $400.00 I then asked her who was her supervisor that night and she replied "Richard Dick". A few years back I had flown his wife out of Basswood Lake Canadian Customs station in serious pain in the middle of the night to the Ely hospital. He came out of the office and said "Pat Magie, what are you doing here?". I explained that I had bought an aircraft out east and was on my way back to Alaska, but blew an engine in Northern British Columbia. I showed him the blue entry slip I got at Sandpoint Lake upon entering Canada with the plane and it was for 5 days and would expire that night. Within minutes we had an INTRANSIT slip for the engine seeing as we would install the engine to fly it on to Alaska and a fresh 10 day entry slip for the aircraft. I thanked him saying to say "hello" to his wife and we were on our way to Kenora where we spent the rest of the night. Three days later we were in Fort St. John where I connected with a Canadian aircraft mechanic who had a Cessna 180 on floats. We made a date for him to come over in three days and we would have the bad engine ready to come off the aircraft. I also got permission from a logging company to drive in on their private logging road. It took us another day to negotiate the logging road, but when our fly - in mechanic showed up we had the cowling off, all of the engine components removed and a log tripod set in place ready to lift the engine off. He showed up at 0900 and when he arrived we hooked up his chain hoist, then removed the bad engine replacing it with the fresh one. The next day at 3:30 p.m. we test flew the airplane. Then we packed up everything including the bad engine which we ended up using it as an anchor for one of our floating cabins on Prince William Sound. Patrick and I got in the air the next morning and flew to Prince Rupert, B.C. for fuel and to check the oil consumption. Next was to Ketchikan, AK for U.S. Customs, then on to Juneau for a night's stay and a good look at the new engine. Then we were in Cordova by noon the next day, and home. When I started I was hoping to do it in three or four days, but it took just over three weeks.

Scott had to back track to Ft. St. John to pick up the Alcan Highway again with three days to Valdez, AK, then catch the ferry for a 6 hour long ride to Cordova. Project done! Meanwhile Dick Folsom back in Greenville, Maine was getting started on floating his DC-3

CHAPTER 33

MOVIE WORK

During the month of June, 1995 I came back to Cordova on Saturday afternoon after a week long tour of the State. My sister, Joan McMillan, was in Alaska helping us out for the summer as well as a couple of her sons. She told me that a fellow had called about using the Twin Beech for a movie. She gave me a phone number to call, but I was flying until dark that night and back in the air at 0700 with another week long tour departing Sunday afternoon, so the call never got made. The next weekend I did get a phone call from Kevin LaRosa who was a helicopter pilot and owned a helicopter company out of Van Nuys, California. He also was a well known Aerial Coordinator in TV and movie work. We talked for a while about a project, arousing my interest and agreed to talk again when he had some numbers.

Kevin and I did talk twice the following weekend and I explained that my schedule would keep me pretty well tied up until the end of September. He said that would not be a problem as it normally takes a few months to put it all together. He did say that Paramount Studios would be the filming company as well as giving me a rough idea of the pay scale for the filming. I did tell him that I was very interested and to keep me posted if it was going to happen. I did not hear from him for almost a month until he called asking if I had to spend some time in South East Asia would I still be willing. We did negotiate a price for shipping days for the Twin Beech

18 and he said this would probably all start in early October. I called him during August announcing that I had become engaged to a lady that I had been seeing for the past year and a half. I thought it would be very nice if she could accompany me on these travels. The answer came back "Make sure her passport is current". Towards the end of September Kevin called to tell me to take the Twin Beech down to Pitt Meadows, BC to have the aircraft stripped of its paint and a black lacquer trim added. I went back to Pitt Meadows a week later, picked up the Beech, flew to Seattle, (Customs) then to Lakeport, CA where I picked up my fiancée Debbie. Our next stop was Long Beach Harbor in California. We landed just outside of the bridge where we found two boats in the water flashing lights at us. After a short discussion about our destination we step taxied almost three miles to the dock that they had built for us. It was just getting dark, but we saw a skyline of plywood covered wooden frames that made the buildings into a 1930's New York Harbor. Our boat crew showed up, dropped us at our hotel with orders to be there at 5:00 p.m. the next evening to start filming. This is when I started to recognize the similarity of the military and the movie business — hurry up and wait!

Meanwhile after Debbie found out there was a year long waiting list for a wedding on the Queen Mary she did find a wedding site to make us a legal couple on 10-10-1995! We spent a few days there at Long Beach before our scenic drive back to Lake Port, CA. It was all set up for the Twin Beech to be shipped to Bangkok, Thailand for off loading, but two weeks later Kevin LaRosa called to ask if I could fly the aircraft from Singapore to Thailand. The monsoon season was pretty strong in Bangkok and the harbor was too flooded to off load. I told him to call back in 15 minutes while I checked it out which he did. I told him it was a four hour flight and we had six hours of fuel - - with another hour's fuel in cans in the cabin so we would make it easily. Two days later Debbie and I flew from San Francisco to Tokyo, changed aircraft for another six hours landing in Singapore just before midnight. Two mechanics showed up the next day and spent several days re-assembling the plane and getting it back in the water. We spent a week in meetings with the Singapore government but they would not give us permission to fly out of their harbor. So I told them I would taxi three miles to Malaysia and fly from there. By the time I got back to the hotel they had sent me a five page fax saying that I had to have a marine captain's license to taxi out of their harbor, so the decision was made to barge the airplane to Phuket, Thailand for $15,000.00 instead of flying. This was an additional 6 day trip so once the barge was out of sight Debbie and I jumped a flight to Phuket via Bangkok. At Phuket we were picked up by a van from the film company with a young Thai driver for the two hour ride to Krabi. This was undoubtedly one of the most frightening happenings of my life. The driver was probably 20 years of age and I could not understand how he lived that long. I have flown in a lot of bad weather and tough terrain and never been scared, but he was in the left lane passing another vehicle when topping hills or passing on corners, some times driving off road to pass. Unbelievably we made it, but had a serious discussion with the people running the production saying we would never do that again. But five days later the aircraft was to arrive in the harbor at Phuket and I had to be there to fly it back to Krabi. One person of the marine office had to go to Phuket that day also with his van and driver, but he convinced me that he would be riding the front RH seat and would not allow any foolish moves. They did get me there so I settled in awaiting the barge.

There was a south wind blowing right into the dock with a seven foot sea when the barge arrived and I told the harbor master that we could not off load the aircraft with that kind of wind and water. The Beech was on it's beaching gear which required it to be in the water to remove the gear. I did call the office in Krabi who told me there was a boat leaving Phuket for Krabi in another hour with the harbor master of New Zealand. I made connections with him and we started east bound in a fairly heavy rain. It was a 25 or 26 foot twin engine vessel with two young Thai fellows up front. It really was too rough riding to sit, so the two of us were standing up and hanging on. I could not help noticing that our wake was always in a curved line behind us. After a hour and a half the two up front admitted they were lost just as a large freighter showed up out of the mist. They flagged down the vessel with a lot of shouting going on until someone pointed out the directions to Krabi - which we found a half hour later. Being very wet and sore made a drink like a piece of Heaven that night!

The next day the weather improved, so I hopped a ride with one of the vans, got the plane off loaded and flew it back to Krabi landing on the river. Paramount had taken over an entire resort just outside of Krabi, so it did not take to long to get to know everyone. We were on the second floor overlooking a large swimming pool with the jungle past that. Catherine Zeta Jones was in the room on our left side with stunt pilot Corky Fornoff on our right side. Corky was flying a pair of Grumman Ag-Cats on floats that were leased from an Australian company. He would often come back to his room late in the day and climb over the railing to our room to have a cocktail while telling flying stories. Catherine was playing the part of a villainous seaplane pilot flying one of the Ag-Cats. Twice I had to wear a wig and dress like her while she was supposedly flying the Twin Beech (Drax's Aircraft). I do not think there are many men who have been a body double for Catherine Zeta Jones! It was hot and humid in Thailand — in the early fall and she was costumed wearing a heavy wool suit. Twice after wearing that all day, she would come back to her room, strip off the suit and come out on the balcony to breath some fresh air sans clothing. Both times it happened when we were playing gin rummy with Catherine behind Debbie's back, but being on an extended honeymoon I did not think it proper to go around pointing out a naked woman. I did tell her about it later, when she said she now understood why I started losing at the gin rummy game occasionally.

We spent seven weeks in Thailand and had a lot of fun. Screen Actor Billy Zane wore the purple suit of the "The Phantom" while Kristy Swanson played the role of "Diana Palmer" — the heroine. Treat Williams became the bad guy "Xander Drax" who had a desire to take over the world with his own airforce of the Grumman Ag-Cats. Treat Williams said several times the he hoped the movie would sell well so he could sell his Cessna 310 and buy a Cessna Citation jet. Simon Wincer was the director and we got to know him pretty well. We did quite a bit of filming northwest of Krabi which was almost a three hour boat ride each way, but it was a beautiful spot. Several times when we were all leaving about the same time I would ask Simon if he would like to ride back with me making it a 20 minute ride — and he was very receptive. He would invite Debbie and I up to his suite for cocktails and to watch what they called the "dailies" of the film they shot that day. Then it would all get edited as to how it would be in the film. Then of course Kevin LaRosa was the aerial coordinator who handled all of the aerial maneuvering while flying the camera equipment helicopter. And he was good at it - - he would tell me to fly directly at him as he was hovering. Automatically I would climb a little as we closed in and he would be on the radio yelling "NO, NO". He did finally break me into to keep flying right at him, then he would adjust the collective and drop right below me.

One day we were filming a little south of Krabi in the Phi Phi Islands which was a very pretty spot. It was only a few minutes flying time for me so when I got there the filming barge and a gaggle of boats were anchored just off of the entrance to Phi Phi Don Island. I got a call on the radio to land right there.

I swung around into the wind, landed and pulled up to the filming barrage where they fitted a small inflatable Zodiac boat between the floats to tow me inside the entrance. The bay was about a quarter of a mile across with sheer limestone cliffs rising out of the water 1,200 to 1,500 feet. I taxied around the bay for a few minutes while they were filming, 1 then I came alongside the barge and I suggested that they position themselves where they could get a good shot of me landing through the entrance.

Kevin said that he did not consider that safe because of a light downwind and the high cliffs in the bay prevented a go-around if needed. I countered saying that we had to do that quite often in Alaska because of large waves on the open water, you are forced to land downwind and touch down in the smoother water. Everyone finally agreed, moved the barge around followed by my landing through the entrance. It was decided that it looked very good and even though it was not in the script it avoided the cut and was in the final filming — I even got a $1,000.00 stunt bonus. Several days after that I had to practice for a scripted stunt by flying a passenger laying on the left float. We took the cabin door off, had the stunt man lay on the float while the stunt director, Billy Burton, sat in the seat right next to the door to watch the stuntman. Debbie sat in the RH front seat watching for signals from the director as to continuing or stopping. We taxied out into the river, applied power and got on the step. Then we ran for almost a mile until the director gave the thumbs up to complete the take-off. When we came off the water I kept it low and slow, circled and landed on the river again. We tied up and talked to the stunt man about what he thought of it. He said "No problem" so we took off again, and climbing to 2,000 feet while flying around for several minutes and then decided it worked for the script scene. We did hit a light rain shower coming back in and he said the rain hitting his face was tough to take. We held off for a couple of days to avoid rain showers, this time to 4,000 feet with the camera helicopter close alongside. The script called for the stuntman to fall off of the top of the float and hang on by one hand — this with no parachute or safety harness — just a piece of 1/8 inch aircraft cable from his belt attached to a float strut. I collected another $1,000.00 stunt bonus, but I am sure his pay was many times more than that. The stunt director's daughter, Heather Burton, was the stunt woman who had to jump from a flying Grumman Ag-Cat to the back of a running horse that is being chased by a white wolf. They had to do many retakes of that scene because that horse would shy away from the plane while she was standing on the float waiting to jump Finally it worked and she landed on the horse while on film. It was rumored that she could purchase a new BMW convertible with the sum of her stunt bonus. Another young gal by the name of Svetla Krastis was also a stunt woman and seeing what some of these people did made it seem rather tame for me to be called a seaplane stunt pilot. Debbie and I went to Hollywood for the premier of "The Phantom" and Catherine Zeta Jones brought up the fact that my name was listed in the credits twice as seaplane pilot and seaplane stunt pilot while she was only named once. All I could say is "your name is a lot larger". It was a lot of fun and if you think of my 10 hours of actual flying for the movie I made $10,000.00 per hour plus a neat trip — one week in Long Beach, two weeks in Singapore and seven weeks in Thailand.

Our invitation to the screening at Paramount Studios

For Thanksgiving the company had several turkeys flown down from Bangkok and contracted to a local restaurant called "Francos" to prepare a holiday meal for the cast and crew. The eatery was owned by Franco who was Italian and his Thai wife. Because Thanksgiving is not observed there, they needed a lot of advice and help as to dressing and cranberry sauce. The restaurant was not very large so quite a few tables and chairs ended out on to the sidewalk. Another neat memory! Almost a year later on a busy Sunday I was on our dock in Cordova, AK loading the Twin Beech with a group of seven fishermen and their gear for our mountain camp when one of the fellows mentioned that he had seen the airplane somewhere before. We had left the "Phantom" paint scheme on it when we got it back to America. After discussing it a bit it turned out that "The Phantom" was the inflight movie on one of the legs that day. My next movie was almost two years later when Kevin LaRosa called about doing the movie "Godzilla" for Sony in Hawaii. Debbie and I had moved to Hawaii late in 1996 to concentrate on getting a permit to operate a seaplane tour business. I then had seven years working on that permit and was told in June, 1997 that it was going to happen. I said to Kevin that we would do the movie and I went back to Seattle to dissemble the Twin Beech to ship it to Hawaii. The wings came off and stowed between the floats. On arrival to Honolulu it was taken to a hanger on the airport, reassembled and got ready, then got craned over the road to the waters of Keehi Lagoon where we had already started construction of a large dock and a floating office. The next day we were scheduled to fly to the other side of Oahu Island to start the filming, but when I taxied out and called the control tower for take-off clearance, I was told that Sealane 8 had been closed several years before and had never been reopened making it not possible to allow me to fly. This was almost the end of August and I had made a $10,000.00 plus check on July 1 which was finally acknowledged in mid August with the permit being issued — but I still cannot fly. I was not very happy when a Honolulu Police Officer came in our door. When he heard the story he went right over to the airport offices and asked how they can accept several months rent, issue a permit to operate while not allowing the flight. He came back very quickly and said that we can make one take-off and landing that day, but must have a meeting the next day before any other flights could be made. So we got the movie started that day and I was at the control tower very early the next morning. I did convince them that I was a 30,000 hour pilot and could very easily handle the easiest flying that I have ever done. Now we could fly and get the movie done.

Kevin was flying a camera equipped helicopter and it went well seeing we had worked together before.

We did most of the flying and filming along the east shore and Kualoa Valley. The valley was part of John Morgan's Ranch with many movies filmed there. Morgan's ranch also had two small fish ponds that I did quite a few landings — in mainly for advertising shoots such as Eddie Bauer, REI. They also owned Secret Beach between the ponds and the ocean and a peaked island called Chinaman's Hat that always had nude sunbathers on top. I do remember one scene where Kevin told me to go just off shore, do a 180 degree turn with a low pass down the mountain valley over a building they had erected for the film— he emphasized this with a reminder to stay low. When I pulled up to go between the mountains Kevin came back on the radio saying "We have to do that one again — not so low this time — they all ran". With a quick discussion we settled on 50 to 100 feet which then worked pretty good, finishing that scene. We flew for almost three weeks with the wax paint job that was starting to look bad by the end because of some rain and the spray from the floats on take-off and landings. 1998 saw our involvement with "Fantasy Island" series. This film used our DHC-2 Beaver which was painted in their paint scheme — a wax paint job for the first few weeks, then they brought in someone to do a normal paint which held up in the water better. We started filming a trial episode on the northwest side of the island of Kauai with Tommy Hauptman of Maui doing the filming with his helicopter. This episode aired in September, 1998 with one day per week of filming until the show ended in January, 1999. We did quite a few days working in John Morgan's fish ponds which were a tight fit in and out. Late in the series I became famous for my first spoken words on the screen when asked what time it was I replied "It's hard to say"!

We did shoot several episodes of the "Bachelor". I think it was two episodes of the U.S. version, one of the French version and one from New Zealand. We also did quite a few advertising shoots — mainly on John Morgan's "Secret Beach". This was a fairly protected spot that we could get in and out at almost anytime which was also equipped with a beautiful sand beach. We worked with Eddie Bauer's company of Seattle, a couple times for REI also of Seattle, Crazy shirts, a large soft drink company from Japan, Trump Waikiki Towers, and a dozen or so other companies. Most of these would be bringing some of there staff and goods with them that created more revenue for Hawaii with their hotel rooms, meals and rental vehicles. But finally the state of Hawaii with their infinite wisdom stopped us from landing there and that activity ceased. It was strange that boats or helicopters could land at the beach, but not a seaplane. We ran into some more of this Hawaiian reasoning later.

During 2003 we worked with Disney Productions filming scenes for their move "Even Stevens". This was staged on John Morgan's Sunset Beach. The following year of 2004 we hosted the cast and crew of "50 First Dates" including the actor Adam Sandler. The filming was done dock side with meals brought in by a caterer.

The filming was done dockside with meals brought in by a caterer.

On August 30th, 2018 we rented the seaplane base to a film company to make a episode of a new TV series called "Magnum P.I." This was going to be a weekly TV program and we had negotiated the rate. We did not book any tours on the filming days as we did not want people wandering around during the filming. The Magnum Helicopter would be landing and taking off our dock all day.

We ended up with them paying us $16,000.00 per day so they would have the run of the place and we were not allowed to use our two aircraft for tours, so part of that was rent on the aircraft. We had our floating chapel attached to our dock, but they said that they would work around the wedding schedule. We did four film shoots before our Airports Manager, Roy Sakata told the movie TV company that they had to give 14 days prior notice before a shoot. Of course, this cannot work with filming because you cannot predict the weather that far out and knowing if you can film. The state again took a lot of money out of our pockets, even though they supposedly wanted us to pay them a lot.

CHAPTER 34

BEARS

I suppose that because I spent a lot of my life in lonely remote places it has given me many stories of bears. It started when I was aged three years and my maternal grandfather shot a bear climbing through a screened window right over me. I was six years when I watched my mother chase a bear out of our kitchen with a broom. I was 14 years when I killed my first bear who was terrorizing our guests at a fishing resort where I worked. I suppose by now I have probably killed 20 bears, but only when they become a problem tearing up equipment or causing a loss of business by chasing off customers. Many people do not believe it when I say that I have been bitten by a bear many times. When I was in my mid twenties I helped raise two black bear cubs - - Blueberry and Cranberry. I was working my last sport how for the season selling canoe trips. It was Easter weekend in Minneapolis and I had permission to have a small cage in the back of my booth. One day I had an appointment to have my bear cubs at WCCO TV station at 3:00 p.m. for a filming. About 2:30 I gathered up the two cubs — they were about the size of a fair sized cat. The TV station was about six blocks from the Convention Center, so with a bear on each shoulder I walked out the front door. Waved down a taxicab, but when he pulled up and saw the bears, he quickly drove off. So with a bear on each shoulder I walked to the station and the pedestrians on the sidewalk gave me a lot of room. Then I ended up walking back to the Convention Center when the filming was finished with a bear on each shoulder.

A year later I was coming off of a ten day canoe trip and we were going to spend our last night at Wheelbarrow Falls on the Basswood River. A bear had taken over that campsite which was costing the outfitters a lot of money in torn up pack sacks and tents. Some parties stopped there on their first night out and they would lose all of their food supplies, then go back to the outfitter and want their money back! So I was purposefully staying there to solve this problem. I put the two A Frame tents for the two couples back away from the normal campsite. I had a almost new light weight 3 foot by 7 foot one man tent with real nylon mosquito netting installed instead of the old heavy cotton netting that had been used for years. I kept my tent down by the river and we had a nice fresh fish dinner. After I did the dishes and cleaned up, I told the guests to stay in their tents if they heard a lot of noise. We had part of a number three Duluth pack with what was left of our food supplies. I put this about five feet from the door of my tent, laid a poncho over the pack sack, put all of the aluminum plates, cups and silverware in a couple of aluminum cooking pots thinking I would be sure to wake up if a bear tried to move it. I had a 9 mm Luger pistol which I put right next to my sleeping bag. Later on I awakened to the loud clatter of cooking ware and sat up. There was a bear picking up the pack sack of food and I came up with the Luger. I was just about to shoot when I remembered my nylon mosquito netting so I reached down to move the zipper up and move the pistol outside. The bear evidently heard the zipper, dropped the pack sack and turned to look at me with both front paws still up in the air like he was giving up. I pulled the trigger as he let out a terrible scream and started to fall or jump into the tent. I was in my sleeping bag trying to slide further back in the tent. His head hit the ground about five inches from the nylon mosquito netting and I emptied the gun with it practically touching his skull — and blew my netting all apart. I got the guests to give me some help to move the carcass away from the tent, patched up my netting with some duct tape and tried to sleep the rest of the night away. In the morning we still had our food to make pancakes and bacon. Then I checked the bear out and decided that my first shot evidently broke his spinal cord and then went through a lung. That meant he just collapsed with that shot — not jumping on me — and the punctured lung had made the hideous scream. When then put the carcass in the water towed it downstream, wired four rocks on his legs split his belly and watched him sink in 15 ft of water. In three weeks or so there would be enough worms so that you would have a excellent fishing hole of your own.

About a month later I had a party of three men whose big interest was in the fishing, so we took a 3.h.p. outboard motor and tied the two canoes side by side with about a three foot gap in the center.

This makes a very steady platform for fishing and while it is not very fast it works out well when traveling large lakes like Basswood. I spent two days in town between trips and a couple of people mentioned to me to avoid camping on Pine Point of the North Bay of Basswood because a bear had just taken it over.

The next day we ran up the Moose Lake Chain, checked in with Canadian Customs at Prairie Portage, then ran another six miles to Bayley Bay and the Canadian Ranger Station. Jerry Payne was the Ontario Ranger and had been there for many years. After we completed the fishing licenses and travel permits, Jerry took me aside and told me about Pine Point of North Basswood and the bear. I told him that I had planned on spending the night there and could possibly cure the problem. Jerry had known for several years that myself and Hollis Latorelle carried pistols and occasionally eliminated a bear that took over a campsite. The lower level of the Canadian government was actually easier to deal with than the U.S Government. It really was illegal to have a handgun in Canada as a tourist, but it was handled quietly to get things done. A Canadian Customs officer, Roy Forsythe at Ottawa Island on Basswood Lake took me aside after my second or third trip into Canada on a middle of the night med-a-vac. He told me that I should not bother landing for clearance and risk an additional night landing — just bring him the injured person's name and address plus the point of landing on the next day. Seeing as night flying VFR as prohibited in Canada this was quite an easement of rules, but I sure appreciated it. On the U.S. side every time the FAA heard about a night flight they issued a violation even if a life was saved.

We pulled into North Bay about 4:00 p.m. The Pine Point Campsite was on the east side of the bay and was long and narrow, but had many large Norway pines with a great view looking to the south. I put up a 7 foot by 9 foot tent for the guests near the south tip. I put my tent up close to the camp because I was sure we would have a hungry bear stopping in for a meal. It was our first night out so I had New York Strip steaks, corn on the cob and baked potatoes (in the coals) topped off with chocolate banana pie. That should certainly encourage a hungry bear to stop in. As soon as the tents were erected, I got started on preparing dinner so everything would be finished by dark. The odors were pretty strong, so we had a quick campfire and went to bed. I told the party that we would probably have a bear problem that night so do not come out of their tent if there was a lot of noise and never go north of the campsite on the trail. We used to carry slab bacon in those days because it was smoked and would not spoil. I cut the rind off the slab and tied it off with fishing line around a hand grenade that had mysteriously showed up in my gear when I got out of the Marine Corps. I placed that package about two hundred feet north of the camp and just off the trail with a string tied from the pin to a tree. I was sure that any hungry bear would get the odor of the bacon rind, but to be sure I put some steak scraps and empty corn cobs with the package. I had been asleep about an hour when I heard a loud explosion and decided I would check it out when it got daylight. Sure enough there was the remains of a bear without a head or shoulders. We did get it down to the water, attached four rocks and sunk it in 15 feet of water where there should be some hellgramites waiting to feed on what was left.

When I moved to Alaska later on, I got rid of the 9mm Luger and picked up a .44 Magnum short barreled semi-automatic Ruger Rifle. The brown bears (Grizzlies) were considerably larger than the black bears of the Midwest. A sawed off 12 gauge pump shotgun loaded with 00 buckshot and slugs was also another favored weapon. I remember hearing a story about a Fairbanks, Ak moose hunter.

He woke up one morning during the moose season to find a moderate snow fall happening. He immediately called in sick, grabbed his 30-06 rifle, some lunch and drove his pickup out of town. When he got out a few miles he slowed down, radio playing, heater on while watching for fresh moose tracks crossing the road. It was not to long before he found some real fresh tracks crossing from the LH side of the road to the RH side. He stopped, took a good look at the tracks, got his rifle and started into the alders. He went about 150 feet in through very thick alders when a brown bear hit him from behind, knocking his rifle out of his hands and face down on the ground. He must have suffered a lot of pain in the next few minutes because he has several large chunks of his cheeks missing off his LH buttocks and LH thigh and leg plus a broken LH arm. He was wearing a .357 Magnum revolver on his belt and managed to get it out of his holster, stuck the muzzle right into the mouth of the bear and blew its brains out. This killed the Bear, but he fell right on top of the wounded hunter. With his broken arm, blood pouring out of various holes, he could not begin to move the carcass and finally passed out.

Luckily two more "sickly moose hunters" drove up in their pickup to find another pick up on the road with the engine running, driver's door open, heater going and radio playing. Of course, they stopped and looked at the tracks, then got their rifles and started following those tracks. It was only minutes until they came on to the bloody scene, got the bear off of the hunter and hauled him back to the road. They took both pick-ups and started back to town and the hospital. Miracles happen.

We stayed in Alaska for 20 years and loved it. One of the last years I flew up to one of our outpost cabins 100 miles north of Cordova on Hanigita Lake. This camp was at the 3,000 foot level of the Wrangell Mountains and would freeze - up within the next two weeks. I wanted to clean up everything making sure no food was left in the propane refrigerator, cooking gear all put away, propane returned to town and pipes with welded roofing nails attached to windows and doors for bear protection. I spent almost two hours inside the cabin and made stacks of things going back to Cordova. I finally picked up a stack of pots and pans and walked out the door. I quickly felt that there was something wrong and stopped about four feet from the door. I looked around finding a brown bear standing up about ten to twelve feet away and looking at me. It was easy to see he was a honest ten footer because our eave on the cabin was eight feet high. In a smooth monotone I told him " you go your way and I will go mine".

With that said he came down to all fours and came about four feet closer to me, stood up again and started clacking his jaws. Now I looked at the Cessna 206 heeled back at the beach about 40 feet away with the RH rear cargo door and the RH front door that we had installed both open with my .44 magnum sitting on the RH front seat. I dropped the pots with a clatter and I know it could not be, but it seemed like my feet only touched ground once. Then I grabbed the rifle and put a round right between his front feet and he decided to look elsewhere for his last meal before hibernation. I was in a National Park and if you kill a brown bear, even if it is required, it gets very tedious with paperwork for a year or so. The bear left, I got everything loaded in the plane, but my rifle stayed in my hand until I taxied out!

Bears were the main reason to carry a firearm in Alaska, but wife Debbie had a timber wolf walk up to within 15 feet of her one foggy morning as she was making the morning coffee. He stood there for 10 - 15 minutes watching her until he finally walked off into the mist. She usually carried a Smith and Wesson model 629 .44 magnum with a 6 inch barrel — and she was good with it. For years we flew our seven day tour of Alaska — usually with six guests, two pilots and a gal cooking. Our guests were mainly couples so we bought the best and lightest A Frame tents we could find. Often Debbie and I folded up the seats in the Twin Beech and that was home. Our second pilot would sleep in the single Otter. Debbie would get up at 0600 every morning, get dressed, pull on her hip boots and wade ashore to start a fire and make coffee. We always erected a couple of tarps the evening before to cover a warmup fire, a two burner gas stove and a folding oven. We would set up a small can of gas to start the fire and use the can to get some 50 weight oil out of two five gallon oil cans which would really get a good fire going. Usually she would open the cabin door on the Beech to stick a cup of coffee inside for me not much after 6:30 a.m. — then I would get up and moving. By 0700 she had hot coffee and rolls ready for the guests as they arose and a full breakfast by 0800 including Eggs Benedict on Thursday morning north of the Artic Circle.

One day she was at our rainbow camp on Tebay Lake cooking for a few days and the entire camp of guests and guides were out fishing in another lake for the day so she was alone. While walking down to the lake she passed some very thick underbrush and she heard the brush crackling as if something was moving towards her. It is very hard to outrun a bear, so she got her .44 magnum ready to go, but then a very large lumbering porcupine walked out into the open not knowing how close it was to getting shot.

Later on while we were at a sport show during the winter we looked at a Desert Eagle .50 caliber semi- automatic for her, but she was not impressed with the weight.

CHAPTER 35

MY FAVORITE AIRCRAFT

Over 63 years and almost 41,000 hours of accident free hours of flying time I have flown many different aircraft and had lots of people ask what was my favorite seaplane. Quite emphatically I have to reply the "Beech 18". During WWII the U.S. military asked Beechcraft to equip some of the Beech 18 C-18s-with the primary seaplane fittings in the fuselage to allow the usage as a Air/Sea rescue craft. Being the military no flight testing or certification was required so Edo did manufacture some 7850 floats to complete the usage. In the late 1930"s several A-18s and B-18s were floated and sold on Edo 7170 floats with Lycoming engines then the C-18S came out with the Edo 7850 floats. I only heard of a couple of the C-18s floated in Alaska by the military, so after the war some of these 7850 floats ended up in surplus sales.

The story goes that in the late 1950's there was an aircraft parts auction on the East coast and Ben Wiplinger of St. Paul, Minnesota and Joe Marrs of Lake Placid, Florida met at the sale site. There were 12 sets of brand new Edo 3430 floats with Cessna 195 attach gear being offered and another set of a 11 new large Edo floats, but no other description. They both wanted the 3430's but realized that they would just raise the price bidding against each other. They decided to flip a coin and the winner would have the bid on the 3430's and the loser would bid the 11 sets of large floats. Ben Wiplinger won the toss and got the 12 sets for $450 each set of his floats.

Joe Marrs did not know what aircraft his floats were for but he thought he could make some boating catamarans and put fairly large outboards on them and sell them. He was reported to bid $700 per set and of course no one else bid on these. A month or so later the floats showed up in Lake Placid and one of the mechanics opened a crate.

Then he went to Joe with the info that these were for a Twin Beech C-18 and were complete with struts and drawings. Joe told him that they had two of those Beeches in the yard and the crew could make a spare time project by putting one on floats. When it was flying everyone was impressed by how well it handled so Joe approached the FAA about getting a STC. Amazingly it got handled very quickly and he got the approval certificate from the New York office. In 1961 I saw an add in Trade -A-Plane with a picture of a Twin Beech on floats that he had for sale. I saw that and decided that I had to have one. I even made a 2"x4" frame in the hanger with cardboard siding as a mockup of a Twin Beech and figured that I could get two canoes inside the fuselage by installing the Beech cargo door kit.

I bought my first Twin Beech form Joe Mars in May of 1964. This was the seventh one he sold and the first on to stay U.S. registered as the first six had gone to Canada for registration. I paid $27,500 for N6799C with a brand new set of Edo 7850 floats, two zero time engines and props, extended wing tips, new paint and a military interior – six seats bolted to the floor. I traded in a 1955 Cessna 180, N4636B, for $13,500 credit on the purchase price. I had bought N4636B in 1960 for $12,500 and put quite a few hours on it and took in quite a few dollars which made it a good deal for me. I learned a lot with this aircraft and it had always been one of my favorite C180's and is still flying on Flathead Lake in Kalispell, Montana today.

I had one full time pilot and one part time. Each of these two had multi-engine land ratings but not a MES and I had no multi time of any kind. I made a deal with Joe Marrs to find a ferry pilot to fly the B-18 from Florida to Ely, Minnesota. He came up with Joe Michaud who operated a seaplane training OP in Opa Locka Florida with a Super Cub on amphibs and a Grumman Widgeon amphib. He was also a designated pilot examiner (DPE) and got permission from the FAA to do two multi-engine seaplane (MES) check out rides if the applicant had a multi engine land (MEL). Dave Hangartner was flying full time and Steve Gheen, a USFS pilot was flying part. They both had MEL and got the MES check rides. I got a hour of dual instruction in the Beech and loved it.

I had given a lot of thought to setting up the aircraft to hauling two canoes inside the fuselage, but now we were into the busy season and I could not afford the money or time to start that project. Our primary business at that time was flying canoe parties to a drop off point and they would paddle a week or two back to Ely or sometimes would get picked up a 100 miles or so from their starting point for the return to Ely. We also had several fly-in resorts on the Canadian side and a 90 mile flight to a lake just north of the Duluth, Minnesota for airport connections. We made a lot of pick-ups there for many of the customers of the various canoe outfitters and all of the resorts around Ely. Once word got around about the Twin Beech we started getting inquiries about multi sea training and a year later I got a Part 141 flight school approval from the FAA so we could qualify for training GI Bill trainees. These were pilots that the VA paid for 90 percent of their training costs to make them better pilots and more employable.

Our Twin Beech 18 doing MES training in California where we would winter during our Alaska years.

In 1970 Joe Mars had sold off all of his 7850 floats, but Bristol Aero space in Winnipeg, Manitoba had started manufacturing new and improved floats approved for the later model D-18s. These floats had a .064 thousandth bottoms instead of the .040 thousandth bottom of the military version, Much stronger. The D18S was 600 pounds heavier empty weight than the C-18s, but had a dual fuel selector, feathering props and a higher gross weight of 8,725 pounds. Bristol was receiving inquiries from people in the U.S. who thought they might be interested in a Twin Beech on floats. I had been operating N6799C for several years by then and was very happy with it. In Lake Placid a few years before Joe Marr's operation had a Beech that lost an engine on take-off and crashed into the bank in a canal with considerable damage. He ended up selling it to Charles Grognet of Houghton Michigan who rebuilt it and started hauling passengers from there to Isle Royale on Lake Superior.

During 1964 we simply tied one canoe under each engine nacelle and loaded four to six passengers and their gear in the cabin. This worked pretty well. After we bent several flaps we learned to manually extend the flaps so you could feel when the flaps and canoe met each other. Using the electrical flap exerted a little too much pressure on the flaps. During the winter of 1964 -65 I heard that the Canadian Mounties were waiting to arrest us for flying two canoes outside with passengers. So during the spring of 1965 we flew the Beech down to St. Paul and landed in the Mississippi River the day the ice went out.

We got the aircraft out of the water on its beaching gear and in a hanger and then bought a cargo door kit and arranged for an annual inspection. We got the aircraft back a couple weeks later – just after the ice had gone out in Ely. We quickly got it in the hanger there and worked on the canoe problem. We removed all of the existing cargo compartment, added heavy duty 1" Angle aluminum running to the back end and laid down a folding plywood panel that would allow the inspection of the elevator and rudder cables. The headliner would come out and be replaced with .020 aluminum sheeting with a white vinyl covering. I found a company in Miami that was making a four or five place folding bench seat of Aluminum and canvas and got a pair and removed the bolted in single seats. We then tried to fit a canoe inside the fuselage. We found that a 15 footer would almost make it, but did not come close to a 17 footer – which was the most common size that the canoe outfitters used. There were several thousand rental canoes available in the Ely area and that is where most of our business came from.

We then widened the entryway between the cockpit and the cabin by six inches and hacksawed off a metal piece on top of the instrument panel holding the fuel pressure warning lights and moved these to the lower panel. Presto! A 17 foot canoe would go through the cargo door standing up on its side and the forward end would end up just above the instrument panel and would be less than one inch short of touching the windshield. Then the canoe would be moved to the rear still on its side and up on the angled plywood ramp protecting the control cables. A second canoe then could be put in the same way until it was almost hitting the windshield, then moved to the rear but turned upside down and rested on the first one. It was also tied up to two eyehooks in the ceiling. Now the left hand folding bench seat could be lowered and locked in place. The camping gear and equipment goes in the lower canoe which is standing on its side and under the LH bench. The benches and cargo hooks are held by Brownline track. The LH bench would seat five passengers and another in the RH front seat made it possible to carry six passengers, their gear, and two 17 foot canoes with a cruise at 160 mph with a 5 ½ hour range if you had the large nose tank. The roof hatch was part of the installation and allowed the pilot to get out to either wing and jump off onto the dock to catch the aircraft to tie it up. It took a fairly agile pilot to fly the Beech on floats. For departure you loaded the aircraft with passengers and freight, untied it, pushed the nose out to open space, jumped on the float, climbed the ladder and up to the wing, moved forward to enter thru the roof hatch and immediately start the engines before you drifted into something. If you had a strong current or wind you would have the engines primed, master switch and magnetos on before you pushed off. 98 % of the time you would start the left engine first to get you away from the dock or beach quickly.

I bought my first Twin Beech in 1964 and sold it in 1971 for $32,500. 1970 I bought N6561D and I started a certification process for the D-18s which took the better part of a year to finish and sold it almost 10 years later for $45,500. I had paid $12,500 for the aircraft and $32,000 for the floats, part of a sweetheart deal to get the U.S. certification. During the mid 1970's I had a doctor from Wisconsin call me and ask if I were interested in buying a cheap C-18 Beech that had the fuselage float fittings. When I asked what he called cheap, he answered 6 or 7 thousand dollars. I told him to bring it up to Ely and I would check the float fittings. He answered that he would be there that afternoon and I told him to call me at Sandy Point Seaplane Base on 122.8 so I could meet him at the airport. We had a 2,400 foot grass strip at that time and I was there to watch him land using less than half of it which impressed me.

It only took a few minutes looking at the aircraft, then I told him to come down to the lake and our office and I would check the serial number against a list of C 18's built by Beech with float fittings. If the serial number showed up I would give him a $5,000 check. 30 minutes later I owned another Beech 18 - N44573 which turned out to be my favorite. It was a C model which was much lighter, but it had the feathering props and dual fuel selectors. It usually would true out at almost 170 mph if flown properly at 4,000feet with a 46 gallon per hour fuel burn and was just a nice flying aircraft. Several phone calls and a couple of days later we flew it down to Janesville, Wisconsin and one of the better known shops for maintaining Beech 18s. There we got a cargo door installed plus paint job - $20,000. Then to Winnipeg, Manitoba and Bristol Aerospace for float install - $64,000. I now could appreciate the $32,000 sweetheart deal on N6561D for the float approval. Once it was on floats it came back to Ely and into the hanger for a two piece windshield, Beech extended wing tips, L&R folding bench seats and all the mods to allow two 17 foot canoes to be carried inside the fuselage.

I have flown 11,500 hours in Twin Beech 18s on floats, but never did fly one on wheels. I did one take-off and landing in a Twin Beech on skis at Sioux Lookout, Ontario. Orville Wieben of Superior Airways had gotten an approval of a straight ski for a DeHavilland DHC-3 on the Beech 18 and offered me a set for $7,500. I did fly up to Sioux Lookout, Ontario and tried flying it but passed on it because we did not have enough winter traffic to justify the spring and fall change over. I have picked up another couple hundred hours in Gruman Widgeon, Goose, Mallard, Cessna T50 (Bamboo Bomber) and Piper Aztec. The hull aircraft did not offer much opportunity to haul external loads and they draw more water when tailing it back on a beach to load or unload. The T-50 could not hold altitude on one engine which really put it in the category of a single engine aircraft with an extended glide range. I really liked the Piper Aztec (Nomad) on floats, but it really was not an external load carrier. Being a bush operator means you have customers that count on you to bring them whatever they need. So the basic rule was "if it did not fit inside, tie it on outside". The Twin Beech and the single Otter would handle most of this freight inside – I could put 50 sheets of ½" plywood in the Beech standing it up on edge and shoehorn the last eight or ten sheets in. But if we had only six or eight sheets to go we could not justify a Beech or Otter and would lay them flat on the spreader bars and tie it down cris – crossed with rope and put a C clamp on the leading edge to keep it from separating in flight. You did have to watch your flare on landing because occasionally it would blank out the elevators — so no steep approaches. Twenty foot dimension lumber definitely was tied on the top of the floats as well as some refrigerators, freezers, long couches, doors and windows. And I would like to have a dollar for every 55 gallon barrel of fuel that I have flown. That was another plus of the Twin Beech – the floats had a wide stance without spreader bars so you could just roll a barrel out of the door into the water, and roll it ashore. With the Beech we would haul 8 drums on short hauls or 6 barrels on long flights. The Beaver would carry 4 drums and the Otter 6 to 8, but for the Beaver or Otter you had to have a long 2"x12" plank to roll it down or a pump and hose to transfer the product to another empty drum. I have seen many floats that have gotten smashed by dropping a full barrel on it. The Norseman would carry 6 or 7 barrels, but was a little harder to off load.

Freight was a large part of our business. People would buy some property on a fly-in lake then come to us to fly the materials and crew in to do the construction. We would usually try to do this in early May if the ice went out early enough so we did not disturb our summer business. I remember one May we had the materials for three different cabins stacked up our parking lot. This would be almost 1,000 sheets of plywood, hundreds of studs and boards plus cement mix, windows and doors, nails and tools.

Then we usually started hauling all of the furnishings in by late summer. External loads were a big part of our flying. I have over 8,000 flying with external loads – mostly boats and canoes. I remember one trip in a Norseman MKV with 4 passengers and a 16 foot boat a 20 hp outboard motor, all of their tents, food, camp gear and a 55 gallon drum of fuel. It ran for a while on the take-offs, but got to where we were going. The Norseman was a useful and interesting aircraft. It was designed by Robert Noordyn in 1933 and first built in 1935 with 903 total built. The U.S. military bought 749 during WWII and most of these were returned to civil use after the war. The last one sold was in 1959. A 600 h.p. P&W engine was the primary power plant. The aircraft had a 52 foot wingspan and was one of the first to have ailerons that deployed with the flaps. I have about 1,000 hours in a Norseman and can probably attribute a lot of my hearing loss to that.

Back to the Beech 18 with its dual rudders. It had a fairly low silhouette when taxing on the water, wide stance on the floats and differential power which all made it pretty controllable taxiing in strong winds. The DeHavilland Otter with its long fuselage, high rudder and ventral fin was one of the worst to control on the water if windy. The Beech 18s two Pratt and Whitney R985's gave you 900 h.p. making getting off upwind, downwind, or crosswind pretty simple. The single Otter had a high lift wing that would make flight rather wobbly in strong winds, while the Beech would take it smoothly. In mid-September of 1995 I was scheduled for a noon pick up of four fishermen at our salmon camp on the Tsiu River 100 miles down the coast and they were to catch the Alaska Airlines afternoon flight to Seattle. It was raining pretty hard in Cordova so I called the camp on the HF radio and they said "do not think about it. Winds are gusting to almost 100 and we have less than a mile visibility in heavy rain". The next morning there was not a cloud in the sky and glassy water in Cordova. So I gathered up some supplies that had to go to the camp, fired up the Twin Beech (N1042H) and started down the coast. Arriving at the Tsiu River I found broken clouds at 2,000 feet, good visibility but a very strong SE wind. After circling a couple of times people started coming out of the tents, but I could see that they had 30-40 degree lean into the wind. The river was about 100 feet wide and three to four feet deep with almost 1/3 of a mile long stretch right into the wind before it turned and headed north. The banks were all sand right there, so I decided to try it. The landing went very well although I noticed that I was traveling pretty slow. Beech stall speed on floats is 80 knots and you just cannot get it more than 2 or 3 knots lower at touch down. With that horse power though you can yank it out of the water at 55 knots, put your nose down for a very few seconds and you have VMC. We did not have docks in the camp because we would get such high winds there at times, but the sand banks dropped right off so we just buried a couple of logs, "dead men," and tied ropes off to make tie-downs. When I pulled up to this spot I was RH side to the bank and we could not turn it round as we normally did because of the strong wind. I saw the airspeed indicator locked on 60 knots as I went out through the roof hatch. We quickly unloaded the freight and I did not get much response when I told the guests to bring their gear over to the plane. The group of three persons said they did not want to fly in this wind, but the single fellow was from Minnesota who said that he had flown with me several times back there and this was his second trip to Alaska and had never been worried. He said that probably he would make it back in time to go to work the next day. I explained to everyone that we would just sail backwards in the river and then take off and we would be flying in not much more than1/2 a minute. Cordova was dead calm and perfectly clear and I would turn out over the ocean within the first minute. There should be no turbulence all the way except maybe a bump or two passing around Suckling Hills. That convinced everyone, they grabbed their belongings and we were on our way and it was as advertised. I would not have tried it in any other aircraft — another plus for the Beech 18.

CHAPTER 36

ENGINE FAILURES

My first engine failure was in a brand-new Cessna 206 (N2457U) that had just barely 27 hours on its Continental IO-520 (300h.p.) when the crank shaft snapped into two pieces. I had picked this airplane up in Wichita and flown it back to Ely. The next day one of the flight instructors took two students and a Lycoming engine that needed overhaul and went to Oklahoma and back. It was the last week of April and I suggested to my wife that we take the four kids out of school for a couple of days and fly down to the new Disney World in Florida. I knew the ice would be going out in the next ten days or so and I would not have another day off until freeze-up in late November. We settled on leaving right after school on Friday. I was scheduled to fly a wolf survey for the U.S. Fish and Wildlife on skis, but usually that work was done by 1:00 p.m. or so. We normally had ten to twelve Timber Wolves that we live trapped, put a radio collar on their neck, then followed them by air about three times a week. This allowed the wildlife people to know how much ground they would cover and how many deer they would kill. This particular Friday we picked up a signal of a wolf that we lost over a month before. When we tracked down the signal it was halfway to Minneapolis — most unusual! We did stick around until we got a visual spotting on him to make sure he was alive and not a collar in the back of some one's pickup.

This made the day stretch out and we did not get into the air towards

Florida until 7:00 p.m. and dark. About 9:30 p.m. we could see the lights of Chicago behind our left wing with a large rising moon right off our bow. Suddenly we saw a large glob of oil on our windshield and I picked out a flashing beacon just ahead. This was Terre Haute, Indiana and a good spot to overnight. I told the line crew to top off the tanks, but do not wash the windshield so I can see where that oil was coming from. The next morning we were back to the aircraft early, found the fuel tanks filled and a spotless windshield. I ran the engine up awhile, added a quart of oil and we took to the air again but keeping our eye out for open land just in case. By the time we were near Atlanta we had quite a bit of oil on the windshield again so decided to land at Newnan where one of my ex-pilots was managing a FBO (Fixed Base Operator) on the airport. It was Saturday and his two mechanics were off, but we put the Cessna in his hanger and de-cowled it. He lived right on the airport with his wife and kids, and the two families knew each other. Wiley and I changed the oil, cleaned the engine thoroughly and did find that two nose case bolts were very loose.

They evidently got out of the factory without being torqued down — which we did and then gooped them up. Feeling better about this we got back into the air again and got near Gainsville when we ran into a thunderstorm just after dark. A small airport with a lighted runway showed up right when we needed it. The kids really liked this because the operator had a big finned pink Cadillac for a courtesy car. The next morning we finally got to Kissimmee, Florida and started to enjoy Disney World. We even had a clean windshield.

Three days later we loaded up the Cessna 206 planning that with an early start we would be home that night. We stopped in Chattanooga, Tennessee for fuel with a quick bathroom break. Back in the air and we found it very bumpy, so I filled IFR (Instrument Flight Rules) to VFR on top. We broke out about 7,000 feet above sea level (MSL) and smoothly proceeded to Rockford, Illinois for another fuel stop and rest room break. Still no oil showing on the windshield, but I added a quart of oil to the engine. We had shot an instrument approach (IFR) into Rockford and broke out with an 1,800 foot ceiling, so I decided to stay VFR below the clouds on departure. This was before the computer life and it usually took 30 minutes or more to get an IFR clearance, so I would air file when I got to Madison, Wisconsin. The stretch in Northern Wisconsin and Duluth, Minnesota were pretty low to get through safely VFR after dark. We were in the air a few minutes later going north in pretty smooth air and good visibility when the engine hiccupped and I saw the oil pressure going down, then the engine began shaking. I immediately reduced the power telling everyone that we were going to make an emergency landing.

This brought the kids to life, "Land in this field Daddy, lots of cows". Then "Land in this field over here, more cows". Then my wife said "Runway" and pointed ahead on the right. By then I knew I had to shut the engine off before it shook itself off the airframe, but it looked like I could make it. I probably touched down on the first fifty feet of the runway and rolled to a stop. I did not know what airport it was, so I just called on 121.5 MC (Emergency) and told the tower that I could see that we were down on their runway Five and needed a tow truck. This started quite a flap while the tower kept telling me that I could not land without a clearance while I was trying to tell him that I had an engine failure and had no good choice except the runway. After five minutes of this I turned the radio off and the six of us started to push the airplane down the runway when a pickup with two fellows and a piece of rope showed up saying that "they were the tow truck I requested". We got the plane over to their hanger and found out that the propeller was almost off. Of course the aircraft was brand new still covered by warranty, so we just called a nearby motel, got a van sent over and we settled in. The next morning I spent a couple of hours on the telephone with Cessna and Continental Engines who both promised a brand new engine shipped out that day. Then we grabbed a North Central Airlines flight to Duluth, Minnesota where one of our crew met us. A week later we picked up the Cessna there in Jamesville, Wisconsin and brought it back for the float installation. We flew the plane 335 hours, started having oil pressure problems again and when we pulled the oil screen it was plugged with metal pieces. Another few conversations with Cessna and Continental Engines and they agreed to another new engine — which I refused saying I was tired of changing their brand new engine every few months, so send me a factory overhauled engine so I could see how that works. We put the OH engine on and finished up the season. Later during the winter I sold the plane to a lawyer in Anchorage, Alaska and ferried the aircraft up there on wheels. I saw the plane often and know that he flew that engine to overhaul with no problems.

I had another Continental 0-520 fail on me one day in the fall. I had purchased the aircraft about three months earlier, but we had only flown it just over 100 hours. We were just opening up our salmon camp 100 miles down the coast from Cordova, Alaska. The weather had been pretty lousy for a couple of days and we had quite a bit of food and gear that did not get down there with almost 20 fishermen scheduled to fly down there that afternoon. It was a Sunday morning and everyone of our planes were flying moving our guests to several different locations. I took all the seats out of the Cessna 206 except the pilot's seat. I then loaded it right to the ceiling plus two compartments in the floats that had cargo hatches. I knew I had an overload, but I did not have to climb very high going down the coast to the Tsiu River. It took a little longer to get off the water, but it flew fine. Cordova, Alaska has the Pacific Ocean (Prince William Sound) on the west side and Eyak Lake on the east side. To leave Eyak Lake east bound you pass through two mountains a little over 2,000 feet high and a pass that is 1/3 of a mile wide, but the terrain is only about 15 feet above sea level and called "The Gap". The airport is at the 13 mile marker and a bridge crossing a tributary of the Copper River is at 27 mile. I leveled off at 500 feet crossed the Copper River and just east of the river the engine made a loud "Bang" while throwing smoke and flames from the front left side of the cowling. I rolled over to the left and turned back for Eyak Lake about

35 miles away. I did pick up the orange tail of our DeHavilland Beaver just turning north bound on the Copper River. I knew it was piloted by John Davis who had a party of four headed for our lodge on Tebay Lake. I called him on the radio, told him that I had just lost a cylinder and was on my way back to town. He replied that he was turning around and will keep me in sight until I made it back to the lake. I just got across the Copper River and got another "Bang" from the engine compartment and lost a couple hundred feet of altitude. I passed this on to John and he said he was behind and above me. There was a strong North wind blowing down the Copper River that made it hard to hold my altitude which made me think it would be a mess if I had to land on the gravel downwind and went upside down. I was now down to 250 feet and could barely hold 80 mph. I went just south of the airport heading for the Gap when I got my third "Bang" and the electrical system went out. I already had the propeller all the way forward to keep the RPM's up and 10 degree of flap down just trying to stay in the air — there was a small lake just off my right so I just turned in and landed. Just as I came over the trees I noticed a small cabin and dock on the north shore which was probably someone's duck hunting camp. I got my paddle out and paddled over to the dock and tied up. John Davis circled, but I could not talk to him on the radio and he turned to the Gap and Eyak Lake. He dropped his passengers off back at our dock and then came to pick me up. Then he got his passengers loaded again and on their way to Tebay Lake. While he was gone I took the Cessna 172XP and flew back to the 206, pulled the cowling off and found three blown cylinders — all on the same side. The last and third one melted the battery cable causing the loss of electrical power. We had bought this as a rebuilt aircraft and engine a few months earlier and the seller had done an excellent job on the airframe, but when I checked the engine logbook I found that the six cylinders were overhauled by one of the cheapest companies in the U.S. I ordered three cylinders the next morning and it took two days for

installation, but it was only a six or seven minute flight to the aircraft. Later on the other three cylinders were replaced.

John Davis and myself had several happenings together. For 10 winters we took all of our airplanes down from Cordova to Lakeport, California. We quite often rented a large house right on Clear Lake with a large dock — the owners usually went south to Phoenix, Arizona for the winter while we came south from Cordova, Alaska. We would do quite a bit of maintenance, both single -engine and multi - engine seaplane training while moving around the U. S. doing sport shows selling our Alaska trips. We usually moved the planes south during late October and November with the north bound flights during April and early May. We got some of the aircraft flown north one spring when I came up with some severe stomach pain and spent two days in the hospital followed by two days bed rest at the house we had rented. The pain had stopped and I felt fine, but had no idea what caused it. As matter of interest in the next five years or so I was hospitalized three times (including the Mayo Clinic) and never found out the cause of it and never had it again. My daughter Katie said they were going to send John Davis down rather than me flying the Twin Beech alone and have that stomach problem come up again. Two days later John showed up in Santa Rosa, CA and Tom Wasson hopped over the hill with his Piper Cherokee and picked him up. By then I had packed up and fueled the Beech so we could get an early start the next morning. At 0800 we were in the air heading west with a RH turn when the ocean showed up. We followed the coast line all the way to Westport, Washington where we turned right again and headed for American Lake. A friend, John Kittelson, had a seaplane base there with a couple of DeHavilland Beavers and that was our next fuel stop. We got almost to Summit Lake and ran into clouds right to the ground that forced us to turn back. We got back to Gray's Harbor at Westport and swung around to land when the left engine quit. Mixtures, props, throttles, dead foot, dead engine, feather the engine, shut off the fuel and land. The landing was great, so we taxied into the marina and found a spot to dock. Then we found the harbor master, got his ok on our parking and when we mentioned needing fuel he recommended that we do that after 9:30 in the morning seeing it was a weekend. After that we got a room and a couple of dungeness crabs for dinner. The morning saw us making a forty minute flight to American Lake. By 11:00 a.m. we started to Nanaimo, B.C. for Canadian Customs and then up the coast to Ketchikan, Alaska for U.S. Customs and overnight. That put us in Cordova midday the third day.

Another time that I ran out of fuel was early May and the ice had just gone out a couple of days earlier. I was on a Fish and Wildlife wolf survey and we located a wolf that we lost three weeks earlier.

We really wanted to get a visual on the animal and extended our flight time somewhat. We were flying a Cessna 172 with a 180 h.p. engine up grade, constant speed propeller and a set of Pee Kay 2300 floats — a performer but the fuel burn was increased while the tankage stayed the same. I started a descent when we thought the wolf was right in front of us, but the engine hiccupped and I realized that we were low on fuel. Most aircraft make the hose from the tank to the engine located toward the rear of the tank. I immediately pulled up into a gradual climb and reduced power a bit. We were about 20 miles from our base, so I started for it keeping water under me all the way. When we got back to Sandy Point I put my nose down to land which made the engine quit again. No problem — we landed about a half mile short of our dock — so I raised the office on the radio to have a canoe bring two gallons of gas for us.

Running out of fuel counts as a pilot failure, not an engine failure and these two instances were the only fuel quantity problem I ever had.

Every spring I would have a dozen or so new Cessna's coming off the production line in Wichita. We ordered them with our specs 90 days before expected final completion, then when finished we had seven days to pay for and move the unit from the delivery center. It was right about the first of May one spring I received three finals for pickup. A few days earlier I had talked to another dealer from south Minneapolis and told him that I was going to Wichita that week and probably fly three of my people down in a Aero Commander I had, then he asked if I could take his pilot /mechanic along to pick up a unit he had just been invoiced for. Then he called me back to ask if I would fly his Piper Aztec he had taken in on trade several months back and it had been sitting in the back of his hanger all winter. He wanted to put a few hours on it and get it sold. I said that was fine and the four of us would be there the next afternoon. Right after lunch the next day, the four of us got into a Cessna 172 to pick up the Aztec at Airlake Airport just south of Minneapolis. We found it blowing 30 knots right across the runway with occasional guest to 40 knots. The landing went alright, but was busy, so we decided to spend the night there and get an early start the next morning. This worked out fine — the wind had disappeared and we had a 1,500 foot ceiling with good visibility and we climbed to 1,000 feet AGL, flaps up, gear up, established cruise power. A few minutes later I started thinking that this was the slowest Aztec I had ever flown — which was not many as it had not been approved on floats yet. Then I spotted the mirrors that told me the landing gear was still down. Bill Gooch's pilot/mechanic was in the RH front seat so he dug out the manual and pumped the gear up. That was better as I watched the speed come up. But within five minutes the LH engine and propeller went to "Feather" position which meant we had two engines running, but only one delivering any power. Seeing as our copilot lived and flew around here I asked him where the closest runway was — he pointed to the left and said "15 miles". We were down to 800 feet AGL now and I could pick up the runway. This meant we had to pump down the landing gear and prepare for the landing. The runway was 3,000 feet long and I naturally carried a little too much altitude until I started my descent. I was probably 600 feet to 800 feet down the runway on touch down, but I got on the brakes — NO BRAKES! I cut both mixtures and got someone to open the door and stared at the end of the runway coming up. We stopped with about five feet of runway left in front of the nosewheel. We manually turned the plane, then called Bill Gooch back at Airlake Airport and he came down and picked us up in a van. He said he would have a couple of his people go down to straighten out the problems — and sold the AC a month later. He was also a dealer for the Bellanca Viking 300 and gave us a new demonstrator to finish up our Wichita pick up. I dropped the Viking off the next day and Bill Gooch told me that the hydraulic fluid must have leaked out quite a bit during the winter and pumping the gear up and down did not help. He said that propeller system had a hydrogen tank and that was too low to make it do what is was supposed to do.

At one time a few years ago I received a small plaque from Viking Air Ltd. Of Sidney, British Columbia for having 10,000 hours flying time in a DeHavilland DHC-2 Beaver. I have added about another 1,500 hours in a Beaver, but in all of those hours I have only had one engine failure. That happened in Keehi Lagoon in Honolulu, Hawaii on a nice sunny day with a 12 to 15 knot SE wind — almost a everyday occurrence. A party of four Germans walked into the office saying they wanted to take a hour long tour of Oahu in a seaplane — preferably a Beaver. They were two couples, spoke good English and one was a Boeing 737 Captain in Germany. Usually a party of that size we could handle with either a Cessna 206 or the Beaver, but with no hesitation I went out to start fueling up the Beaver while my wife Debbie would do the paperwork and a briefing on the map giving them an idea of what they would see. I was ready when they came out of the office and they walked up a mobile ramp we had into the aircraft. The Boeing 737 pilot sat in the front right seat and we talked of the Class Bravo airspace we operated in. I lined up with a bit of a crosswind on Sealane 4 and added the power when the control tower cleared me. Climbing out I turned to the SE and started a shallow climb to 1,500 feet above sea level. We usually went down Waikiki Beach at 1,000 feet right offshore and then 1,500 feet by the time we reached Diamondhead Crater. At about 800 feet the engine hiccupped once making me take notice of a 10 foot swell piling up on the beach in front of us. A few seconds later the engine quit and I started a fairly steep descending turn to the right. I could not see it behind me at the time of failure, but I knew there was a channel about 60 to 70 feet wide going back to Keehi Lagoon. I had about 200 feet of altitude when I got lined up with the channel for a downwind, crosswind coming from the right side. I had my RH float lowered quite a bit making the touchdown really pretty smooth and my run out taking us into Sealane 8- 26. As I fell off the step I had to strongly step on the LH rudder to avoid running into the shoreline and going aground. Of course, the aircraft started weather cocking into the wind as I tried to start the engine again — with no start. I was going to call the control tower for assistance when a small boat with two fishermen pulled up and asked if they could help. I pulled out a rope and asked if they could tow me back to our base. My wife Debbie got a surprise when a boat came in towing me less than ten minutes after I started my takeoff. I was surprised that I never did hear from the tower. We did offer the group a ride in the Cessna 206, but I guess they had enough adventure for the day. We dug right into what caused the engine to quit and found a magneto drive gear failed.

I had two crankshaft failures — both on Twin Beeches. The one caused a lot of grief and trouble and my son and I had to taxi for 24 hours in the middle of nowhere. The other one happened on Clear Lake in Northern California. I had two students there for a few days getting multi - engine seaplane ratings in the Twin Beech. One was a good friend, Warren Kregness, who owned a bank in Tower, Minnesota and we had chased down the fellow who robbed his bank one day. I met Warren one day when he came in our office asking about learning how to fly. He started that fall, on floats and took his Private Pilot's checkride on skis that winter. His son also got into the act and got his license shortly behind his father's finish. A few days later Warren called me and said to come to Tower for lunch. He wanted me to bring my Cessna order book so we could order a new Cessna 180 with floats and skis for him. I told him that I would come for lunch, but he was not ready for a Cessna 180. We had lunch that next day and I told him that I would sell him a used 1969 (current year) Cessna 172, with floats and skis also both he and his son could build their experience level. Then I would give him the same price for trade in that he had paid for it now — barring any damage. About eight months later we made a deal and took the Cessna 172 (N79571) back on trade for a Cessna 180, I did not believe a 40 to 50 hour pilot should be flying a Cessna 180 in some of the weather you run into while flying the bush where you cannot get weather reports most of the time. It worked well — over the years I sold him the Cessna 172 one new Cessna 180, two new Cessna 185's, two Cessna 206's and half of a Cessna Twin Engine 310. I trained Warren and the other fellow in the Beech for several days with one flying and the other observing. I liked doing it that way when I could. I got both of them ready so we went out and did a practice check ride flight. It takes about one hour, loose an engine on take-off just before flight, climb to altitude for slow flight, engine out procedure and stalls. Then glassy water, rough water and cross wind take offs and landings, followed by step taxi, step turns and docking. Warren completed his with minor correction and the two swapped seats. We did exactly the same things and the second to last landing was a single engine landing followed by staying on the step and take off back to our dock. When he applied power for the last take off the RH crank shaft broke. He did not correct for that and we started making a pretty tight turn on the water with the LH engine putting out full power. Just before we started going sideways I reached out and pulled both mixtures off. Then we had a two mile taxi back to our dock where I called the FAA to cancel the check rides for the next day — and ordered a fresh engine from Paul Abbott at Covington Engines in Oklahoma. It took a couple weeks to get the engine, then changed and we had a busy season going in Alaska had to get up there as quick as we could, so the check rides never did happen.

Thanksgiving Day, November 26, 1982 I took off from Guntersville

Lake in Northern Alabama headed for Fort Myers, Florida in a DeHavilland DHC-3 Otter to have Thanksgiving dinner with my daughter Katie and her husband Tom. I climbed to 4,000 feet MSL for awhile while I crossed the foot of the Appalachian Mountains and picked up a couple of rough spots of the engine. As I started to descend toward the Georgia border those rumblings showed up again and I started thinking that I would land on the La Grange Reservoir and see if I could spot anything that might be causing the odd noise. I was now down to 3,000 feet above sea level when there was a pretty noisy explosion followed by black smoke, flames and a lot of oil coming over the cowling making a mess of the windshield. l had just passed a lake next to a town, so I immediately started a 180 degree left turn while shutting the engine and fuel off. I could not see much through the wind shield, so I opened up my sliding side window and stuck my head part way out so I could see to land. It was downwind, but the landing was pretty smooth. Once I fell of the step the aircraft weather cocked 180 degrees into the wind while I jumped down to the float to see if I had a fire that would make me evacuate. There were no more flames, but a lot of smoke caused by oil on the hot engine. The lake was probably a mile and a half long and I was coming up on the downwind side fairly fast. I could not see anything but trees coming right up to the water's edge and certainly would cause some damage. I could see a large dead tree sticking out over the water on my LH side so I climbed back into the cock pit and started sailing towards it. Most people are surprised that you can be fairly accurate sailing backwards by using your rudder and ailerons. As I came up on the dead tree I climbed up on the roof, then out on the wing and got a rope around the tree as I drifted by. I pulled it in behind the tree and tied off pretty securely as long as the wind did not switch direction. Now I had to put my hip boots on to get ashore and walk down to the highway at the far end of the lake. I was born and raised in Northern Minnesota and we only had a few garter snakes — the 40 degree below zero kept them down in numbers. But here there were rattle snakes, water moccasins, coral snakes and copper heads and I have to walk through a mile and half of thick brush without stepping on one of them. Just as I was going to step into the water I noticed flashing red lights half way down the lake. A fire truck drove into sight followed by a police car and a pickup. Two men got out of the pickup and started to walk down the shoreline headed for me. When they got to me they said there was boat coming to tow me to the other end of the lake. This worked out nice. There was a small beach that we heeled the plane on and got it securely tied off. The Chief of Police was there and asked what I needed. I had checked out the engine and found that one half of the number one cylinder was completely missing. That is what caused all of the smoke, flames and spraying oil. It turned out that a young fellow in the town of Roanoke, Alabama had actually seen the top half of the cylinder come off and land in his yard. The next day his father brought him and the missing piece over to me at the Otter. It seems that a good share of town folks had seen the event when it happened. By the time that we had tied down the Otter there must have been 30 some cars there watching. I did tell the Chief of Police that I needed a telephone so that I could call my daughter to tell her that I would not make it for dinner. He took me to his office and while I was talking to Katie a woman came in the office with a Thanksgiving turkey dinner for me. Before I had eaten that another woman came in with another dinner for me. I asked the Chief of Police if he could recommend a motel or hotel that I could get a room and a drink. He replied that it was a dry county, but maybe he could send a deputy over the county line to pick something up for me. I told him that I had a bottle of bourbon in my bag and could just get by with a room. Then he picked up his phone and called someone, he then told me he had a room set up in a house next to the airport. The fellow's name was McDonald and he was a retired Marine and was a Private Pilot. He and his wife were very nice so I spent the night. The next afternoon my son-in-law, Tom Prijatel, showed up and we started driving around the state looking for a replacement cylinder for a Pratt and Whitney R1340.

There were quite a few agricultural sprayer operations that used the 600 h.p. engines on Grumman Ag-cats. It took a day and a half and we found an operation in Selma, Alabama that had three Ag-cats and five overhauled cylinders on the shelf and he sold us one. We were back two days later taking the cowling off of the Otter when a car pulled up and it turned out to be an aircraft mechanic, who had maintained a Grumman Mallard using the same engine for several years. With his help we were ready to go again in a couple of days.

Then on to Fort Myers, Florida where we wintered offering all day tours from Sanibel Island to Fort Jefferson on Dry Tortugas Island which many years before had been a prison. On the way back we stopped in Key West Harbor for lunch and sightseeing, followed by a flight over the coastal Everglades.

John Davis stopped in for breakfast in Honolulu
en route to Australia by G5

CHAPTER 37

THE GOOD THE BAD
AND THE UGLY

With 63 years invested in an aviation career I met a lot of very interesting people and a few that were not. During August of 1968 I hosted the first National Fly in of the Seaplane Pilots Association in Ely. I seem to remember that the organization was then based at Little Ferry, N.J. with an airline pilot acting as President. I did meet a fellow named Alan (A.C.) McDonald the first day who was FAA and wanted to buy a seaplane rating. He was there with his young son and a pickup camper in our parking lot. We had taken our Twin Beech, N6799C, to St. Paul, Minnesota for the fore runner of the Beech mid- section X-Ray, but while the center section was fine, we did find a small crack in the RH wing spar. We got a ferry permit from the FAA to fly the plane back to Ely. I bought a brand-new wing for $300.00 (Surplus) and another $100.00 for paint. We had to wait for the shipment, so we put the Beech in the hanger to remove the RH wing in preparation for the switch. Two years later we found out that Alan McDonald was sent to Ely to ensure that we did not fly the Beech that weekend. He did get his seaplane rating — which qualified him to be our Principal Inspector Operations (PIO).

The following summer we got a FAA contract to instruct A.C. McDonald and Dorvin Hagen for multi - engine seaplane ratings in the

Twin Beech. Just before they arrived my only instructor in the Beech, Wiley Hautala, said he did not want to train the two FAA students. I told him that I was counting on him to do it because I was not a CFI. Not only was it a nice piece of income, but we needed to have easier availability of multi-engine sea Part 135 check rides. Wiley did say that he would do it if he could have a week's vacation the week before the training - which I approved. The morning the training was to start, Wiley called saying he was stuck in Anchorage, Alaska and could not make it back. l immediately called Ray Walberg in Duluth who had been a PBY pilot during WWII and Bill Leithold in Wisconsin who was flying a Grumman Mallard for Gold Bond Stamps. They both said they were willing to sign off the training, but did not feel qualified to train in the Beech that they had not flown. The FAA applicants showed up a few minutes later so I could explain that I did not have a Certified Flight Instructor (CFI) to do the training. They both agreed that they would rather have me do the training with my experience in the Beech and have Roy Walberg sign off on the training. We worked on that the next few days and had some fun, A.C. McDonald was so fast on single engine procedures that your eyes could not keep up with his hand — but his landings were more like arrivals. On the other hand, you could see Dorvin Hagen's single engine work while hardly feeling his landings. The FAA sent one of their people up to do the two check rides with ten hours of training each. They left the office just before 5:00 p.m. and Alan told me to be at his room at 7:00p.m. to write the CFI written exam — both parts of the Fundamentals of Flight and the Fundamentals of Instruction with no studying. We did manage to get both done by 10:00 p.m. by working together. This was before the computer age making you mail in the written test and getting your results three weeks later. Alan McDonald did call three weeks later to ask how I did. I told him that I passed my Fundamentals of Flight, but he did not do well on his Fundamentals of Instruction— which hardly makes sense anyway, you just study until you get it. He said that he would be in the northern part of the state the next week, so plan on being in his room Thursday night to re-do the second written. By the time these answers were back we were pushing freeze-up with the check ride postponed to ski season.

I did get a call from Alan in mid-December saying that he would be in Ely for my check ride the next day. He arrived about noon on a clear day, but about 10 degrees below zero. So he asked if any aircraft were warmed up. I pointed at a Cessna 180 with skis sitting on the ice 30 feet in front of the door telling him that I had landed that one just a few minutes before. I took the RH front seat and checked him out on his first ski flight, followed by him checking me out in a half loop followed by a half roll. The next few months I did add an Instrument instructor rating (CFI-II) and a multi-engine instructor rating (MEI). I found it very handy when it was all finished.

I dealt with Alan McDonald for several years after that and it went very smoothly. I remember hearing a story after he moved to Denver that the Minnesota office got a new man that wanted to go to Ely on the opening day of fishing season, anchor off our Sandy Point base and close us down for hauling canoes and external loads. Alan bluntly told him to leave that seaplane operation alone — they are not having accidents and run a really safe business. We did have a neighbor that lived down the lake about a mile from us that was continually complaining about our aircraft making too much noise. His name was Matt Marolt and he was a low level USFS employee — so he did not make any complaints about the three Forest Service Beavers that were based just past his house on the west side. They took off and landed right in front of his house quite a bit while we tended to follow the north shore of the lake. One day during the summer Alan McDonald's voice came up on the Unicom saying he was landing at the airport and wanted to borrow our van for an hour. I sent one of the dock hands right up there then they dropped the young fellow off back at our dock and drove away. A hour later the van came back and Alan asked if I would drive the two of them back to the airport so he could talk to me. He then told me that he was at Matt Marolt's because the Governor was leaning on the FAA. He said that the first thing he saw walking into the house was a pair of 10 power binoculars laying on the windowsill. He said that explains the aircraft "N" numbers being reported all of the time. While he was standing there he watched one of our planes taking off along the north shore without offensive noise. Then a few minutes later a USFS Beaver landed about 100 yards in front of Matt's house. He did say the north shore departures were almost a mile away and not overbearing because most of the time the first power reduction was already made when passing Matt Marolt's house. I got back to our base just as their Bonanza was climbing out, nosing down with the propeller in low gear while passing over Mr. Marolt's house at 50 feet and full power. We never did get another complaint. Alan McDonald was a great guy and had common sense which is often missing in government people.

While we operated in Alaska, we spent ten winters in Lakeport, California located on Clear Lake. We would bring all of our aircraft down the coast in late October and November, do our maintenance inspections along with both single-engine and multi-engine seaplane ratings. We did quite a bit of training for FAA people from all over the United States — usually for both ratings. When I started that I communicated with the Sacramento, California office as they were the closest FSDO. They decided that they had one inspector with a single engine sea rating who they would send over for multi-engine sea training. Two weeks later Inspector Daniel Abdon showed up and got his multi-engine sea rating. Our insurance company — and myself — said that he basically was a low time pilot with hardly any seaplane experience and that I would have to give the final exam ride with Dan observing. We were used to that with many FAA examiners requesting that themselves. If you are smart, safety is the key — which is me having several thousand hours in a Twin Beech on floats compared to very little time for these people.

We did quite a bit of advertising and were doing about ten multi - sea ratings per month. If we could arrange two or more check rides per day, Dan would drive the 90 miles to Lakeport, but if there were just one ride per day we would meet him at the south end of Berryessa Lake which was a 25 miles drive for him.

This did cause some problems because Dan was driving a government car and there was no way he was going to let a civilian ride in that car. We would land at a state dock to tie up with Dan meeting us with the applicant. Then we would walk a mile to a small Park area with a table to do the oral exam.

We would walk while Dan would drive, with the same to return to the airplane. We had a good pilot John Davis flying for us in Alaska for the summer as well as Lakeport during the winter. That really aggravated John and he kept saying the car belonged to the taxpayers. I would get aggravated at Dan when making the final docking at the conclusion of the exam. He would be standing in the hatchway leaning over my shoulder watching my feet saying that if one of my feet touched a rudder pedal he was flunking the student. I told him that was of little concern. If I thought I could prevent any damage to the aircraft or floats, not having to replace a bow section of a float, that would tie the plane up for a couple of weeks and several thousand dollars with all of the parts coming from Winnipeg, Manitoba.

After the second winter he said he would not do check rides any more unless he was in the right seat.

No way that was going to happen with Dan Abdon. The next fall when we came down, the Sacramento Office set us up with Swede Gamble from the Los Angeles Office and they had to pay for his time and expenses. He was a fine careful pilot which made a good operation. The way of the government!

When we moved to Honolulu with the seaplanes, we started getting inquiries about people getting single engine seaplane ratings. I made a trip to the local FAA FSDO office to see if they could provide an examiner for the check rides. They said they could, so we started training in our Cessna 206 once it was inspected by the FAA. Our first applicant was a Japanese pilot living in Hawaii who had a U.S. Private Pilot license with an instrument and multi-engine rating. He really enjoyed the water work enough to talk about adding a commercial license after finishing up this rating Our FAA examiner decided however that he did not like the way he spoke English in spite of the ratings he already had and issued a pink slip — failure. Our second student was a young lady with a Commercial license and a flight instructor rating, but she got a pink slip because the examiner did not like the way she dressed. She did come back the following week to take another try and passed this time wearing long pants. Our third applicant was a woman who went right through the training plus the check ride slicker than a whistle only to ride home with the examiner — her husband. Things eased up after that with several applicants completing the rating complete with a check ride, but then a new obstacle showed up. Our current examiner was supposed to monitor airline pilots and not do seaplane check rides. I have always wondered about that — a FAA person gets type rated in an airline aircraft and then monitors someone who will have several thousand hours in the aircraft. The Honolulu office did actually tell one of their people to walk one city block to our base and get a seaplane rating. This was Dave Ryon who trained in our Cessna 206 and also checked out in the DeHavilland Beaver so he was qualified in both. We had some pilots who bought Beavers on floats and came to Honolulu to get their rating and a week of intensive flight training in a Beaver which made it easy on them and their insurance company. I have a plaque from Viking Air of Vancouver, B.C. who owns all the STC's of DeHavilland aircraft that attests to my having over 10,000 accident free flight hours in Beavers on floats with 16 Beavers owned over the years. The insurance companies really like that. Dave Ryon did our seaplane check rides for a couple of years with no big problems. He was another fellow to have that uncommon common sense. This worked well for a couple of years, until

Dave had a 3:00 p.m. check ride with a young Naval officer for his original certified flight Instructor (CFI) check ride in the Beaver. It was a Kona (westerly wind) and they taxied to sealane 22 for takeoff. This would be a right hand turn out to north over Pearl Harbor followed by a turn to the east to go to Kaneohe Bay Marine Corps air station for the water work seeing as Honolulu was Class B Airspace.

They got their clearance from Clearance Delivery and then switched to the control tower. A hour later — and quite a few inquiries to the tower that were answered with "Hold". They taxied back to our dock a little after 4:00 p.m. with Dave saying it was too late to start the exam. They said they would try again the next week. Two days later Dave Ryon had another single engine seaplane check ride with a ATP pilot. They completed the ride at the Kaneohe base and started a return to Keehi Lagoon in the Class B airspace utilizing a short straight in approach through Pali Pass headed west. They called Approach requesting clearance into Class Bravo, but did not get an answer. After two calls so they veered off to the North along the mountains. By then the control tower had called the Honolulu FAA FSDO with notice of a violation and were somewhat flustered to find that a FAA inspector was the pilot in command.

Meanwhile one of the people working Honolulu Center walked by and was told of the violation against the Beaver. He had gotten a seaplane rating from us the year before, but told them that they should look closer at the track on the screen to see that the aircraft did not actually enter Class Bravo Airspace.

The supposed violation was never actually filed, but I did state that this looked like a "Get even event" after I had complained to the Western Region office in Los Angeles of the happening of two days earlier when the Beaver did not get a take-off clearance. I did mention to our pilots that they could shut their communication radio off, squawk 7600 on their transponder and come into Class Bravo if they did not get a answer to two or three calls for clearance. You have to do something when your government runs amok. The sad thing of all this was that Dave Ryon very quickly transferred to California.

One morning shortly before Dave Ryon did actually leave the Honolulu office on his transfer to California we had a group of five passengers go out on a one hour tour in the Beaver. The pilot was Valorie Reis who did a great job in both the Cessna and the Beaver. It was a 0900 departure which put her back at 1000, then Debbie drove the passengers back to Waikiki while Valorie cleaned up the Beaver and went to a flight school to give an hour of instruction. Two people walked down the ramp into our office, one of them I recognized as a Mr. Lee who was an avionics specialist and the other was also a FAA inspector, but I did not know him. They announced themselves saying that our Beaver was seen flying below 1,500 feet. I asked when and where they saw this. They said they did not see it, someone else had told them about it and it was within the past hour. I commented than that in all the years I have been flying that it is hard to tell looking at an aircraft a mile or so away if it is at 1,400 feet or 1,500 feet. I also said that Special Federal Air Regulation #71 had expired seven months before and I had not seen anything that renewed it. This SFAR#71 was for Hawaii only establishing a minimum of 1,500 feet for all tour aircraft. Them seemed to think it was a recent ruling, so I picked up a current Airman's Information Manual (AIM) and asked the regulation number so I could look it up. Edwin Lee said he thought it was either Part 146 or 147. I said that could not be because all Part 140's concern Maintenance, not Airspace regs. After several minutes of their wild guesses, the other fellow said it would be in our Letter of Authorization for Part 91 air tours. I told him that it was not in there and I would not give him my copy of the letter. I said that years before in another place I had given a FAA inspector a copy of my Part 135 Certificate when asked only to have him tear it up while saying I was out of business. This was illegal, I got mad and hit him — which was a new kettle of worms — but it was quickly decided that any individual FAA inspector cannot go around closing down businesses on his say so. Now this fellow with Edwin Lee got hot under the collar and he said "Step out on the dock and I will beat you to a bloody pulp". In exactly those words. I replied that if anything I had learned in life it was not to get physical with someone half my age. I was 83 years at that time while I put him around the 40 year mark. Three times he made the same statement — each time Edwin Lee backed a little further away from the counter and closer to the door. They did leave shortly so I called Dave Ryon to ask who this inspector was. Dave told me his name saying that he was a new hire and after this was exposed he probably would not last long — not even in Hawaii. Another interesting item came up when Valorie Reis got a letter on September 17, 2013 from Darrett Kanayamu of the Honolulu FAA office which spent 7 pages talking about flight operations that seem to cover Part 135 operations. What I found interesting is that Valorie got this correspondence sent to her home while myself or our business never did get this notification.

With Dave Ryon leaving this made the Honolulu FSDO reach out for a seaplane examiner and they came up with a fellow from Juneau, Alaska where seaplanes out number land planes. He made about three trips to Hawaii for our checkrides for two or three days before agreeing to transfer to Honolulu FSDO. The abundance of sunshine and easy flight conditions would look good to anyone from Juneau after a while. He did spend almost six months in Hawaii before he requested a transfer to Montana — the Honolulu FSDO was a strange place that ran everything their own way. A woman named K.C. Yakamara took over the Honolulu FSDO about that time and solved the problem of seaplane check rides by simply saying that Honolulu would not offer flight exams for seaplanes anymore — period. I immediately got on with fighting this saying it is a FAA rule that you must have a check ride to become a pilot in command so the FAA should have to provide the exam service. What would happen to aviation if all check rides were stopped? One of the founding principles of the FAA was the helping to promote aviation, but was later removed though. I did get quite a bit of support from a FAA official from the Western Region Office in Los Angeles, but then he retired. I never did get any reply at all from Washington, D.C. This went on for almost a year and approximately a $100,000.00 loss of revenue, then someone made the decision to make me a DPE (Designated Pilot Examiner). This was probably justified seeing that at that time I had about 30,000 accident free hours in seaplanes. I was allowed to do five flight exams before I had to attend the FAA School at Oklahoma City which I finally did. This solved the problem of checkrides until my flight medical went away. Even after my medical ran out I could still give some seaplane dual if the person had a seaplane rating and wanted some advanced training.

Now the Honolulu FSDO had to come up with another seaplane rated examiner. This time they chose one of their own people and sent him to a FAA approved seaplane training school in Florida. Florida does have several seaplane operations, but there is not much experience there — other than Jon Brown's — which is practically all Piper J-3 Cubs on floats. I will never forget one day I was driving into John's operation on Jessie Lake just outside of Winter Haven, Florida. It was a warm sunny day as is normal in that part of the world and my windows were all rolled down. I noticed a clatter of noise and glanced to my left — then decided to hold for traffic and stopped. I then watched Jon Brown slide in front of me on a crossroad in a 150 h.p. Piper Apache with the engines shut down and the gear up after loosing one engine on take-off. It slid down the street past me with the wings connecting with a couple of porches of houses trailers. I don't think he replaced that aircraft.

Back to the training of Honolulu's FAA seaplane examiner was completed in a few days when Kyle Bartler returned to do his duty. Scheduling was a large problem the first few weeks. One checkride that we had booked two weeks in advance never got done because he was too busy. This problem of getting rides got me into a lot of trouble with our Mr. Kyle Bartler. We had a pilot from Alaska who came down for a couple of months during the winter to get reacquainted with the sun. He did train a low time Private Pilot for a single engine seaplane rating and signed off his recommendation form, but then he went back to Alaska. We had been trying for a month to get a check ride. Now we finally got a checkride scheduled for the next week, but the applicant came into our office saying that he was not sure if he felt qualified after a five week period of not flying the Cessna 206 on floats. He had just under 70 hours total flight time with practically all in the Cessna 150. Without even thinking about it I said that I would go out with him for a quick run around the block and make things safer. He did well and did pass his check ride with no problem, but two days later I received a certified letter from Kyle Bartler charging me with a violation of flying without a medical certificate. This was sent on to the Renton, Washington FSDO. A week later I was told to send in my pilot's license or pay a $14,OOO.OO fine. My license was to be revoked for one year, then I could reapply starting from the student permit, private, commercial and each rating SEL, SES, MEL and MES. I had already been without a medical for almost two years then and figured that I was basically done flying after 63 years. I did go to a local medical examiner and took a third class medical exam and the doctor said I passed with flying colors, but the paperwork was rejected in Oklahoma City. I was in my later 80's in age and everyone thought I was too old to fly. Then the last straw happened not too much later which made me want to give up on aviation. We had a retiring military pilot who after a 20 year career as a pilot and had the astounding flight time of 2,098 total hours — flying off aircraft carriers. Now he was moving to Alaska which made him want to add a seaplane rating. He did not seem to have any problem with the training. Kyle Bartler came for the check ride.

They did the oral on our dock, taxied out for an easterly departure going to Kaneohe Bay for the water work followed by a return through Pali Pass. I was just walking on the dock as I noticed the aircraft turning final on Sealane 4. I noticed he was a little fast during the final approach.

He did skip on touchdown which made the aircraft rise almost ten feet in the air — no big deal — just add 4 to 5 inches of manifold pressure with a light touch of nose up pressure until the floats actually touch down again.

Immediately though our highly experienced examiner (under 30 hours float time) hit the throttle all the way forward to full power. Because of the low airspeed the rudder could not keep up with the "P" factor of the propeller turning at full speed making the aircraft turn 30 degrees or so to the left. This going sideways definitely restricts the ability to maintain flight which made the Cessna touch the water going sideways with the right bow striking first. There was a large amount of water splashing but the aircraft did not have enough speed to actually flip over. Wife Debbie was sitting in our floating bathroom and heard me shouting to "Shut down the power". It eventually floated right side up and the adventurers taxied up to the dock. We quickly got a float pump going on the float with quite a bit of water coming out. We then ran the plane up on one of our pneumatic ramps to get it out of the water so it would not sink. After pumping the floats dry, we started a damage assessment. There were almost a dozen rivet heads missing, and a slight bend in one of the Keelsons. Three or four hours went to replacing rivets and straightening, then the tram wires had to be loosened along with the float struts and bolts. The entire structure then carefully measured, aligned and retightened, and given a new coat of Poly paint. The check ride was repeated and completed the next week, but I had a problem that Kyle said several times that it was a good thing he was there to prevent a crash. He had no conception of what I was talking about when I mentioned "P factor". I think we lost money on that one! He caused the near crash!!

We spent 23 years in Hawaii after an eight year push to be allowed to work there. Amazing, most states go out of their way to promote business — including small businesses — jobs are needed for the locals. No jobs, no tax revenue. Hawaii though has a entirely different outlook. I have operated in quite a few states with Alaska leading the pack to help businesses grow with low taxes and few interferences.

We did meet some nice people in Hawaii though that still remain friends. Shortly after we got rolling we had a fellow come in and tell us he was a seaplane pilot — which got our attention seeing as there were not any seaplanes in Hawaii except ours. His name was Jay Katz who had flown for John Kelly on the Connecticut River. We talked a couple of times and then went out flying. We ended up offering him a part time job — as he did not want to give up his employment with Continental Airlines flying a Jet. His home base was in Honolulu so, he could spend some time flying for us. This worked well for a while until Continental closed their Honolulu Base and he had to choose between Guam or Newark, New Jersey. He went to Guam. As fine a man as you will ever meet.

Another fellow by the name of Clay Eveland (his uncle Harry Clark was a DC-3 flying legend in Hawaii) came in one day and said he was a seaplane pilot. He had gotten his rating in a Lake amphib in Oklahoma. He was working across the street as a mechanic and got involved in maintenance on our Beaver. He flew for us a couple of years (even made a few trips back to fly for us after he moved to America), married his wife Eve (who got her seaplane rating with us) and had their rousing reception on our floating dock. New flying job offers took he and his wife to the mainland. One summer he went to Ketchikan, Alaska to fly for Pro Mech Air on floats. He had lots of great stories and we still see and talk to both of them often to catch up on their new adventures flying jets. Growing up a Arkansas farm boy you could always count on Clay to get stuff done what ever it was, and always with a smile on his face. Clay and Eve are still good friends and in contact on a regular basis, Marco Alletto was born and raised in Italy where his brother died and left him $1,000,000.00. He migrated to the U.S. He was an avid scuba diver and he ran into Susie Cooper who also was a serious diver. They ended up getting married, buying a tri -maran sailboat in Mexico and sailing it to Hawaii.

Stopped by to visit Clay and Eve in Pennsylvania
after a trip to an air show on the east coast

Then he enrolled in a Private Pilot course at a flight school. He noticed our seaplanes one day and talked to us. Water was a big thing in his life and when he left he said he would start his seaplane rating the day he got his private license. Which he did. A week after he got his seaplane rating he told me he wanted to buy a Cessna 206 on floats. I gave him a copy of "Trade - A- Plane" and told him to look for an amphibian to make storage easier in Hawaii. It was not long before he was back with photos and specifications of a Cessna 206 on amphibs. Everything looked good and the price was right. So he went to Seattle to buy it, containerized it and shipped it back to Hawaii.

Later on we shot another movie at our dock "50 First Dates" and they paid Marco $2,000.00 to park his airplane at our dock, overnight along with ours. When they had the premier of the movie in Honolulu and on the first showing of all the aircraft, Marco jumped up yelling " Thatsa my plane". A few months later he took a flying job in King Salmon, Alaska. I told him that he would do better to start in Ketchikan where the terrain was a little easier. He did not last long in King Salmon and disappeared with a Beaver in the Shelikof Straights where it can often blow 70 knots or so. He had talked to another company aircraft shortly before saying the weather was low on the south end so he was going to try the Kamishak River to the north. A few parts were found in the water about a month later that were known to be from that Beaver. Tom Moss was a Hawaiian Airlines Captain who could not get enough flying.

He also was a member of the Civil Air Patrol as well as doing some instruction for one of the flight schools. He showed up at our office shortly after we arrived in Hawaii and got a seaplane rating. Then he also flew for us for quite a few years and was a very good pilot. One day when I was giving him dual for his rating we got held up by ATC returning through Pali Pass and were higher than we wanted. We had to make a steep descent with low fuel when the engine quit. I told Tom that I had it and made the landing while overshooting the dock. We had informed the tower and by the time I sailed close to the dock there were FAA personal standing on the dock. It was pretty breezy which blew me up to the shoreline about 30 feet before I reached the dock. Wife Debbie immediately waded out waist deep in the water to keep the floats from hitting the rocks. Then one of the FAA fellows came and helped her making it possible to safely tie it up. The other two just stood there holding their brief cases. Evidently the helping hand got in trouble at the FSDO office afterward and left less than a month later. He did stop in to tell us that he could not work anywhere he was not allowed to help someone in trouble.

Mike Hudgens was another pilot who walked down the ramp of our floating seaplane base in Honolulu saying he wanted to be a seaplane pilot. That was easy and we had him checked out pretty quickly. He was a Boeing 747 captain for Japan Air Lines (JAL) based in Honolulu, so he started as a part time pilot. Awhile later Japan Airlines laid off their U.S. 747 pilots based in Honolulu replacing them with Japanese pilots. Mike then became a full-time seaplane pilot and started fixing up his house in Kaneohe.

After a few years flying seaplanes for us Mike finnaly reached his dream of becoming a Alaska Seaplane Pilot.

Later on Alaska called and he went to Ketchikan for the summer — which ended up being seven summers. He always said that his dream in life was being a bush pilot. He started off with Pro Mech Air flying Beavers and then moved down the street to Turbine Otters at Taquan Air. Before he went to Alaska, I checked him out on how to hand prop a Beaver on floats. He had a big smile on his face when it started. After that he and his wife moved to Key West, Florida there they owned a house from Mike's time as a pilot in the Navy.

I believe that our former seaplane pilots who went on to flying wheel aircraft of any sort, worked out to be better pilots due to their time flying seaplanes which taught them to use all their senses and to think out of the box. It was my pleasure to help mentor these younger aviators to live their dreams.

CHAPTER 38

THE END - ALMOST

I flew for 63 years for a total of 40,800 flight hours without an accident. Just over 33,000 of those hours were on floats, 6,000 hours were on skis on frozen lakes and rivers. That leaves less than 2,000 hours on wheels with most of that not on paved airports. A lot of sand beach landings at low tide, gravel roads and paved highways, 600 foot runways, one 800 foot runway with a 45 degree bend in it and one 1,800 foot gravel runway where the bottom end was 400 feet lower than the top — land uphill, take off downhill. I owned 488 aircraft in that 63 years and had over 300 pilots flying for me, but I am proud to say that I never had a passenger so much as cut a finger in all that flying — most of it pretty hard flying. I personally had seven complete engine failures, but never put a mark on an airplane. I did put some holes in my floats though. Quite a few lakes and rivers had some dark colored water that made it hard to spot under water obstructions — or fast currents. I learned early to carry some patching material — several small pieces of aluminum, a Yankee drill, some sheet metal screws, small bolts with nuts and a ½ pint of roofing tar to heat for sealant. Later on some one came out with a two part epoxy that you mixed, slapped it on and waited for it to harden. We called it "super goop". It did make seaplane flying in the bush a little easier. There were quite a few changes during that 63 years, but the whole thing was a lot of fun. I would not have missed it for anything.

When I started there was basically one aviation fuel — 80/87 octane and almost every engine manufacturer offered a brand new radial engine. There is nothing of either available nowadays. In the 1950's there were few turbine engines, but many to choose from today. Myself, I still find it more fun to fly round engines and I still fly for fun! I made my last flight late in November of 2018 at the age of 88. I was going to taxi our Beaver from our base at Keehi Lagoon in Honolulu to a marine center at end of the lagoon where Debbie and I were going to dismantle it to put into a container. I guess it dawned on me that I probably would not fly again, so I took off flew five feet off the water to the marina — about four minutes — and the Tower did not notice.

My father started flying in 1920 and had pilot license #8 signed by Wilbur and Orville Wright. He was grounded for awhile during 1923 when he flew under the aerial bridge in the Duluth, Minnesota Harbor in a Jenny when it was raised to let a ship in. His last license was #229 in 1930. He had two Lockheed Vegas on floats that he used for delivering mail around the shores of Lake Superior, but that folded up in the Great Depression. He then flew a short stint with the U.S. mail based out of Wausau, Wisconsin, but in 1932 he took a job with FDR's Civilian Conservation Corps (CCC).

I raised four children — two boys and two girls — and they all ended up being very involved in aviation. My oldest son made a mistake when he went for a ride with someone else and died in February, 2018. He was a good pilot with 27,000 hours total flight time and 22,000 hours of seaplane flight time. He also was the only seaplane pilot I knew that had flown a seaplane on every continent on this earth — except Antartica where seaplanes are not used. He went for a ride with a fellow who ended up in the St. Johns River in Florida in a Kodiak Quest aircraft on wheels after dark. He was in the RH seat on the third attempt to land on a grass airfield where the pilot lived.

Wife Debbie has been a "cannot do without" through many ups

and downs. I hired a fellow to strip a DeHavilland Beaver for a repaint, but after half a day he quit — too messy and too much work. Debbie stepped right up and said that she would do it — and she did. Even lost her fingerprints for a while. But now I can say that I married a "Stripper"! Along with being a terrific traveling companion.

I will be 90 years shortly (April 29, 2020), but hope to start a small fishing camp in Alaska to finish up my working years and then retire for the last years. It has been a wonderful life so far, but I would like to do some more hunting and fishing before it is too late. If you like wilderness fishing for all five species of Pacific Salmon, plus Halibut, Cod, Pink Snapper, Rainbows, Steelhead, Dolly Varden, Cutthroat Trout, Artic Grayling, Dungeness Crab Shrimp plus some other bottom fish with good limits, you can realize a generous discount by telling us you have read this book. Just e-mail me at seaplaneservice@aol.com.

Alaska Airlines comes in twice a day, but seaplanes are not needed to go fishing. Looking forward to hearing from you and to helping you live your adventure.

Be sure to watch for my next book Titled "101 Ways to start a seaplane business" coming soon which tells how, where and how much.

APPENDIX

The appendix section covers several time consuming battles with government agencies. The first part was about the attack on 9/11/2001. We were given a 100 day shutdown by the White House and FAA which makes us the longest shut down flight operation in the U.S. Everyone else was flying again within two and one half weeks. We documented cancellations of $107,000.00 of flights and were promised restitution by the government. However the White House (even after two bills being passed to pay us) decided they could not afford to pay us. There is also mention of two different times that the FAA proposed making all Part 91 operators go FAR Part 135. This was mainly a ploy on their part to control more commercial operators and get a larger budget. We proved several times that Part 91 operators had a better safety record. Then we had 23 years of fighting with the State of Hawaii Airports Division about payments we had already made, but got charged interest up to a years time because they did not credit our account. One time we mailed a cashier's check for $8,000.00 which did not get cashed for a month and to this day never showed up as a credit to our account. For 23 years we leased a 50 foot by 300 foot piece of man made land so that we could build a floating office, home and 225 feet of floating dock. After 23 years they raised our rent from $28,000.00 to $91,000.00 annually (with less than a 30 day notice), so we gave up. I made my last flight at the age of 88. Whatta Life!

GPO's PDF version of this bill	References to this bill in the Congressional Record	Link to the Bill Summary & Status file.	*Full Display* - 7,901 bytes.[Help]

General Aviation Industry Reparations Act of 2001 (Introduced in the House)

HR 3347 IH

107th CONGRESS

1st Session

H. R. 3347

To provide economic relief to general aviation entities that have suffered substantial economic injury as a result of the terrorist attacks perpetrated against the United States on September 11, 2001.

IN THE HOUSE OF REPRESENTATIVES

November 27, 2001

Mr. MICA (for himself, Mr. YOUNG of Alaska, and Mr. SHUSTER) introduced the following bill; which was referred to the Committee on Transportation and Infrastructure, and in addition to the Committees on Financial Services and the Budget, for a period to be subsequently determined by the Speaker, in each case for consideration of such provisions as fall within the jurisdiction of the committee concerned

A BILL

To provide economic relief to general aviation entities that have suffered substantial economic injury as a result of the terrorist attacks perpetrated against the United States on September 11, 2001.

Be it enacted by the Senate and House of Representatives of the United States of America in Congress assembled,

SECTION 1. SHORT TITLE.

This Act may be cited as the 'General Aviation Industry Reparations Act of 2001'.

SEC. 2. GENERAL AVIATION INDUSTRY REPARATIONS.

MINORITY WHIP-AT-LARGE

DEMOCRATIC CAUCUS
EDUCATION TASK FORCE
CO-CHAIR

COMMITTEES:
EDUCATION AND THE
WORKFORCE

SUBCOMMITTEES:
21ST CENTURY COMPETITIVENESS
RANKING MEMBER

WORKFORCE PROTECTION

GOVERNMENT REFORM

SUBCOMMITTEES:
ENERGY POLICY, NATURAL RESOURCES
AND REGULATORY AFFAIRS
TECHNOLOGY AND PROCUREMENT POLICY

Patsy T. Mink
Congress of the United States
2nd District, Hawaii

WASHINGTON, DC OFFICE:
2210 RAYBURN HOUSE OFFICE BUILDING
WASHINGTON, DC 20515-1102
PHONE: (202) 225-4906
FAX: (202) 225-4987

http://www.house.gov/writerep/
WEB:http//www.house.gov/mink

HAWAII OFFICE:
5104 PRINCE KUHIO FEDERAL BUILDING
HONOLULU, HI 96850-4977
PHONE: (808) 541-1986
FAX: (808) 538-0233

BIG ISLAND: 935-3756
MAUI: 242-1818
KAUAI: 245-1951

February 20, 2002

Pat And Debbie Magie
Owners
Island Seaplane Service
P.O. Box 30685
Honolulu HI 96820

Dear Pat and Debbie:

I enclose a letter to Secretary Mineta inquiring what relief is available to you due to the excessive federal mandated grounding of your business.

I am also happy to cosponsor H.R. 3347, the General Aviation Industry Reparations Act of 2001. My name will appear on the cosponsor list along with 30 of my colleagues when the House goes back into session on February 26, 2002. I am informed that the bill's sponsor, Representative Mica, the Chairman on the House Subcommittee on Aviation has reported H.R. 3347 out of his subcommittee to the full Transportation Committee.

I remain hopeful that H.R. 3347 will immediately pass and that the Department of Transportation is immediately able to offer you financial relief.

Very truly yours,

PATSY T. MINK
Member of Congress

MINORITY WHIP-AT-LARGE

DEMOCRATIC CAUCUS
EDUCATION TASK FORCE
CO-CHAIR

COMMITTEES:
EDUCATION AND THE
WORKFORCE

SUBCOMMITTEES:
21ST CENTURY COMPETITIVENESS
RANKING MEMBER

WORKFORCE PROTECTION

GOVERNMENT REFORM

SUBCOMMITTEES:
ENERGY POLICY, NATURAL RESOURCES
AND REGULATORY AFFAIRS
TECHNOLOGY AND PROCUREMENT POLICY

Patsy T. Mink
Congress of the United States
2nd District, Hawaii

2210 RAYBURN HOUSE OFFICE BUILDING
WASHINGTON, DC 20515-1102
PHONE: (202) 225-4906
FAX: (202) 225-4987

http://www.house.gov/writerep/
WEB:http/www.house.gov/mink

HAWAII OFFICE:
5104 PRINCE KUHIO FEDERAL BUILDING
HONOLULU, HI 96850-4977
PHONE: (808) 541-1986
FAX: (808) 538-0233

BIG ISLAND: 935-3756
MAUI: 242-1818
KAUAI: 245-1951

February 20, 2002

The Honorable Norman Mineta
Secretary
U.S. Department of Transportation
400 7th St. SW
Washington DC 20590

Fax: (202) 366-7202

COPY

Dear Secretary Mineta:

I write to inquire what relief the federal government can offer to small charter plane or helicopter (Part 91 operators) businesses that were forced to shut down after the tragic events of September 11, 2001.

In Hawaii, Island Seaplane Service Inc. was not allowed to fly from September 11, 2001, until December 19, 2001. This is outrageous!

Since the federal government mandated that they were not allowed to fly, they should be entitled to federal relief!

Their insurance premiums jumped up $4,000 a month and their fixed costs total $1,000 a day. No business can survive with these costs when they are not allowed to work.

Please advise what relief is available to Part 91 operators who were shut down by the federal government for an excessive period of time.

Your prompt attention to this inquiry will be appreciated.

Very truly yours,

PATSY T. MINK
Member of Congress

286

U.S. House of Representatives
Committee on Transportation and Infrastructure
Washington, DC 20515

May 1, 2002

Compensate general aviation!!!
Support H.R. 3347

Dear Colleague:

In the aftermath of the September 11th attack, the federal government ordered all aviation grounded. Commercial aviation was grounded for **four days**. General aviation was grounded even longer. This action was necessary to protect the public safety. Congress enacted legislation to provide compensation for the four days of direct losses suffered by the big commercial airlines and also provided a loan program to keep troubled air carriers operating. This was the right thing to do and it was instrumental in saving our aviation transportation system. We now need to provide the same fair compensation for the small general aviation businesses who were grounded, in some cases, for several months.

The closure of all general aviation businesses resulted in the loss of millions of dollars and thousands of jobs. The General Aviation industry responded in a truly patriotic way by working with the federal government and Congress to protect the safety and well being of the public. However, they are now the forgotten victims of this tragedy. These businesses did not lose money because they chose to shut down – they were ordered to shut down by the federal government.

I believe that it is wrong for the federal government to take away any person's private business for benefit of the general public and then fail to fairly compensate that person as provided in the 5th Amendment of the U.S. Constitution.

On February 27, 2002 the Committee on Transportation and Infrastructure, by voice vote, reported H.R. 3347, a bill that provides relief to those general aviation businesses that were ordered to be grounded by the federal government in the months after September 11th. The bill provides both compensation for direct losses which must be supported by documentation and also a loan guarantee program for troubled businesses. The bill has bipartisan support.

Unfortunately, there are those who oppose the bill because "it costs money." Doing the right thing and respecting the spirit of the U.S. Constitution frequently will "cost money.". However, the precedent of allowing a federal agency to unilaterally shut down a business for several months without any accountability and without requiring the payment of any compensation is one that should concern all of us.

I urge you to join with me in contacting the leadership of both parties to schedule H.R. 3347 for further action in the House of Representatives. Let's do the right thing again.

Sincerely,

DON YOUNG
Chairman

island seaplane service inc.

85 Lagoon Drive • Honolulu, HI 96819 • Tel (808) 836-6273 • Fax (808) 836-7861 • Mailing Address: P.O. Box 30685, Honolulu, HI 96820

May 16, 2002

George W. Bush, President
The White House
1600 Pennsylvania Avenue NW
Washington, DC 20500

A Story of Small Business vs. Big Government

I have been in Aviation for over 40 years, accumulated over 35,000 of accident free flying time, served in the Marine Corps during the Korean conflict and raised four children who are all active in Aviation. My wife and I moved from Alaska to Hawaii in 1996 and invested nearly a million dollars in starting a seaplane sightseeing tour business. During 1998, 1999, and 2000 we lost money, but 2001 saw a turnaround and we started making a profit. We were the only air tour in <u>all</u> of Hawaii recommended by the National Geographic Traveler Guide for the years 2001 and 2002 and the only one on the Island of Oahu recommended by Frommer's Travel Guides for 2000, 2001, and 2002. Then, following the September 11th disaster, we were shut down completely by a knee jerk government action. We were not allowed to work again until 4:00pm December 19th when the shut down order died a natural death. For 100 days the government, George Bush, Condeleesa Rice and the FAA refused to let us make a living.

Now these governmental agencies and the same people do not want to make any repayment of the monies that we lost due to their action. How can the government legally deprive us of our way of making a living and not be compelled to pay us back our losses? They are trying to prevent HR 3347 from coming before Congress. This is the House bill introduced by John L. Mica (D-FL) that was designed to give some restitution to small general aviation companies that were not re-imbursed as the airlines and Part 135 operators were. Part 91 operators in Class B airspace fell into a large crack somewhere --- the only operators being shut down for 100 days and then being the only operators not receiving any financial restitution.

 seaplane tours

288

island seaplane service inc.

85 Lagoon Drive • Honolulu, HI 96819 • Tel (808) 836-6273 • Fax (808) 836-7861 • Mailing Address: P.O. Box 30685, Honolulu, HI 96820

somewhere — the only operators being shut down for 100 days and then being the only operators not receiving any financial restitution.

In a letter (04-30-02) to Don Young (R-AK) Norman Mineta (Sec.-DOT) made the statement that the government is financially hurting because of the September 11th disaster and cannot afford to repay businesses that they forced to close. Don Young answered (05-01-02) that Amendment #5 of the Constitution actually prohibits the government form depriving people of their property (business) without repaying them. In spite of the government's supposed financial shortage, each member of Congress received a substantial pay raise this fall and also Congress is proposing to pay farmers 180 _billion_ dollars not to grow crops. We would be happy not to grow anything if we could get paid!!

We would not even be asking for restitutions if we had been allowed to go back to work within the first three weeks like all of the other operators ---FAR Part 121 and FAR Part 135. However the government deemed us a national security risk and kept us closed down for 100 days!! Thus we feel that we are entitled to get back the expense money we were forced to spend to stay here until we were allowed to operate again. We are not talking about profits that we could have made — just the expense monies required to stay open.

We urgently need the passage of HR 3347 very quickly or we will go out of business and lose our investment and retirement. We have done everything possible to avoid this. We even took in a partner to survive this long, but our days are numbered now. We need this legislation enacted. SOME TIMES _DOING THE RIGHT THING_ DOES COST MONEY!

Sincerely yours,

Pat Magie, President
ISLAND SEAPLANE SERVICE INC.

 seaplane tours

island seaplane service inc.

85 Lagoon Drive • Honolulu, HI 96819 • Tel (808) 836-6273 • Fax (808) 836-7861 • Mailing Address: P.O. Box 30685, Honolulu, HI 96820

George W. Bush, President   *June 26, 2002*

Dear Mr. President,

Thank you for your letter of June 6th. To me your reply sounds like that of a politician who wants to avoid saying anything. I thought my letter May 16th to you was fairly concise as to my thoughts and concerns of needing financial restitution of income your administration took away from our business.

I have enclosed a copy of my last letter as well as your unrelated reply. I was looking for support of H.R. Bill 3347 and S. Bill 2007 both of which were authored to provide relief for small aircraft operators that work under Federal Air Regulations Part 91. We suffered direct losses of approximately $100,000.00 with a Federally mandated shut down of 100 days following September 11th. It required about $1,000.00 per day to cover insurance expenses, aircraft and vehicle payments, rents, permit costs and other expenses to stay here until we were allowed to work again.

Now your administration has asked Congress to refrain from reimbursing us for our losses that were incurred by your shut down because the Government cannot afford to pay us. Last week I did see in the newspapers that you are proposing to give away millions of dollars to poor people that cannot accumulate enough funds to make a down payment on a home purchase. Because of our large investment in our business we have not been able to make a down payment on our own house either. Maybe we will qualify for your government giveaway on this program.

I would really appreciate a reply with your thoughts on the administration forcing our business closure and not re-paying us . This definitely should be unconstitutional and certainly is unconscionable.

Your letter stated that government should be limited and not overbearing, but we still feel that your shut down will put us out of business if we are not reimbursed. We do consider that 100 day closure and no payback was overbearing.

> *Sincerely yours,*
> *Pat Magie, President*

ISLAND SEAPLANE SERVICE INC.

 seaplane tours

February 24, 2004

George W. Bush, President
The White House
1600 Pennsylvania Avenue NW
Washington D.C. 20500

Dear President Bush,

Our governmental system is very disappointing. We were ordered to close our doors on September 11, 2001 by government order and were forced to remain shut down for 100 days with no compensation for the $100,000 in expenses we had to spend to sit here. We wrote hundreds of letters to the Administration, other officials and members of Congress with barely any replies. Congressman John Mica and Senator James Inhofe sponsored H.R. 3347 early in 2002 that would have provided us financial aid, but the Administration asked Congress to kill the bill and the bill died. Our main response from Washington D.C. has been from several attorneys from DOT saying that they feel it is entirely legal for the government to close down U.S. businesses without compensating them.

Last spring H.R. 2115 surfaced, sponsored by Congressman John Mica again, that would provide economic relief for Far Part 91 operators and other aviation businesses financially hurt by September 11, 2001 Closures. This bill was passed by the House and Senate last fall and signed into law -- Public Law 108-176--when President Bush signed it December 12, 2003. Then the ball got dropped again in January, 2004 when no funds were appropriated to meet the terms of the law.

Many aviation businesses have closed up since the knee jerk shut down of 9-11.. A few weeks after 9-11 flight instruction in Enhanced Class B airspace was allowed again. Then I could legally give flight instruction to a student pilot and the student pilot even could fly solo in the Class B airspace but I as a Certified Flight Instructor with 36,000 hours of accident - free flight time could not fly solo in this same airspace. Who can understand this ?

Our nation has recently spent billions of dollars blowing up Iraq and is now spending billions more rebuilding Iraq- but citizens of our own country cannot get repaid for unfair and unjust government shut-downs. Who needs a government like this ? We need your support in righting this wrong and move to get funding for the aviation operators hurt by 9-11 and were supposed to receive restitutions with Public law 108-176.

Sincerely Yours,

Pat Magie, President
ISLAND SEAPLANE SERVICE INC.

DANIEL K. INOUYE
HAWAII

APPROPRIATIONS
Subcommittee on Defense -- Ranking Member

COMMERCE, SCIENCE, AND TRANSPORTATION
Subcommittee on Surface Transportation and
Merchant Marine

COMMITTEE ON INDIAN AFFAIRS---Vice Chairman

DEMOCRATIC STEERING AND COORDINATION
COMMITTEE

COMMITTEE ON RULES AND ADMINISTRATION

United States Senate
SUITE 722, HART SENATE OFFICE BUILDING
WASHINGTON, DC 20510--1102
(202) 224-3934
FAX (202) 224-6747

PRINCE KUHIO FEDERAL BUILDING
ROOM 7-212, 300 ALA MOANA BOULEVARD
HONOLULU, HI 96850-4975
(808) 541-2542
FAX (808) 541-2549

101 AUPUNI STREET, NO. 206
HILO, HI 96720
(808) 935-0844
FAX (808) 961-6163

March 10, 2004

Mr. Pat Magie
President
Island Seaplane Service, Inc.
85 Lagoon Drive
Honolulu, Hawaii 96819

Dear Mr. Magie:

Thank you for your letter regarding the economic hardship you continue to experience due to the limitations placed on general aviation operations after the terrorist attack on September 11, 2001.

I share your frustration that general aviation businesses did not receive any financial relief from the federal government. Therefore, I was pleased that, as a first step, the Aviation Reauthorization bill, Public Law 108-176, enacted earlier this year authorized payments to certain businesses harmed by the restrictions placed on FAR Part 91 Operators, including a provision I requested to provide relief to air tour operators. This legislation provides the legal authority for the Department of Transportation to make such payments. The payments can not be made until funds have been appropriated by the Congress for that purpose. In addition, once funds are provided, the Administration must develop regulations governing the disbursement of those funds.

Unfortunately, the Aviation Reauthorization bill was approved too late in the year to secure funding in the Fiscal Year 2004 Appropriations Bill. Please be assured that I will request funding for this reimbursement program in the Fiscal Year 2005 Departments of Transportation and Treasury, and Related Agencies Appropriations Bill. I know it will give you not comfort to hear that this is an exceptionally difficult budgetary year. You can be assured however, that I will do my best.

Mr. Pat Magie
March 10, 2004
Page 2

Thank you for taking the time to share your concerns with me. I will keep them in mind as my colleagues and I work to develop the Fiscal year 2005 Appropriations Bills.

Aloha,

DANIEL K. INOUYE
United States Senator

DKI:cae

STATE OF HAWAII
DEPARTMENT OF TRANSPORTATION
AIRPORTS DIVISION -- OAHU DISTRICT
HONOLULU INTERNATIONAL AIRPORT
300 RODGERS BOULEVARD, #12
HONOLULU, HAWAII 96819-1830

BRENNON T. MORIOKA
DIRECTOR

Deputy Directors
MICHAEL D. FORMBY
FRANCIS PAUL KEENO
BRIAN H. SEKIGUCHI
JIRO A. SUMADA

IN REPLY REFER TO:

AIR-OL
09.0099

December 22, 2009

TO: ALL CONCERNED

FROM: JAMES W. PRATT
          ACTING OAHU DISTRICT AIRPORTS MANAGER

SUBJECT: INCREASE IN WATER/SEWER FEES AT HONOLULU INTERNATIONAL
          AIRPORT

The City and County of Honolulu and Board of Water Supply have increased water and sewer
fees for the Honolulu International Airport and our surrounding properties as follows:

Water Charge	=	$2.98 (per 1,000 gallons)
Power Cost Adjustment	=	$0.058 (per 1,000 gallons)
TOTAL WATER CHARGES	=	$3.038 (per 1,000 gallons)
TOTAL SEWER CHARGE	=	$8.66 (per 1,000 gallons)
TOTAL WATER/SEWER CHARGE	**=**	**$11.698 (per 1,000 gallons)**

[handwritten annotation: 5.98 / 2.98 / -2.68 over check / per 100]

As a result of recent increases, Honolulu International Airport invoices shall reflect the new rate
of $11.698 (per 1,000 gallons) effective November 1, 2009.

Should you have any questions, please contact Mr. Deane Kadokawa, Landside Operations
Manager, at 836-6522.

island seaplane service inc.

13

85 Lagoon Drive • Honolulu, HI 96819 • Tel (808) 836-6273 • Fax (808) 836-7861
Mailing Address: P.O. Box 30685, Honolulu, HI 96820 • E-mail: seaplaneservice@aol.com • www.islandseaplane.com

December 24, 2009

James Pratt
State of Hawaii - Airports Division
Honolulu International Airport
300 Rodgers Boulevard, #12
Honolulu, HI 96819-1830

Aloha Jim,

Per our phone conversation a few minutes ago about the water charges. We received your letter yesterday about the increase in fees for water charges. I am not complaining ~about the increase in fees, but I did notice the rate per 1000 gallons is rising from $2.98 per unit to $3.038. This caught my attention as we have been paying $5.66 per 1000 gallons for the past 13 years.

I have been talking to your people about the water bills and the fact that we would like to see the meter readings on the bill each month. I have enclosed copies of the May, 2009 and June, 2009 billings. You will notice the billing amount on each bill is $141.50, but the amount of water gallon age is considerably different. It took months to get this squared away - they simply wrote out a new billing statement to make it work out. We would still like to see the meter reading on each bill like everyone else does. Also we do not have a sewer hookup.

Sincerely yours,

Pat Magie, Owner
Island Seaplane Service Inc.

seaplane tours

BRENNON T. MORIOKA
DIRECTOR

Deputy Directors
MICHAEL D. FORMBY
FRANCIS PAUL KEENO
BRIAN H. SEKIGUCHI
JIRO A. SUMADA

IN REPLY REFER TO:

AIR-OL
10.0002

STATE OF HAWAII
DEPARTMENT OF TRANSPORTATION
AIRPORTS DIVISION – OAHU DISTRICT
HONOLULU INTERNATIONAL AIRPORT
300 RODGERS BOULEVARD, #12
HONOLULU, HAWAII 96819-1830

January 6, 2010

Mr. Pat Magie
ISLAND SEAPLANE SERVICE, INC.
P.O. Box 30685
Honolulu, Hawaii 96820

Dear Mr. Magie:

This letter is in response to your letter dated December 24, 2009.

We are pleased to advise you that the Airports Division's Fiscal Office is moving forward on your request to include water meter readings on invoices.

As far as not being able to provide you with reasonable access to the airport's main sewer line, we decided to stop charging Island Seaplane Service sewer fees.

Mr. Deane Kadokawa, Landside Operations Manager, will reconcile your account and inform you of our findings.

If you have any questions, please feel free to contact Mr. Kadokawa at 836-6522.

Sincerely,

James W. Pratt
Acting Manager
Oahu District Airports

island seaplane service inc.

85 Lagoon Drive • Honolulu, HI 96819 • Tel (808) 836-6273 • Fax (808) 836-7861
Mailing Address: P.O. Box 30685, Honolulu, HI 96820 • E-mail: seaplaneservice@aol.com • www.islandseaplane.com

March 23 2010

James Pratt
Acting Manager Oahu District Airports
State of Hawaii - Airports Division
Honolulu International Airport
300 Rodgers Boulevard, # 12
Honolulu, Hawaii 96819-1830

Dear Jim,

First, I would like to thank you for the assistance in alerting the Sheriff Department March 1ˢᵗ when we held our press conference here at the seaplane base. That was certainly appreciated.

Second, I am still trying to get to the bottom of our water usage billings. I spoke to Deane Kadokawa the afternoon of December 23, 2009 about it and he said he would get back to me Monday, December 28ᵗʰ, 2009regarding the increase of water rates to$3.038 per 1000 gallons of water effective November 1, 2009. My concerns then were that we have been billed $5.66 per 1000 gallons for the past 13 years. I did write you on December 24ᵗʰ,2009 about this and you answered January 6, 2010 that you were not going to charge us sewer chares seeing as we do not have a sewer line. I currently have water bills from October, November and December that are billed wrong, and do not want to pay these until the proper amounts are billed.

Just now as I write, Deane Kdokawa called and we spoke of these things. I faxed him copies of the last three billings and he said he would get back to me . Happily, we are now getting meter readings on the bill.

> *Warm Aloha's*
> *Pat Magie*

 ## seaplane tours

LINDA LINGLE
GOVERNOR

MARK J. BENNETT
ATTORNEY GENERAL

LISA M. GINOZA
FIRST DEPUTY ATTORNEY GENERAL

STATE OF HAWAII
DEPARTMENT OF THE ATTORNEY GENERAL
Civil Recoveries Division
425 QUEEN STREET
HONOLULU, HAWAII 96813
(808) 586-1100 Tel
(808) 586-1111 Fax

April 26, 2010

<u>**VIA FACSIMILE NO: 836-7861**</u>

Mr. Pat Magie
c/o Island Seaplane Service Inc.
85 Lagoon Drive
Honolulu, HI 96819

RE: <u>Sewer System Credit</u>

Dear Mr. Magie:

Thank you for your letter of last week regarding overcharges on the water. As it turns out, Airports Division fiscal has been working on this accounting which goes back to 1998 and it appears that you have a credit in excess of $6,000.00.

Airports Division proposes to close out your payment plan indebtedness ($4,000.00 plus) by applying the credit as set off. Details to follow.

Very truly yours,

JOHN P. GILLMOR
Deputy Attorney General

JPG:gv

cc: Dean Kadokawa, Airports Division
    Julene Hiruya, Airports Division, Fiscal
    Chris Ferrera, Esq.

island seaplane service inc.

85 Lagoon Drive • Honolulu, HI 96819 • Tel (808) 836-6273 • Fax (808) 836-7861

Mailing Address: P.O. Box 30685, Honolulu, HI 96820 • E-mail: seaplaneservice@aol.com • www.islandseaplane.com

April 28, 2010

State of Hawaii
Department of Attorney General
Attn: John Gillmor
425 Queen street
Honolulu, Hawaii 96813

Aloha John,

We seen to be getting close to ending the "Saga of water charges". Airports tells me we have a credit of $6,782.20 due and I assume that interest will be added to that and, of course, more interest for each day that it still drags on.

Excuse my passion about this interest, but I keep getting charged for interest without ever being told what it is for. I have enclosed a bill received a couple of weeks ago that has 22 amounts charged as "interest", but I have no idea of what it is for. Interest on this one monthly statement totaled $595.34 with no explanation of what it is for. The statement also does not show ay payment on account. The billing for 03/01/2010 was paid on 03/19/10 and the billing on 04/01/10 was paid on 04/07/10, but they do not show up as being paid. We also paid the three water billings of $181.12, $66.84 and $115.44 on 04/16/10 after waiting to get them corrected for several months. It does not show up on the statement, but we did make payments totaling $5141.40 during the statement period.

I would like to finish up this affair as soon as possible, but I feel that we should have a meeting to straighten out all these interest charges.

Sincerely yours

Pat Magie

seaplane tours

300

island seaplane service inc.

85 Lagoon Drive • Honolulu, HI 96819 • Tel (808) 836-6273 • Fax (808) 836-7861
Mailing Address: P.O. Box 30685, Honolulu, HI 96820 • E-mail: seaplaneservice@aol.com • www.islandseaplane.com

May 28, 2010

State of Hawaii
Department of the Attorney General
Attn: John Gillmor
425 Queen Street
Honolulu, Hawaii 96813

Dear John,

This is almost poetic being this is hopefully a "Dear John" letter. All that is left now is to straighten out the arithmetic.

Per your letter of May 11th, the following should happen

5/11	Rent Account due (including 11/08)	$4,778.00
5/11	Repay plan due (to 5/11)	+ 4,836.89
		9,614.89
5/11	Paid Repay plan	- 1,000.00
		8,614.89
5/8	Paid Rent Account (check #1607, cashed 5/13)	- 2,389.00
		6,225.89
	Minus Interest credit (per your letter 5/10)	- 604.13
		5,621.76
	Minus Water over pay credit	- 6,782.20
	Plus balance Island Seaplane Credit	+$1,160.44

Thus our credit should be $1,160.44 not $569.11. It looks like the interest credit of $604.13 was left out of the tally. Please verify this, so we can make our June rent payment.

Sincerely yours
Pat Magie

CC: Dean Kadokawa, Airports Division
Julene Hiruya, Airports Division, Fiscal
Chris Ferrera, Esq.

 seaplane tours

LINDA LINGLE
GOVERNOR

MARK J. BENNETT
ATTORNEY GENERAL

RUSSELL A. SUZUKI
FIRST DEPUTY ATTORNEY GENERAL

STATE OF HAWAII
DEPARTMENT OF THE ATTORNEY GENERAL
Civil Recoveries Division
425 QUEEN STREET
HONOLULU, HAWAII 96813
(808) 586-1100 Tel
(808) 586-1111 Fax

June 14, 2010

Pat Magie
Island Seaplane Service, Inc.
P.O. Box 30685
Honolulu, HI 96820

  RE: Island Seaplane Service, Inc.

Dear Mr. Magie:

  Thank you for your letter of May 28, 2010. It has taken me a few days to figure out what has happened. The problem is that there is an error in my May 11, 2010 letter to you. The amount of both credits ($604.13 interest credit and $6,782.20 water credit) is correct. However, the $4,778.00 current amount balance is incorrect. That figure is the actual current balance of $5,382.13 less the interest credit of $604.13. With respect to the accounting shown on your letter of May 28, this would mean that the interest credit was taken twice. There is also the matter of an additional credit for interest for May of 12.80. The correct May 28, 2010 balance would be $569.11, after taking all credits.

  With respect to June, 2010, there is a water charge of $230.88 in addition to monthly rent of $2,389.00. After applying the credit balance carried over from May 2010, total amount due for June 2010 is $2,050.77.

  I like to be of assistance whenever I can in facilitating discussions between tenants and Airports Division. In this case, however, I erred in stating the actual amount of the balance due on the current account ($5,382.13, not $4,778.00) and for that I apologize.

         Very truly yours,

         JOHN P. GILLMOR
         Deputy Attorney General

JPG:ls

cc: Ross Higashi , DOT, Airports Division, Fiscal
  Julene Hiruya, Airports Division, Fiscal
  Christopher D. Ferrara, Esq.

island seaplane service inc.

85 Lagoon Drive • Honolulu, HI 96819 • Tel (808) 836-6273 • Fax (808) 836-7861
Mailing Address: P.O. Box 30685, Honolulu, HI 96820 • E-mail: seaplaneservice@aol.com • www.islandseaplane.com

June 19, 2010

State of Hawaii
Dept. Of Attorney General
Attn: John Gillmor
425 Queen St, Room 212 DOT
Honolulu, Hawaii 96813

Aloha John,

I give up - I keep hearing different number as to what we owe on such and such a day. We did pay the three monthly water bills for February, March and April that we received on June 2 and the bank shows them paid on June 11. So I added the $230.88 back into the credit of $569.11 making a total credit of $799.99. I have enclosed a copy of our check for $1,589.01 to cover June rent and really would appreciate notice if it is applied elsewhere.

We do like the fact that we are finally getting meter readings on our water bills. Now it would be nice to get a water bill each month instead of lumping several of them together.

Sincerely yours

Pat Magie, President
Island Seaplane Service Inc.

CC: State Of Hawaii DOT Airports Division
Accounts Receivable
Honolulu International Airport
400 Rodgers Boulevard Suite 700
Honolulu, Hawaii 96819-1880

 seaplane tours

island seaplane service inc.

85 Lagoon Drive • Honolulu, HI 96819 • Tel (808) 836-6273 • Fax (808) 836-7861
Mailing Address: P.O. Box 30685, Honolulu, HI 96820 • E-mail: seaplaneservice@aol.com • www.islandseaplane.com

July 12, 2010

State of Hawaii
Department of Attorney General
Attn: John Gillmor
425 Queen St., Room 212 DOT
Honolulu, Hawaii 96813

Dear John,

I really thought we were done with all of this, but we received a statement on Saturday, July 10 that shows we were in arrears $230.88 for over 30 days. This amount previously showed up as the total amount of the water bills for February, March and April of 2010. We received the billings on May 30, 2010 and paid for the three months on June 5, 2010 and the checks were cashed on June 11, 2010.

Per our conversation on June 19, 2010 (enclosed) we agreed upon our final credit of $799.99 which we applied to our June rent of making out a check for $1,589.01 and mailing it that day. I really thought we were even that day. Now that same amount of $230.88 shows up again, but now as part of our June rent payment.

I spoke to three women from fiscal today, but did not get an answer that I could understand. Twice I asked if there was someone there that could speak English well enough so that I could understand. I did try to call Julene, but got a recording at 3:50 p.m.. I will try again tomorrow.

Sincerely yours

Pat Magie, President

Cc: *Jim Pratt ????* AIRPORTS Director
  Christopher D. Ferrara, Esq.
  Jelene Hiruya, Airports Division, Fiscal

 seaplane tours

LINDA LINGLE
GOVERNOR

MARK J. BENNETT
ATTORNEY GENERAL

Russell A. Suzuki
FIRST DEPUTY ATTORNEY GENERAL

STATE OF HAWAII
DEPARTMENT OF THE ATTORNEY GENERAL
Civil Recoveries Division
425 QUEEN STREET
HONOLULU, HAWAII 96813
(808) 586-1100 Tel
(808) 586-1111 Fax

July 30, 2010

VIA FACSIMILE NO.: 836-7861

Mr. Pat Magie
President
Island Seaplane Service Inc.
85 Lagoon Drive
Honolulu, HI 96819

    RE: Island Seaplane Service Inc.

Dear Mr. Magie:

    In response to your letter of July 12, 2010, I have enclosed a calculation sheet and a reconciliation ledger from Airports Division.

    The calculation sheet is a review of the payments and credits that was discussed at our last meeting at Airports Division.

    Should you have any questions, please feel free to contact me.

                Very truly yours,

                Gwen Valparaiso, Paralegal
                FOR: JOHN P. GILLMOR
                     Deputy Attorney General

GV:
Enclosure

5/10/10	Rent with Interest	$5,382.13	
5/11/10	Interest credit was generated and applied to open interest charges on 5/10/10	$ (604.13) $4,778.00	
5/11/10	Rent	$4,778.00	
5/11/10	Payment Plan	$4,836.89	
	Subtotal	$9,614.89	
5/11/10	Payment	($1,000.00)	
	Subtotal	$8,614.89	
5/8/10	Rent Paid	($2,389.00)	
	Subtotal	$6,225.89	
4/30/10	Sewer Credit	($6,782.20)	
	Subtotal	$ 556.31	CREDIT
5/31/09	Open Credit	$12.80	CREDIT
	Subtotal	$ 569.11	CREDIT
5/28/10	Three Water Charges	$(230.88) *	
	TOTAL	$ 338.23	CREDIT
6/10	Rent	$2,389.00	
	Apply Credit of	($ 338.23)	
	Total Owed For June Rent	$2,050.77	

*The three (3) water charges were deducted from the sewer credit as shown above calculation. Amount due of $230.88 is a result of making the payment for the three (3) water charges then applying the payment of $230.88 as a credit.

ISLAND SEAPLANE SERVICE INC.

85 LAGOON DR.
HONOLULU, HI 96819

6143

59-102/1213
85

DATE 6-5-10

PAY TO THE ORDER OF _State of Hawaii Dot_ | $ 54.68

Fifty Four + 68/100 DOLLARS

Bank of Hawaii
MAPUNAPUNA BRANCH
HONOLULU, HAWAII 96819

FOR _Water Bill_ UW 10209482

Feb

Debra A. Magie

⑈006143⑈ ⑆121301028⑆ 0081⑈560625⑈

Proc Date 06-10-2010   Account # 81560625   Amount 54.68

ISLAND SEAPLANE SERVICE INC.
65 LAGOON DR.
HONOLULU, HI 96819

6144

DATE 6-5-10

59-102/1213

PAY TO THE ORDER OF _State of Hawaii Dot_ | $ 88.10

Eight Eight & 10/100 ————————— DOLLARS

Bank of Hawaii
MAPUNAPUNA BRANCH
HONOLULU, HAWAII 96819

FOR _WATER Bill_ MARCH u W10209566

Debra A. Mogil

⑈006144⑈ ⑆121301028⑈ 0081⑈560625⑈

Proc Date 06-10-2010   Account # 61560625   Amount 88.10

26

ISLAND SEAPLANE SERVICE INC.
85 LAGOON DR.
HONOLULU, HI 90819

6145

59-102/1213
05

DATE 6-5-10

PAY TO THE ORDER OF _State of Hawaii DoT_ $ 88.10

Eighty Eight & 10/100 DOLLARS

h Bank of Hawaii
KAIPONAPUNA BRANCH
HONOLULU HAWAII 96816

Water

FOR _April_ uw10209619

Deba G. Mage

⑉006145⑉ ⑈121301028⑈ 008⑉560625⑉

Proc Date 06-10-2010   Account # 81560625   Amount 88.10

309

recieved July 10'

STATE OF HAWAII - DEPARTMENT OF TRANSPORTATION
OPEN ITEMS STATEMENT OF ACCOUNT

Date: 07/01/2010

DOT-AIRPORTS DIVISION
ACCOUNTS RECEIVABLE
HONOLULU INTERNATIONAL AIRPORT
400 RODGERS BOULEVARD SUITE 700
HONOLULU, HI 96819-1880

WILLIAM H. MAGIE
ISLAND SEAPLANE SERVICE INC-FC
PO BOX 30685
HONOLULU, HI 96820-0685

Account No: 71408-01
Tenant: ISLAND SEAPLANE SERVICE INC-FC

Transaction Date	Reference Number	Transaction Description	Original Amount	Transaction Balance	Cumulative Balance
Open Invoices:					
HNL					
06/01/2010	F10209063	Inv: Fixed Charges-RP-5585	$2,389.00	$230.88	$230.88
06/30/2010	UW10212446	Inv: Utilities - Water-Misc Billing	$78.99	$78.99	$309.87
07/01/2010	F11211586	Inv: Fixed Charges-RP-5585	$2,389.00	$2,389.00	$2,698.87
			Open Item Balance:		$2,698.87

Summary of Aging Status

Company: 71408-01
Campus: ALL

As of: 07/01/2010

	Days Since Invoice			
	1-30	31-60	61-90	91+
Total Unpaid:	$2,467.99	$230.88	$0.00	$0.00

Please disregard Open Item Balance if payment has already been made.

An interest charge of 12% per annum will be applied to agreement(s) that are more than 30 days past due. For billing inquiries, please call (808) 838-8649 between the hours of 07:45 AM and 04:30 PM, Monday through Friday, except holidays. Please submit the attached remittance statement when making payments. If no indications are made, payment will first be applied to interest and then the earliest outstanding invoice(s). Remittance should be made payable to:

DEPARTMENT OF TRANSPORTATION-AIRPORTS DIVISION

cashed 6-11 *Pd 6-5 √# 6143 Feb — 54.68*
 # 6144 march — 88.10
 # 6145 April — 88.10

Page 1 of 2

Transaction Date	Number	Doc No	PO Number	Class	Original Amount	Adj	Balance Due	Status	Customer	Customer Name
12-May-10	8519521	144198		Payment	(1,000.00)	(430.89)	(569.11)	Open	71408-01	ISLAND SEAPLANE SERVICE INC-FC
1-Jun-10	F10209063		RP-5585	Invoice	2,389.00		2,389.00	Open	71408-01	ISLAND SEAPLANE SERVICE INC-FC
				June 2010 rent:	2,389.00					
28-May-10	UW10209482			Misc Billing Invoice	54.68		54.68	Open	71408-01	ISLAND SEAPLANE SERVICE INC-FC
28-May-10	UW10208566			Misc Billing Invoice	88.10		88.10	Open	71408-01	ISLAND SEAPLANE SERVICE INC-FC
28-May-10	UW10209619			Misc Billing Invoice	88.10		88.10	Open	71408-01	ISLAND SEAPLANE SERVICE INC-FC
				Water charges:			230.88			
				June 2010 rent:	2,389.00					
				Water charges:	230.88					
				Subtotal:	2,619.88					
				Less credit:	(569.11)					
				Total due:	2,050.77					

311

island seaplane service inc.

85 Lagoon Drive • Honolulu, HI 96819 • Tel (808) 836-6273 • Fax (808) 836-7861
Mailing Address: P.O. Box 30685, Honolulu, HI 96820 • E-mail: seaplaneservice@aol.com • www.islandseaplane.com

August 3, 2010

State of Hawaii
Department of the Attorney General
Attn: John Gillmor
425 Queen St., Room 212 DOT
Honolulu, Hawaii

Dear John,

I guess it will never end! I thought we were all paid up, but I did not consider the mentality of some of the people involved..

Your "paralegal" came up with this schedule of payments. It shows that on May 31 we had a total credit of $569.11. On May 28 they took $230.88 of that credit away and applied it to water charges for February, March and April totaling $230.88. This is what I have complained about for years - taking monies away and applying them where they wish. On June 1 we were billed for these same water charges of $230.88 which we paid on June 5 for the second time. These checks were paid by the bank on June 11. If we had been advised by airport on May 28 of this shuffle everything would have been fine, but they billed us and we paid up for the second time. Now we are currently being billed $230.88 plus interest for the third time. Will the well ever run dry.

Sincerely yours

Pat Magie

seaplane tours

DEPUTY DIRECTOR
MICHAEL D. FORMBY
FRANCIS PAUL KEENO
JIRO A. SUMADA

3𝒥

**STATE OF HAWAII
DEPARTMENT OF TRANSPORTATION
AIRPORTS DIVISION**
400 RODGERS BOULEVARD, SUITE 700
HONOLULU INTERNATIONAL AIRPORT - HONOLULU, HAWAII 96819-1880

IN REPLY REFER TO:
AIR-AF 10.0234

August 19, 2010

ISLAND SEAPLANE SERVICE INC-FC
PO BOX 30685
HONOLULU HI 96820-0685

Dear Sir/Madam:

Notice Of Delinquency
Account Number 71408-01

A review of your account discloses that a debt due the Airports Division in the amount of $230.88, including interest and service charges, which is past due.

We request your immediate attention and payment of the outstanding amount within five (5) business days from the date of receipt of this notice. If the delinquency is not cleared by the end of the month, your account will be referred to the State of Hawaii, Attorney General, Civil Recoveries Division.

Should you disagree with the amount due, please call Ms. Joanne Lui at (808) 838-8660.

If you have already made payment, please disregard this notice.

Very truly yours,

SIDNEY A. HAYAKAWA
ADMINISTRATIVE OFFICER

CC: Oahu

island seaplane service inc.

85 Lagoon Drive • Honolulu, HI 96819 • Tel (808) 836-6273 • Fax (808) 836-7861
Mailing Address: P.O. Box 30685, Honolulu, HI 96820 • E-mail: seaplaneservice@aol.com • www.islandseaplane.com

September 3, 2010

State of Hawaii DOT
Attn: Sidney A. Hayakawa
400 Rodgers Boulevard, Suite 700
Honolulu, Hawaii 96819

Dear Mr. Hayakawa,,

Per your letter of August 19, I have enclosed an history of this $230.88. I have also enclosed copies of three cancelled checks that we wrote in June that covered these three water bills for February, March and April of 2010 which we received on June 3rd and show that your department cashed them. There is also a letter of history of our account with you that states you appropriated $230.88 from our credit account on May 28th and did not notify us, but instead sent us a bill on June 1st billing us for water for February, March and April. We paid this on June 5th thinking we still owed the bill - because we were never told that the monies were taken from our account. By the way, this credit came from the fact that we were over-charged for water for thirteen years and we never received the interest that you people are so quick to charge us.

If you and I cannot resolve this between ourselves, I will request another meeting between us plus John Gillmor from the Attorney General's office, Jim Pratt from your department and our attorney.

Sincerely yours

Pat Magie, Owner
Island Seaplane Service Inc.

Cc: John Gillmor
      James Pratt
      Chris Ferrar

 seaplane tours

island seaplane service inc.

85 Lagoon Drive • Honolulu, HI 96819 • Tel (808) 836-6273 • Fax (808) 836-7861
Mailing Address: P.O. Box 30685, Honolulu, HI 96820 • E-mail: seaplaneservice@aol.com • www.islandseaplane.com

August 29, 2013

Federal Aviation Administration
Western Region
P.O. Box 92007
Los Angeles, CA 90009

Gentlemen,

First to establish my bonafides: I hold commercial certificate #1452340 with SES, SEL, MES, MEL, Instrument, CFI with A, II MEI and have accumulated over 39,000 accident free logged hours. I also held a DPE for a few years and have owned 488 aircraft in my 58 years in aviation and probably hold the world's record of seaplane time with over 32,000 hours. I raised four children who are now all actively involved in aviation and have a copy of one of my father's last licenses (#229 signed by Orville Wright on our counter in our office). My fathers first license was #8 signed by both Orville and Wilbur Wright and he knew Lindbergh and Amelia Erhart. My wife and I have operated a seaplane operation in HNL for over 17 years now.

On August 28ʰ at 2:13 p.m. our DeHavilland DHC-2 N110AW taxied away from our dock in Keehi Lagoon in HNL with pilot John Whalen, commercial certificate #3473625 ad pilot in command and FAA Inspector David Ryon from HNL FSDO who was giving John Whalen an original CFI check ride. Mr Whalen is a submariner in the U.S. Navy and had to cancel this check ride the previous Wednesday because the U.S. Navy changed his work schedule at the last minute. They cleared the dock and taxied downwind on Sealane 22 while speaking to Clearance Delivery. Upon turning into the wind, they announced to tower that they were ready for departure on Sealane 22 and were told to "hold"/ An hour later at 3:14 p.m. they arrived back at our dock and said they were canceling the check ride because they could not get a clearance to take-off. They had communicated with the tower several times reminding them of their requested departure, but were reminded to "hold". They said another voice came on from the adjoining airport suggesting that the tower must have forgotten them. The controller acknowledged that and cleared him to take off.

After discussing this with the two pilots, I called the control tower on the phone and asked for the supervisor. The person on the phone acknowledged himself as the supervisor and I asked him what the problem was with the clearance and got the answer that he had just come in and did not know of it and he would call me back. This is a very common reply when you ask a question about ATC procedures - "I just came in, but will check and call you back". I never did get a call back. When this happened the traffic pattern had just changed from east departures to west departures and landing traffic was primarily landing on 26L and there were not many

 seaplane tours

island seaplane service inc.

85 Lagoon Drive • Honolulu, HI 96819 • Tel (808) 836-6273 • Fax (808) 836-7861
Mailing Address: P.O. Box 30685, Honolulu, HI 96820 • E-mail: seaplaneservice@aol.com • www.islandseaplane.com

departures at the time. Our office floats on the water between the runways and we can see or hear all the traffic. When I did not hear the Beaver take - off, I walked out on the dock and watched them taxiing in circles at the end of the sealane a third of a mile away. I thought at first that they had a aircraft problem, but then found out it was a ATC problem. This Class Bravo is used as a training ground for new hires, so we see a lot of poor service. ATC fought hard to keep seaplanes out of Honolulu when we were working on this project 25 years ago - it took eight years to get permission to do this. Myself and at least a dozen different pilots flying for me have had many orders to "hold" and wait 15 to 20 minutes to go. Because we are on the water, our passengers will get queasy bouncing up and down on windy days. My wife and I a few years ago went for a personal flight and gave up after waiting 40 minutes for a take-off clearance.

We lost about $600.00 of revenue because of this last incident, but the main point is that our customer and FSDO inspector have to find another time to do the check ride and he might be some what flustered thinking it could happen again.

Whoever was working the control tower at that time certainly cannot be qualified to be an airtraffic controller. I would have to say the same for whoever answered the phone and identified himself as the supervisor.

Sincerely Yours

William H. Magie

 seaplane tours

Wm Magie complaint letter

To: William H. Magie -

Your letter dated August 29, 2013, was received in our office on Friday,
and it has been forwarded to Linda Pellegrini, the Manager of the Honolulu
Air Traffic Control facility and district manager responsible for
operations in the ATC facility you wrote about. I have confirmed with Ms.
Pellegrini her receipt of your letter, and she will provide you a response
once she has had an opportunity to look into it.

Thank you for writing,

Naomi Tsuda, AWP-7
Regional Counsel
Western Pacific Region
(310) 725-7101 / FAX: (310) 725-6816

IMPORTANT: This message, and any attachments thereto, is intended solely
for specific recipients. If you are not an intended recipient of this
communication, you are not authorized to read, print, retain, copy or
disseminate this message or any part of it. This message may be
confidential, an attorney-client communication, part of the agency's
deliberative process, or attorney-work product and must not be forwarded or
otherwise shared without express permission. If you have received this
e-mail in error, please notify me immediately by e-mail or telephone,
discard any paper copies and delete all electronic files of this e-mail.

island seaplane service inc.

85 Lagoon Drive • Honolulu, HI 96819 • Tel (808) 836-6273 • Fax (808) 836-7861
Mailing Address: P.O. Box 30685, Honolulu, HI 96820 • E-mail: seaplaneservice@aol.com • www.islandseaplane.com

August 29, 2013

Federal Aviation Administration
Western Region
P.O. Box 92007
Los Angeles, CA 90009

Gentlemen,

First to establish my bonafides: I hold commercial certificate #1452340 with SES, SEL, MES, MEL, Instrument, CFI with A, II MEI and have accumulated over 39,000 accident free logged hours. I also held a DPE for a few years and have owned 488 aircraft in my 58 years in aviation and probably hold the world's record of seaplane time with over 32,000 hours. I raised four children who are now all actively involved in aviation and have a copy of one of my father's last licenses (#229 signed by Orville Wright on our counter in our office). My fathers first license was #8 signed by both Orville and Wilbur Wright and he knew Lindbergh and Amelia Erhart. My wife and I have operated a seaplane operation in HNL for over 17 years now.

On August 28th at 2:13 p.m. our DeHavilland DHC-2 N110AW taxied away from our dock in Keehi Lagoon in HNL with pilot John Whalen, commercial certificate #3473625 ad pilot in command and FAA Inspector David Ryon from HNL FSDO who was giving John Whalen an original CFI check ride. Mr Whalen is a submariner in the U.S. Navy and had to cancel this check ride the previous Wednesday because the U.S. Navy changed his work schedule at the last minute. They cleared the dock and taxied downwind on Sealane 22 while speaking to Clearance Delivery. Upon turning into the wind, they announced to tower that they were ready for departure on Sealane 22 and were told to "hold"/ An hour later at 3:14 p.m. they arrived back at our dock and said they were canceling the check ride because they could not get a clearance to take-off. They had communicated with the tower several times reminding them of their requested departure, but were reminded to "hold". They said another voice came on from the adjoining airport suggesting that the tower must have forgotten them. The controller acknowledged that and cleared him to take off.

After discussing this with the two pilots, I called the control tower on the phone and asked for the supervisor. The person on the phone acknowledged himself as the supervisor and I asked him what the problem was with the clearance and got the answer that he had just come in and did not know of it and he would call me back. This is a very common reply when you ask a question about ATC procedures - "I just came in, but will check and call you back". I never did get a call back. When this happened the traffic pattern had just changed from east departures to west departures and landing traffic was primarily landing on 26L and there were not many

 seaplane tours

island seaplane service inc.

85 Lagoon Drive • Honolulu, HI 96819 • Tel (808) 836-6273 • Fax (808) 836-7861
Mailing Address: P.O. Box 30685, Honolulu, HI 96820 • E-mail: seaplaneservice@aol.com • www.islandseaplane.com

departures at the time. Our office floats on the water between the runways and we can see or hear all the traffic. When I did not hear the Beaver take - off, I walked out on the dock and watched them taxiing in circles at the end of the sealane a third of a mile away. I thought at first that they had a aircraft problem, but then found out it was a ATC problem. This Class Bravo is used as a training ground for new hires, so we see a lot of poor service. ATC fought hard to keep seaplanes out of Honolulu when we were working on this project 25 years ago - it took eight years to get permission to do this. Myself and at least a dozen different pilots flying for me have had many orders to "hold" and wait 15 to 20 minutes to go. Because we are on the water, our passengers will get queasy bouncing up and down on windy days. My wife and I a few years ago went for a personal flight and gave up after waiting 40 minutes for a take-off clearance.

We lost about $600.00 of revenue because of this last incident, but the main point is that our customer and FSDO inspector have to find another time to do the check ride and he might be some what flustered thinking it could happen again.

Whoever was working the control tower at that time certainly cannot be qualified to be an airtraffic controller. I would have to say the same for whoever answered the phone and identified himself as the supervisor.

Sincerely Yours

William H. Magie

 seaplane tours

island seaplane service inc.

85 Lagoon Drive • Honolulu, HI 96819 • Tel (808) 836-6273 • Fax (808) 836-7861
Mailing Address: P.O. Box 30685, Honolulu, HI 96820 • E-mail: seaplaneservice@aol.com • www.islandseaplane.com

September 12, 2013

Naomi Tsuda, AWP-7
Regional Counsel
Western Pacific Region
P.O. Box 92007
Los Angeles, CA 90009

Aloha Ms. Tsuda,

I wrote you on August 29th and the letter was received in your office on Thursday, September 5th. A copy of this letter is enclosed. I was asking a very simple question as to why my aircraft N110AW was held for one hour awaiting take-off clearance. On August 28th I did speak on the phone to one of the so-called supervisors who was going to get back to me and never did. I am still working on this and probably will have to go to the Washington office.

A follow - up on August 30 at just about noon the same Beaver N110AW was returning to HNL Seaplane base via Pali Pass from Kanehoe after a check ride. The pilot, Gary L. Brizendine, ATP, #20800225 was just finishing his commercial add on SES rating administered by the same FSDO inspector David Ryon who was involved in the August 28th incident. Mr. Brizendine made several calls to approach on 119.1 without reply and then turned right along the mountains. The controller on approach immediately initiated the procedure for a violation of entering a Class Bravo entry without a clearance. When they phoned the FSDO office to report the violation they evidently found out that a FSDO flight inspector was in the aircraft. Meanwhile one of the Center people from downstairs was called to look at the chart, but he told them to look close and the aircraft did not actually enter Class Bravo airspace. Being a simple 39,000 hour pilot I assume that the slow response from ATC would open the door for a "get even" violation. I have had no choice but to tell all of our pilots that if they do not receive a reply after two calls, squawk 7600 and proceed. We are seaplanes and cannot land elsewhere.

I would appreciate some response to these problems and if I am told that is all due to sequester, I will probably have to move to Canada.

Sincerely yours
William Magie

 seaplane tours

**Federal Aviation
Administration**

Honolulu Control Facility
760 Worchester Avenue
Honolulu, HI 96818
P: 808-840-6100
F: 808-840-6110

September 18, 2013

William H. Magie
Island Seaplane Service, Inc.
P.O. Box 30685
Honolulu, HI 96820

Dear Mr. Magie:

Thank you very much for taking the time to write us regarding the experience your check-ride client had on August 28, 2013. It is important that individuals and companies that operate out of Honolulu International Airport let us know of their experiences, whether negative or positive. Those of us not directly connected with day-to-day operations may not always be aware of situations where we as a facility may not have fulfilled our mission to the best of our ability.

After receiving your letter, I immediately tasked our staff support specialists to look into what led to the poor service your client experienced that day.

As you noted in your letter, the airport was in a Kona wind or RY22/26 configuration. This greatly reduces the airport's arrival and departure capacity by restricting IFR arrivals to one runway, Runway 26L, and restricting overseas departing flights to one runway as well, Runway 22L. This also affects the complexity of the operation, since we now have departing IFR traffic, many times heavy jets, crossing over Runway 26L, which we normally avoid by having parallel arrival/departure operations utilizing Runway 8L and Runway 8R.

At the time that N110AW called Local Control and advised that they were ready for departure, there were three (3) small aircraft inbound for Runway 22R, three (3) jets lined up on the Runway 26L final and five (5) more being vectored for the Runway 26L LDA approach. On the airport were seven (7) oceanic departures waiting for Runway 22L, three (3) waiting for Runway 26R from intersections west of RY22R and one (1) aircraft waiting for Runway 26R at Taxiway C.

Because your aircraft would be departing to the south, conflicting with arrivals on the LDA RY26L approach, it was much more difficult to find a departure slot. Wake turbulence considerations from heavy aircraft departing on Runway 22L as well as landing on Runway 26L, further add to the difficulty. On a Tradewind or Runway 4/8 configuration, wake turbulence normally does not affect sea lane operations because the aircraft departs to the north, away from the heavy departures on Runway 8R.

Analysis of the airport surveillance radar, the ASDE (airport surface radar) and audio for Local Control indicated very few opportunities for N0AW to depart. The aircraft that was holding for Runway 26R at Taxiway C waited from 1421 to 1454 to depart, which equates to a 33 minute wait. We also had an oceanic departure taxi back to the gate for more fuel after a 30 minute wait for Runway 22L. When that aircraft initially taxied to RY22R, there were 7 other aircraft ahead of him. This was just a very busy hour.

We do appreciate that it can be very uncomfortable to be waiting on a choppy sea lane and we will impress upon the controllers the importance of ensuring that we treat general aviation aircraft with the same "first come – first served" status as all other airport users, contingent upon factors such as wake turbulence, of course.

We do apologize for the lack of response to your initial phone call to the tower cab supervisor. We will be sure to emphasize to the supervisor the importance of following up on all public inquiries and complaints, regardless of his instant knowledge of the events leading to the phone call.

As you are probably aware, the FAA is very interested in gathering as much data as possible to improve the services that we provide to our customers and inquiries such as yours are very important to the process of triggering an analysis and adding to our knowledge. We apologize that the delay resulted in the cancellation of your rating flight.

Please do not hesitate to contact us again in the future, either through the Service Area as you did, or directly through the address or phone number listed at the top of this letter.

Sincerely,

Linda Pellegrini,
Air Traffic Manager

September 24, 2013

Linda Pellegrini
Air Traffic Manager
HCF
760 Worchester Avenue
Honolulu, HI 96818

Dear Ms. Pellegrini,

Thank you for your letter of September 18, but tomorrow will be _four_ weeks since I asked the question of Honolulu Control tower why my aircraft waited one hour for take-off clearance on Sealane 22 on August 28th before giving up and taxiing back to our dock. I did talk to a "Supervisor" immediately and was told he would get back to me - and I am still waiting.

I think you have a problem with your staff "specialists" because you gave me a some what tedious explanation that was not truthful. Mr. John Whalen, the pilot in command, requested a "West Loch Three" departure which required a right turn-out to the North. We had discussed these procedures years ago with the managers of the tower and all agreed that by turning North midway down 22L and 26R we would be passing over west bound aircraft while they would still be on the ground on their take-off run and over landing aircraft taxiing in after their touchdown. There is no problem with wake turbulence either way. I have over 39,000 hours and 58 years of accident free flying and transported many thousands of passengers and never had a passenger so much as cut a finger. You have to believe that we are more interested in the safety of our aircraft then your people are. I never had a close call of a mid-air until coming to Hawaii and a few years back I had three almost mid-airs in one 30 minute flight while under control each time. The first one involved a H-53 helicopter within Kaneohe's class Delta airspace and the second a helicopter in Pali Pass under HNL approach and the third involved a JAL DC-10 under control of HNL tower.

I have enclosed copies of previous correspondence with the Western Region office concerning the incident on another student getting a check ride with Dave Ryon on board as the inspector of the HNL FSDO. I really believe that both of these incidents are a "get the seaplane" program.

Sincerely yours
Pat Magie

PILOT of the YEAR

Bush pilots as a group are renowned for determination in the face of adversity, willingness to take risks for the sake of others, uncanny skill, and ingenuity. Pat Magie—by all accounts a classic bush pilot—is the Seaplane Pilots Association's 2000 Seaplane Pilot of the Year.

Magie's aviation career stretches back to the late 1950s when Pat bought a J-4 Cub late in the short Minnesota season. The cub was a meager performer, a characteristic only compounded by the wrong type of prop hanging off the front end. Eager to learn how to fly, Pat enlisted Chick Beel, a U.S. Forest Service pilot. With winter coming on fast and the ice making its annual advance, Pat figured he would head down the Mississippi as the winter bore on, picking up instructors along the way. As it turned out, Chick had no trouble getting Pat through his first solo and well on his way before winter could intervene. "He was a natural pilot," says Chick of Pat. "I never had to demonstrate anything to him twice."

Within the next few years, Magie upgraded to a 165-hp Stinson 108-3, and by the early '60s had founded Wilderness Wings. Based at Sandy Point Seaplane Base on Shagawa Lake, just north of Ely, Minnesota, Wilderness Wings prospered on the aviation staples of training, selling airplanes, and flying charters to the Canadian wilderness for canoe trips and hunting. Before long Pat was running just about every model of Cessna, with a couple of Twin Beeches and a Beaver thrown in for good measure. Students streamed in from around the country for seaplane training, many taking advantage of the GI bill, others fascinated by the unique equipment and dazzling wilderness. Multi-engine seaplane ratings were one of Pat's specialties, a task for which he employed the popular Beech 18.

Pat Magie
By Michael Volk

Pat Magie on wing,
John Parish standing

Pat Magie Seaplane Pilot of the Year

Printed in the United States
By Bookmasters